外 国 哲 学

第 十 七 辑

商务印书馆
2005年·北京

主办：中华人民共和国教育部人文社科基地北京大学外国哲学研究所
协办：中华全国外国哲学史学会
　　　中国现代外国哲学学会

编 辑 委 员 会

主编：赵敦华　靳希平

执行主编：徐向东

学 术 委 员 会

（以姓氏拼音为序）

卞崇道（中国社会科学院）	白彤东（美国泽维尔大学）
陈嘉映（华东师范大学）	陈小文（商务印书馆）
程　炼（北京大学）	邓晓芒（武汉大学）
杜小真（北京大学）	冯　俊（中国人民大学）
傅有德（山东大学）	韩林合（北京大学）
韩水法（北京大学）	韩　震（北京师范大学）
贾泽林（中国社会科学院）	江　怡（中国社会科学院）
靳希平（北京大学）	刘　闯（美国佛罗里达大学）
倪梁康（中山大学）	尚新建（北京大学）
唐热风（中国社会科学院）	孙永平（北京大学）
谢地坤（中国社会科学院）	王树人（中国社会科学院）
姚卫群（北京大学）	翟振明（中山大学）
张汝伦（复旦大学）	张祥龙（北京大学）
张志林（中山大学）	赵敦华（北京大学）

卷 首 语

《外国哲学》于1984年由商务印书馆创办，至1998年共出版十四辑，开创了改革开放后中国研究外国哲学的新学风、新传统，在学术界具有广泛的影响。经与商务印书馆商议，从第十五辑开始，北京大学外国哲学研究所负责承担《外国哲学》的组稿、编辑工作。

为了进一步提高《外国哲学》稿件的学术水准，我们采取了国际学术刊物通行的"双盲"审稿制度。除了继续发表对外国哲学历史和经典的诠释性论文外，本刊将特别注重发表史论结合、批判性评论、中外哲学比较等方面的佳作。我们衷心希望全国同仁鼎力襄助，不吝赐稿，把《外国哲学》办成群贤毕至、百家争鸣的学术园地。

《外国哲学》编辑部
2002年4月

目 录

涛慕思·W. 博格　康德的权利论是一个"全面的自由主义"吗？………………………………（1）

谭安奎　政治的概念与政治自由主义 ……………（32）

李凤华　证明与计算：契约论的两种方法
　　　　——罗尔斯与布坎南的政治哲学比较………（69）

卢华萍　苏格拉底与亚里士多德论意志软弱 ………（86）

朱清华　海德格尔的因缘和亚里士多德的"为了善"…（112）

叶　闯　判定真的标准与塔尔斯基真定义在概念上的
　　　　区分 ………………………………………（128）

朱　菁　论意图的聚合原则 ………………………（146）

孟令朋　不是"世界的图画"而是"语言游戏"
　　　　——从《哲学研究》看维特根斯坦Ⅱ的语言观…（161）

David Stern　*Philosophical Investigations* §§1—693：
　　　　An Elementary Exposition ………………（179）

徐向东　Kripke's Paradox, Humean Solution and the
　　　　Nature of Normativity ……………………（207）

刘　闯　Idealization: Getting Scientific Laws by Carving
　　　　Nature at its Joints ………………………（251）

埃德蒙多·胡塞尔　回忆布伦塔诺 ………………（280）

康德的权利论是一个"全面的自由主义"吗？*

- 涛慕思·W.博格（著）
- 卢华萍（译）

从1985年开始,约翰·罗尔斯就一再强调,应该按照一个政治的正义观念来组织多元的现代社会。他从那时起就坚持把他自己的自由主义理解为政治的,以对比于康德和密尔的全面的(comprehensive)自由主义。虽然罗尔斯对他本人立场的这一精细的改进已经被许多人讨论过,他把康德的自由主义描述成全面的这个做法在有关文献中却尚未得到批判性的考察。我在此首开这样的考察,关注的焦点完全是康德。我的主导思想是,通过使康德的"权利论"对照罗尔斯在两个世纪后阐发的区分,我们可以更好地理解前者。

一、导论

从1985年开始,[①]约翰·罗尔斯就一再强调,应该按照一个政治的正义观念来组织多元的现代社会。他从那时起就坚持把他自己的自由主义理解为政治的,以对比于康德和密尔的全面的(comprehen-

---

* 在修改这篇文章时,我从它在孟斐斯、劳伦斯和上海已经激起的活跃讨论中深得教益。同时也十分感谢 Rüdiger Bittner, Ernesto Garcia, Samuel Kerstein 和张双利（复旦大学）,感谢他们高质量的、相当有启发的批评和建议。此外,也特别感谢本文的中文译者卢华萍的优秀的翻译。

① 约翰·罗尔斯,"作为公平的正义:政治的而非形而上学的",《哲学与公共事务》,14(1985),第223—252页。

sive)①自由主义。② 虽然罗尔斯对他本人立场的这一精细的改进已经被许多人讨论过,他把康德的自由主义描述成全面的这个做法在有关文献中却尚未得到批判性的考察。我在此首开这样的考察,关注的焦点完全是康德。我的主导思想是,通过使康德的"权利论"对照罗尔斯在两个世纪后阐发的区分,我们可以更好地理解前者。③

罗尔斯把一个社会正义观念称为全面的,是指这个观念依赖于"人生价值的观念,以及个人美德和品格的理想,这些观念和理想要在很大程度上教导我们的非政治行为"(《政治自由主义》,第 175 页;参看第 13 页)。他声言,"康德的学说是一个全面的道德观,在其中,自律理想对整个生活起一种规导作用"④;此外,更慎重些,"让我们假定,康德观点中的个人和社会的基

---

① "comprehensive"一词在罗尔斯那里主要有两个含义。"comprehensive^1"适用于道德观念(道德理论),指它们包含或者涵盖大多数或者所有的道德论题。"comprehensive^2"适用于社会正义的观念(以及,更明确地,适用于各个自由主义),指它们以如下的方式,是在第一种意义上全面的一个道德观念的一个必不可少的(integral)组成部分:它们以那个道德观念的其他部分为先决条件,或者依赖那些部分。本文在第二种意义上考察康德的权利论是不是一个"全面的"自由主义。——译注

② 罗尔斯这里批评他过去在《正义论》(Cambridge, MA: Harvard University Press, 1971)中描述他自己的观念的那种方式。他评论说,他在那部早期的著作中"没有在道德哲学和政治哲学之间作任何区分",也"没有在全面的哲学和道德学说与限于政治学领域的那些观念之间作任何对比……尽管《正义论》没有讨论一个政治的正义观念和一个全面的哲学学说之间的区别,但问题一旦被提出来,我认为《正义论》显然还是把正义即公平和功利主义视为全面的或部分全面的学说"[约翰·罗尔斯,《政治自由主义》,(New York: Columbia University Press, 1993),第 xv—xvi 页,以下引为 PL]。

③ 我将把康德《道德形而上学》[*Metaphysik der Sitten*,(6:203—228)]的导论内容引为 MS,把第一部分"权利论的形而上学原理"['Metaphysische Anfangsgründe der Rechtslehre',(6:229—372)]引为 RL,把第二部分"美德论的形而上学原理"['Metaphysische Anfangsgründe der Tugendlehre',(6:373—493)]引为 TL。在引用或引述这些材料时,我也会在合适的地方附上行号。所有对康德原话的翻译都是我自己的。["Sitten"在德文中对应所有的社会规则(social rules),包括法律的、道德的和习俗的。所以,英文和中文把"Sitten"分别翻译成"morals"和"道德"可能都太狭窄了。不过我们在此仍然沿用已经通行的译名。除了"导论"外,《道德形而上学》这本书包括两个部分,第一部分是"权利论的形而上学原理"(在本译文中有时也简写为"权利论"),第二部分是"美德论的形而上学原理"(在本译文中有时也简写为"美德论")。——译注]

④ 《政治自由主义》,第 99 页,参看第 78 页——罗尔斯在那里认为,康德的全面性自由主义表达了"自律的伦理价值"。

本观念在他的先验唯心论中有一个基础"(《政治自由主义》,第100页)。

提及以赛亚·伯林,罗尔斯指出全面性社会正义观念的一个主要缺点是可能造成社会的不和,例如它们对待公共教育的方式:"康德和密尔的自由主义可能导向设计一些规定来培养自律和个性的价值,以作为理想来支配大部分生活——如果不是支配整个生活的话"(《政治自由主义》,第199页)。但是,给定罗尔斯所谓的"压迫的事实",即"只有通过压迫性地使用国家权力,才能维持对某一个全面性宗教学说、哲学学说或道德学说的持续共享的理解"(《政治自由主义》,第37页),那么这样一些规定就会导向一个致命的二难困境。只有通过违反它们自己的反对使用国家压迫的原则,康德和密尔的全面性自由主义才能维持它们自己的社会卓越性(《政治自由主义》,第37页注释39)。

罗尔斯并没有把政治的社会正义观念仅仅定义为非全面的或者独立不依的(freestanding)。而是,他在他的定义中又加了两个要素:政治的社会正义观念适用于、而且仅仅适用于一个封闭又自足的社会的基本结构(《政治自由主义》,第11—12页);它们"是用某些被视为隐含在一个民主社会的公共政治文化中的基本理念来表达的"。① 为了避免罗尔斯指出的问题,康德的自由主义只须是独立不倚的,而不必是政治的;因此,我不考虑这两个附加的要素。简单地说,这样我们的问题就是:康德的"权利论"是独立不倚的——还是受惠于他的哲学整体的其他部分,从而偏向那些部分,例如他的善良意志理论和自律理论,或者他的先验唯心论。

让我们从一些简单的要点入手。难以置疑,康德确实支持和发展了先验唯心论和一个自律理想。但这不可能解答我们的问题。因为,一个社会正义观念的缔造者同时持有和表达一些更广泛的宗教观、道德观或哲学观——罗尔斯本人显然也持有这样一些观点,而且可能还表达了它们——这个事实并不表明他所阐发的那个社会正义观念以某种方式依赖这些更广

---

① 《政治自由主义》,第13页。这样,他对全面的社会正义观念和政治的社会正义观念所作的区分不是穷尽的,虽然这两个标签的确相斥。

泛的观点。

指出康德声明他的"权利论"契合他的批判哲学的更广泛的世界观,或者点明康德把他的整个哲学展现为由某些核心的术语、命题和方法统一起来的一个体系,也都不可能解答我们的问题。因为,从一个社会正义观念契合一个全面的世界观这个事实,推不出它仅仅契合这一个全面的世界观,或者它不能也可以"在被表述的同时不谈论、不知晓或不胡乱猜测哪些这样的学说它可能于其归属或者受其支持"(《政治自由主义》,第12—13页)。我们可以从下面的考虑中清楚地看到这一点:罗尔斯把他自己的政治的社会正义观念表述为"一个组件(module),一个重要的组成部分,它契合各种合理的全面性学说并能得到它们的支持"(《政治自由主义》,第12页);他在发展一个交叠共识的范例时甚至声称,他自己的作为公平的正义契合康德的全面的世界观(《政治自由主义》,第145页和第169页)。

因此,要使康德的自由主义因其全面性而不合格,必须表明的不是:康德的自由主义是他的更广泛的哲学体系所必需的,而是相反:康德的更广泛的哲学体系是他的自由主义的先决条件。这个自由主义,如果它除了能被表现为康德的哲学世界观的一个组成部分以外,根本不能被表现,那么它就是全面的。

在本文中,我将为下列假说提供论据:在康德的"权利论"中提出的自由主义不是全面的,既不以康德的道德哲学、也不以他的先验唯心论为先决条件。我不声称这个假说在此被充分地、结论性地证明。但有些人应该答辩这个假说及其论据:这些人抛弃康德的政治哲学,以为它依赖于我们无法指望现代社会的公民自由地赞同的形而上学观点或道德观点。

在全力投诸余文来支持我的假说之前,让我承认,即使康德的自由主义不是全面的,他却不能免于罗尔斯今天认为[1]体现在其早期作品中的讲解上的缺点:康德有时候(错误地)暗示,他的自由主义依赖于他的哲学世界

---

[1] 参看本书第2页注文中所引的罗尔斯的自我批评。

观,因而是全面的。① 康德这样做并不让人吃惊。他深深地确信并坚持他的道德哲学和他的先验唯心论;如果他的自由主义依赖这些理论,而不仅仅得到它们的支持,那么这些理论就会因他的自由主义而获得更加意义深远的证实。②

二、康德的权利(Recht)③定义(§A—§B)

康德在"权利论"中发展的自由主义是由寥寥几个基本要素构成的。其中有些是定义。以这样的方式,康德断言:与一个物相对比,一个"人(person)是其行为能够归于其(imputation)的一个主体"("导论",6:223:24—25)。他继续说:"因此,道德的人格不是任何别的,它是受道德法则约束的一个理性的人的自由……这引出以下结论:一个人只受其(独自地,或者至少与他人共同地)赋予自己的法则的约束"("导论",6:223:25—31)。我对这些话的解读很

---

① 让我引用一个样本段落,这段话暗示,法律上的占有以(内在的)意志自由和绝对命令为先决条件:"没有人该对此感到惊讶:关于我的外在东西和你的外在东西的理论原则逐渐后退到智性(intelligible),而不表现任何扩大了的知识——因为这些原则所依赖的自由概念没有能力演绎出它的可能性,而只能从理性的实践法则(绝对命令)中作为理性的一个事实被推断出来"("权利论",6:252:24—30,参看 6:245:16—21)。我应该补充说,我自己先前对康德政治哲学的理解在这一点上也不太明确。参看我的"康德的正义理论"一文['Kant's Theory of Justice', *Kant-Studien*, 79 (1988), 407—433]。

② 注意康德在发现下面这一点时表现出来的成就感——他发现自己不得不断言,他的道德哲学以他的先验唯心论为先决条件:"实践理性自身,不与思辨理性进行丝毫的串通,就为因果性范畴的一个超感性的对象,即自由,提供了实在性……;也就是说,它通过一个事实证实了在思辨批判那里只能被思维的东西。思辨批判的这个奇怪却又不容置疑的断言——即,思维的主体对其自身来说只是一个在内直观里的现象——此时在实践理性批判中得到了充分的证实"(《实践理性批判》,5:6:7—16)。

③ 在德文中,Recht 至少包括三组含义:法,法规;权,权利,权限;正义。这些含义在康德的"权利论"中均有体现,而首先是指由法则/法律界定、支配和约束的权利/权限。但是,既然在英文和中文中都很难找到一个更好的词来充分而精确地对应 Recht,我就仍然采用目前通行的译法,"权利"(right)。与此相关,它的形容词 recht 可以指恰当的,合法的,公正的,正当的,等等;我在此把它一律翻译成"正当的",虽然也明知其狭隘,而且有点不得要领——最好像博格所提示的那样打个比方,recht 相当于你在下棋的时候遵守棋规,否则就是"不正当的"(unrecht)。——译注

是得益于吕迪格·比特纳(Rüdiger Bittner)和约阿希姆·赫鲁斯卡(Joachim Hruschka),但又不追随二人中的任何一个。解读如下。康德把"道德的"标上着重号,是想昭示这个词限定了"人格"的含义。最可行、同时也将证明"因此"之含义的说明是这样的:具有道德的人格,就意味着是其内在行为能够归于其的一个主体,是具有(先验的)意志自由的一个主体。这是贯穿于康德的道德文论的狭义的、强的人的概念。① 较宽泛、较弱的意义上的人则是这样一些主体:他们的外在行为能够作为他们的意志、选择或意向的表现而被归于他们。康德明确地解释,尽管"美德论"同时涉及内在的和外在的行为与自由,从而必须使用较强的道德人格的概念,"权利论"则只关注人的外在行为与外在自由,从而只须较弱的一般人的概念,或者(可以称为)法律人格(juridical personality)的概念("导论",6:214:13—30)。②

假定有一些人——不是只有一个人,而是一群人。假定他们在同一个空间内按某种方式活动,以至于一个人的行动也许会妨碍另一个人的行动。让我们说,一个人的外在自由所受到的约束,恰恰正至他人妨碍着她的——否则若她选择去做就能做的——行动的程度;一个人的外在自由是不稳当的(insecure),正至他人能够妨碍她否则能做的行动的程度。于是,一个人的外在自由是稳当的(secure),正至他人潜在的妨碍行动本身受到妨碍的程度。一个人的外在自由的稳当性从而要求他人(妨碍她的外在自由)的外在自由必须被约束。所以,只有在这个条件下而且只有稳当至这个程度,即,每个人的外在自由都被约束以使其与所有其他人的被约束的外在自由有一致性,一群人才能有他们的外在自由的稳当性。

康德把"权利"定义为"全部条件,在这些全部条件下,一个人的选择能够与另一个人的选择按照一条普遍的自由法则共存[zusammen vereinigt

---

① 例如,参看《道德形而上学基础》,4:428:21—29,加上 4:446—448;《实践理性批判》,5:87:3—4,5:162:17—20;《单纯理性限度内的宗教》,6:27—28;和"美德论",6:434—435。同时参看《实践理性批判》5:97:6—7 对以道德法则(绝对命令)为据的"归于其"的论述。

② 按照这种解读,康德可能仍然承诺一个综合的、在"权利论"以外提出的主张,即所有人都有道德人格。

werden kann]"("权利论",6:230:24—26)。① 这里的"选择(choice)"是玛丽·格雷戈尔(Mary Gregor)对"Willkür"一词的翻译。只要附上两条说明,这样翻译似乎也不失确当。首先,不应该在决断(decision)的意义上理解"某个人的选择"(如,"她开始为她的选择后悔"),而必须在她的控制范围的意义上理解这个选择(如,"这是她的选择;由她来决定,取决于她")。其次,我们不应该把某个人的选择狭隘地理解为在某个场合取决于她的东西,而必须从总体上把它理解为在她的一生中全部取决于她的东西。我把康德的"外在自由"这个表达解读为等同于这种意义上的选择。也许还可以附上最后一条说明:尽管康德在这里只谈论两个人,他的定义却旨在涵盖无定限的许多人。这样,他把"权利"定义为全部条件,在这些全部条件下,任何人的外在自由能够与其他所有人的外在自由按照一条普遍的自由法则共存。

外在自由各界域(domains)能够共存,当:任何一个人在她的界域内可能做的任何行动都不会使另一个人在他的界域内的行动变得不可能。为了确保选择的这种互相的一致性(mutual consistency),一条普遍的法则需要包含许多不同的限制,因而应该被看作一套法则——这是"法则"一词的通常意思,"基本法(Grundgesetz)"或"习惯法(Common Law)"之类的说法就示范了这种意思。为了确保互相的一致性,这样一套法则必须对所有人适用,必须精确地规定每个人可以做什么,必须做什么,以及不应该做什么。但是,它不必向每个人提出最终是同一的要求来平等地对待所有人。我于是建议,把这里的"普遍的(allgemein)"一词解读为"对所有人适用"这个弱的意义,而不解读为除了弱的意义之外还必须要求在法则之下人人平等的较强的意义。② 诚然,康德的自由主义确实要求法则之下人人平等。但那个要求不是权利在

---

① 在早期的一段类似的话中,康德把权利定义为"根据与每个人的自由共存[Zusammenstimmung]的条件,来限制各人的自由至这个自由按照一条普遍的法则是可能的程度"("论通常的说法",8:289—290)。

② 但是,这难道不正违背了康德在绝对命令的第一条公式中对同一个词的用法吗——那条公式说,"只按照那样一条准则来行为,借此你能够同时意愿它成为一条普遍法则"(《道德形而上学基础》,4:421:7—8)?当然,绝对命令确实包含法则之下的平等这个理念。但这个理念并不蕴含在一条普遍法则这个概念中,而产生于绝对命令如何

定义上是什么的问题,而是康德主张权利应该是什么的问题。权利可能有许多不同的体现方式,其中只有一部分包含法则之下的平等。

我们还须解释,康德用"全部[Inbegriff]条件"来指什么。我认为这个表达具有双重的蕴意。首先,用复数形式谈论条件,康德暗示了权利不仅仅是这样一个单独的条件:有一条普遍法则来限制每个人的外在自由,以确保互相的一致性。这样一条普遍法则对权利来说是不充分的,因为正如常见的人的情形令人信服地显示的,人们可能不重视它。一条普遍法则,只有当它生效时,它才使得人们的选择有可能相互共存;这样,康德的定义中的"全部条件"还必须包括使这条法则生效的条件。这些有效性条件可能包括制度性设施——普遍法则通过这些设施而被权威地制定和公布,权威地解释和适用,并被强制实施。① 因此,权利的一个具体体现(instantiation)可能包含两个成分——在人类中则将包含这两个成分:有一套法则限定每个人的外在自由的界域,并有制度性设施让这套法则生效。

其次,康德把权利和一个完全的(complete)条件集联系在一起,也是在暗示排斥一切多余的限制。这个条件集不仅必须具有包罗性,以便它所包含的条件合在一起是充分的,而且必须具有唯一性,以致对维持互相稳当的

从一个行为主体所仔细考虑过的准则中建构出普遍法则:使一个人想要给自己的那个允许成为普遍的,即,把它扩展到所有的人。参看我的"绝对命令"['The Categorical Imperative', 在 *Grundlegung zur Metaphysik der Sitten. Ein kooperativer Kommentar*, O. Höffe, ed. (Frankfurt: Vittorio Klostermann, 1989), 172—193;重印于 *Critical Essays on Kant's Groundwork of the Metaphysics of Morals*, P. Guyer, ed. (Totowa: Rowman and Littlefield, 1998)]。

① 康德建议,这些有效性条件不受关于人的经验知识的影响:"不管一个人会把人想象得多么秉性优良,遵纪守法,以下这点仍然先验地存在于对这样一个(非法制的)状态的理性观念中:在一个公共的、由法律支配的状态已被建立起来之前,个别的人、人民和国家绝不可能稳当地不受到相互的暴力侵犯,这是由于每个人都有自己的权利(right)完全不考虑他人的意见来做他自己看来是正确的和善的行为"("权利论",6:312;6—12)。我不那么确信,康德能够先验地排除这个可能性:有一类人可能自发地集中于某个单一的规则体系,继而不需要任何进一步的激励就能遵循这些规则。尽管如此,我并不质疑与此相反的这个要点:无法先验地排除这个可能性,即人们可能做不到自发地集中于某个单一的规则体系,继而不需要任何进一步的激励就能遵循这些规则。因此,不可能把康德的"全部条件"化约为仅仅是纯理论性地存在着的一套普遍法则——这套法则若被所有人正确地遵循,就会保障互相的一致性。

外在自由各界域来说,没有一个限制是不必要的。权利排斥任何对如此的互相稳当性没有贡献的限制,从而包含着(用现今的行话来说)一个是帕雷托高效率的外在自由之分配。① 康德在他经典的权利定义的前一段话中相当清楚地表明了这个限定。他说,"权利这个概念……仅仅涉及一个人对另一个人的外在的、实际上是实践的关系,只要他们的行动(actions)——作为[可归于其的]行为(deeds)——能够彼此影响"("权利论",6:230:7—11),而不关心人们的内部状态,诸如他们的愿望,需要,或者目的("权利论",6:230:11—19)。这种情形很可能值得欲求,即人们的行为与他们自己的以及他人的愿望、需要和目的应该相协调。但对康德而言,这是伦理而不是权利所关心的——权利涉及且仅仅涉及互相稳当的外在自由各界域的前提条件。权利解决行为之间的可能的冲突问题,而不理会可能发生在行为、愿望、需要和目的中的所有其他冲突。②

---

① 这句话只是说,这样一些多余的限制不是权利的组成部分;这并不意味着它们与权利(Recht)是不一致的,或者是"不正当的(unrecht)"——尽管,正如我们将看到的,康德倾向于从一个主张滑向另一个。

② 这里,值得纠正康德在这个语境中倾向于犯的三个相互关联的错误。第一个错误是,他倾向于把刚才所阐释的他的权利定义的推论 A 联系于主张 B,即内部状态不可能被作为外在立法的对象。(他在"权利论"正文的开篇就写道,它将关系到"有可能对其进行外在立法的那些法则"——"权利论",6:229:5—6,同时参看"导论",6:220:12—13。)主张 B 超出了权利的定义,而且实际上是错误的。因为显然不是不可能公布一些法则来要求或者禁止特定的内部状态,例如为自己确立某个目标(意向)。同样也不是不可能精确而有效地运用这样的法则——实际上,大多数现存的法律体系在界定罪行(例如谋杀)和分配惩罚时有赖于对故意犯罪意图(mens rea)的裁决。关于这样的外在法则,康德理应不说它们是不可能的,而说它们无所贡献于维持稳当的外在自由各界域,从而不是那些条件中的一部分,即在其下每个人的自由能够与其他所有人的自由按照一条普遍的自由法则共存的条件。这样的法则——其中当然包括支配行为主体对准则进行内部选择的绝对命令——落在康德所界定的权利之外。对权利而言必要的仅仅是人们对法则的外向性服从,是他们的行为的合法性,而不是内部服从,不是道德性。

康德的第二个错误在于混淆了两个论点:一个定义性论点(definitional point),关系到权利所必需的法定限制的内容,以及另一个类似的论点,关系到蕴含在这样一些限制中的标准。前一个论点 A 是,权利的任何一个具体体现所必需的法则都不会约束人们的内部状态。这个论点是正确的。后一个论点 C 是,这样一套法则将仅仅按照外部标准来约束人们的外在行为。这个主张是错误的,这可以通过一个例子容易地看出来。要避免在使用外在对象方面发生冲突,可以借助一套法则来确保每一个对象至多只有一个所有人。但也可以借助另一套法则来避免这样的冲突,这套法则收入了常见的例我对康德的经典定义的阐释把"权利"本质上等同于"Rechtszustand",而后者应该被译作"法制的状态(juridical state)"或"法制的状态(juridical condition)"。① 正如康德在这里界定的,权利不是一个这样的规则体系:如果所有人都正确地遵循这些规则,那就根本没有哪个人的行为会妨碍另一个人的行为。相反,权利是这样一个世界的特性:这个世界中的人们有能力妨碍彼此的行为——或者有能力约束彼此的外在自由。权利在这个世界中得以体现,当且仅当这个世界以这样的方式来组织——人们的外在自由按照一条普遍的法则受到一定程度的约束,以使每个人的受约束的外在自由都是稳当的。权利在人们共存于这样一个有效的法定秩序(legal order)时得到体现:这个秩序限定并维护互相稳当的外在自由各界域。对权利的这个阐释有力地证实了我上面的推测,即必须在弱的意义上解读"普遍的"。即便没有法则之下的平等,一个完全且有效的法定秩序也体现权利或一个法制的状态。这样一个状态所要求的全部东西就是一套持续有效的公共法律,这套法律以可预知的方式约束每个人的自由,从而也可预知地限定每个

外——比如,有些例外允许我使用你的船而禁止你妨碍我使用你的船,如果我们有某些内部状态的话(打个比方,我们都相信另有某个人落水了,而我需要这只船来救她,并且我也打算这样做)。这些法则在例外的情况下限制你使用你的船却反而允许我使用你的船,它们对一个权利体现做了必要的贡献——其必要性不亚于更直接的、仅仅限制我使用你的船的法则对另一个权利体现所做的贡献。一套法则若把内部状态当作标准来使用,它并不因此而超出权利被授之权,即维持互相稳当的外在自由各界域。

有时候,康德把我刚才区分开的两个论点,A 和 C,都混同于第四个论点 D。根据 D,必须唯一地只按照维持互相稳当的外在自由各界域这一目标,来选择法定限制(和制度性设施),以使它们符合权利被授之权。(我们选择一个财产制度而不选择另一个财产制度,其理由必须不能是因为后者会让穷人挨饿——除非这样的饥饿会导致穷人起来造反,从而使人们的外在自由界域不再那么安全。)这个主张 D 区别于别的主张,而且像 B 和 C 一样,不是从权利定义中推论出来的。

① 正如康德通过拉丁文"status iuridicus"所暗示的("论通常的说法",8:292:33;"论永久和平",8:383:13)。康德能够恰当地在德文中使用形容词"rechtlich"和"gesetzlich",只要这两个词分别被理解为"体现权利(Recht)"和"受法律支配"。"正当的"、"依法的"或"合法的"之类的译法是有误解的,因为一个法制的状态很有可能(根据自然法)是不公正的;而且,由于按照制定法它是合法性的组成部分,它本身就不能是依法的,或者合法的。(参看"论永久和平"8:373 注释 30—31 中对"rechtlich"和"rechtmäßig"的比较。)

人的受约束的外在自由并使其稳当。①

如果这就是权利之所是，那么什么是权利论（*Rechtslehre*）呢？这不是一个微不足道的问题，因为"-lehre"这个德文后缀有一种颇具意味的含糊性。在一种意义上，这个后缀表示一个智力学科或研究领域。例如，这种用法出现在"Arzneimittellehre（药物理论）"一词中——该词表示对医药疗法的研究，或药理学。若在这种意义上理解，*Rechtslehre*——或者带有定冠词的 the *Rechtslehre*——将表示对权利（*Recht*）的建立和维持加以思考的一门智力学科，也就是对建立和维持人们之间互相稳当的外在自由各界域进行深思熟虑的这门智力学科。可以认为这个研究领域包括两个分支：经验的权利论——对我们实际地致力于建立和维持权利的历史经验进行反思；哲学的权利论——更抽象地思考权利是否能够、是否应该以及怎样才能、应该如何被建立起来和维持下去。显然，康德的工作会在后面这个哲学的权利论分支内进行。

在另一种意义上，后缀"-lehre"表示某个研究领域内的一个特殊的理论、学说或方法。例如，这种用法出现在短语"Mendelsche Vererbungslehre（门德尔遗传学）"中——这个生物理论对动植物的特征向后代的遗传作出特殊的预测。② 若在这种意义上理解，现在带有不定冠词的 a *Rechtslehre* 将表示一个特殊的权利理论；一个哲学的——或者像康德也许会说的，形而上学的（"权利论"，6:284:9）——权利论则将表示探讨权利是否能够、是否应该以及怎样才能、应该如何被建立起来和维持下去的一个特殊理论。从这里开始，我将在后面这种意义上使用权利论一词，以代替"康德的自由主

---

① 如果对康德的定义的这种阐释是正确的，那么在这个定义中使用的"权利"就既不等于"法律"，也不等于"（社会的）正义"。当法律不完善或者没有效力时，存在着缺乏权利的法律。而当法律完善且有效时，则有可能存在着缺乏正义的权利，例如一个权利对不同的人施加大相迥异的约束。当然，这不是要否认康德也在普通的意义上使用"权利"一词，即表示一个社会的一套法则——当然，康德也在一个更加普通的意义上使用这个词，即"（一个……的）权利"。

② 格雷戈尔·约翰·门德尔（Gregor Johann Mendel，1822—1884）是澳大利亚的一位植物学家。

义"(也以区别于"权利论"的文本)。

　　康德承认这种模糊性,但并不重视它——他强调在每一个研究领域内只能有一个真的理论("导论",6:207:11—29),因此也只能有一个哲学的权利理论,从而对权利的研究应该理想地适合那个唯一真的权利理论的研究和改进。尽管如此,突出区别仍然是有价值的,因为它提供了一个有益的观点来审视康德的事业。我们将能把"权利论"分析为两个主要部分。第一个部分包括康德的权利定义和他对这个定义的分析,这样的分析产生凡是从这个定义中分析地引得出的命题。第二个部分包括康德为了表明权利以及权利的某些体现是可能且可欲的而援引的所有实质性要素。正是这第二个部分,似乎最有理由被疑为以康德的哲学世界观的其他部分为先决条件。

三、康德的权利的普遍原则(§C)

　　在 A、B 两节中阐释过权利和权利论这两个概念后,没有任何过渡,康德就继续阐述他所称的权利的普遍原则。他没有清楚地说明这条原则的经典内容应该是什么,但有两个表达式似乎与此有关。其中一个看上去像定义,在本节的第一段以引文的形式给出;另一个看上去则像命令,在第四段中给出,并被特意地指为权利的普遍法则。第一个表达式是:

　　a) 任何一个行为是正当的[recht],如果它,或者依据其准则(maxim)
　　　　每个人的选择自由,能够与人人的自由按照一条普遍的法则共存
　　　　("权利论",6:230:29—31)。

　　这句话意在为行为的正当性(rightness)规定一个充分且必要的条件,这一点表现在紧接着的下一句话中。下面这个句子推论说,某些行为因为"不能按照普遍的法则共存于自由"("权利论",6:231:1—2),所以犯了一个错误(Unrecht)。

　　第二个表达式要求:

b) 你在外部要这样行动,以使对你的选择的自由使用能够与人人的自由按照一条普遍的法则共存("权利论",6:231:10—12)。

既然康德没有为这两个表达式中的任何一个提出论证,既然至少第二个表达式看起来像绝对命令的一个直接变体或直接运用,这就使人能容易地推定康德在此以他已在《道德形而上学基础》和《实践理性批判》中发展成熟的道德哲学为先决条件。然而,C节的结尾必须被认为是极不利于这个推定的。康德在那里写道,他的原则在第二个表达式中"根本不指望,更不会要求,我自己应当仅仅为了这个义务的缘故而把我的自由限于那些条件;相反,理性只说我的自由在其理念中确实限于那些条件,而且还可以被他人强迫地[tätlich]限于那些条件"("权利论",6:231:13—17;参看 6:231:3—9)。这样,看来好像是对我提出的一条命令,结果是对我的同伴们说出的一个允许——他们可以强迫我在外部这样行动,以使对我的选择的自由使用能够与人人的自由按照一条普遍的法则共存。而且这个允许当然相当一般地存在,而不只关系到我自己:人们可以强迫任何一个人在外部这样行动,以使对他/她的选择的自由使用能够与人人的自由按照一条普遍的法则共存。

有人也许会想,就算第二个表达式的确是一个允许而不是一个命令,它却仍是一个道德的主张,那么推测起来,对它的辩护也就依赖康德的道德哲学。不过,另有一个可选的解释比这可信得多,那个解释为所谈论的允许找的支持并不来自康德哲学整体的其他部分,而来自紧承的上文中对权利的讨论,从而不把这个允许理解为道德的,而理解为法律的。我们在上一节看到,康德把权利定义为有能力妨碍彼此行动的人们所构成的一个世界的特性。现在,康德用这个定义来界定外在行为的特性。这两个特性的相互关系将显示为复杂的,我过一会儿再来处理它。但是,下面这个事实很有说服力地暗示着,这样的相互关系确实存在:权利定义和我们眼前的这两个表达式共享一个主干——"能够按照一条普遍的法则共存……"。① 我于是推

---

① 这一条件的各种表达式相互有别,但区别并不大。我将回到这一点。

测,康德认为行为要么符合、要么不符合权利,而权利,正如我们已经看到的,是人们所构成的一个世界的特定组织方式。那就让我们说,行为满足还是不满足"能够按照一条普遍的法则共存……"这个表达式,决定了它们符合还是不符合权利。C 节的两个表达式现在可以简述如下:

(1a) 任何一个行为,如果它符合权利,它就是正当的,否则就是不正当的。

(2a) 你要在外部这样行动,以使你的行动符合权利(即,是正当的)。

我们已经看到,康德把第二个表达式解读为相等于一个允许:

(2b) 人们可以强迫任何一个人正当地行动,或者:人们可以妨碍不正当的行动。

把"可以"解读为一个法律上的允许,这个想法现在说白了就是把有关人们可以做什么的命题解读为相等于有关他们做什么在(1a)的意义上是正当的命题。这样一个置换把(2b)转变成了

(2c) 强迫一个人正当地行动,这是正当的(即,妨碍不正当的行动,这绝不是不正当的)。

那么,依据对文本的这一重构,(1)结果是适用于行为的一个"正当"(和"不正当")定义;(2)结果是一条定理,它关系到妨碍行为的行为是正当的还是不正当的——这条定理将在 D 节得到验证。[①]

我们还须解释"符合权利"这个谓项。正如可预料的,康德在定义中,也就是在(1)中,给出了最复杂也最精细的阐释。这个阐释包含一个选言。这可能暗示,康德此处是在向人们提供一个选择——在正当地行动的两种不同方式之间进行选择。[②] 但我认为更有说服力的是把他理解为在区分两种

---

① 正是这条定理,康德在"美德论"的导言中称它是"权利论的最高原则",且是一个"分析命题"("美德论",6:396:2, 10—11)。

② Sam Kerstein 指出,这里的"或者"也可以被理解为解释性的。他补充说,尽管很难看出它所连接的两个短语如何可能相互等价,它们却由于自身的含糊性而无法排除这个等价的可能性。三个论点我都承认,但我仍然发现我在文中提出的解释比另外两个选择更有说服力。

情形,暗指:一个行动符合权利这句话的含义,依权利是否在此行为发生的情境中得到体现而定其不同。所以,我提议对(1)作如下翻译:

(1b) 在权利得以体现时,一个行动是正当的,当且仅当它能够与人人的自由按照一条普遍的法则共存(我们必须假定这条法则就是包括在现行的权利体现内的那条普遍法则)。在权利未得体现时,一个行动是正当的,当且仅当依据其准则,每个人的选择自由能够与人人的自由按照一条普遍的法则共存。

那么,这个定义的基本思想就如下。在权利得以体现时(情形一),一个行动若符合现行的法则,就是正当的,否则就是不正当的。这里,行动符合权利,当且仅当它们遵守现行的法则。而在权利未得体现时(情形二),一个行动是正当的,当且仅当它的准则与可能的普遍法则相一致。这里,行动符合权利,当且仅当它们预见(anticipate)到一个可能的权利体现并对其法则遵守在前。

情形二至少在两个方面是有疑难的。第一个问题是,如果在我上文所提倡的那个弱的意义上解读"普遍的"这个词,那么事情看起来就会是:在权利未得体现时,任何(或者几乎任何)行为都可能是法律上允许的——只要行为者的准则预见到权利的某个体现并使行为对其法则遵守在前,而不管那个体现不平等到多么荒唐的地步。① 情形二的第二个问题是,康德聚焦于行为者准则的做法是古怪的,因为他甚至就在这一节中("权利论",6:231:3—5)也如此坚决地强调内部状态的不相干性。他看来并不想容纳这

---

① 这个问题也许看似构成一个理由来认为,至少在这里,"普遍的"一词应该在强的意义上被解读,从而(1b)中设想的互相一致的外在自由各界域必须是平等的界域。我有两个理由反驳这样的解读。首先,"普遍的"这个词在(1)中只出现了一次,同时指涉情形一和情形二。然而,对情形一,康德须要让"普遍的"有其弱的意义,因为他认为不服从任何现存的权利体现都是法律上不允许的,而不管这个体现有没有提供法则之下的平等(参看下面第 26 页的注释②)。其次,如果毕竟有可能的话,我想避免这样的结论:所有人平等的法律地位被偷带了进来,同时,康德回避而非回答了这个问题——为什么预见到一个非平等主义的权利体现并对其法则遵守在前的一个行动,应该算作法律上不正当的(算作不符合权利)。关于这个论题,我在下面将有更多的话要说。

个可能性:某个给定的行为在法律上是正当的还是不正当的,取决于做这个行为时所依据的准则。如果我们严肃地看待康德的这个坚持,①那么我们似乎不得不说,在权利未得体现时,一个行为是正当的,当且仅当它可能(could)按照这样一条准则被做——依据这条准则,每个人的选择自由能够与人人的自由按照一条普遍的法则共存。

这两个问题的一个共同要素是,在权利未得体现时,为法律上正当的行为设置的最低限度结果可能低得令人难以置信。缓解这个困难的一条途径是,对行为怎样才算预见到一个可能的权利体现并对其法则遵守在前加强要求——依如下思路。在权利未得体现时,我的行为是正当的,当且仅当有一个权利体现,(A)它是能实行的,而且我的行为与它一致(若在它之下,将是合法的),并且(B)它能被实际地达到,而且我的行为有助于(或者至少不妨碍)它的实现。也就是说,必须有可能把我的行为理解成出自这样一些准则:这些准则有心于 *exeundum e statu naturali*[必须摆脱自然状态]。有可靠的证据表明,康德实际上的确持有这个观点,并认为目标导向的要素(B)包含在表达式(1)中。在第42节,他写道:"在不可避免的密切相处中,你必须和其他所有人一起摆脱自然状态,向一个法制的状态转变"("权利论",6:307:9—11)。② 他随即说,"这样做的理由能够从权利概念中分析地推演出来"("权利论",6:307:12—13);并且,在阐释这个理由时,他把一个人必须摆脱自然状态和其他人被允许胁迫他这样做看成一回事("权利论",6:307:24;参看《沉思集》,7735,19:503:28—30)。因此康德显然认为,不与他人合作以导向权利的建立,这是法律上不允许的(因为只有那些其行为是法律上不允许的人,才是法律上允许的胁迫的对象)。

让我们整理一下已有的论述。我已经努力表明,康德把他的权利论的核心设想为独立于他的哲学的其他部分。为了生动地理解这个独立性主张

---

① 如果我们容许我们自己来纠正康德的"第二个错误"(详见上面的注释15),那么我们就不需要严肃地看待康德的这个坚持。

② 同时参看"权利论",6:343:23—25,6:350:6—8;以及"论永久和平",8:349 注释16—24。

的意味,我们可以把康德的权利论设想成一个游戏,不过,这样做在以下范围内容易令人误解:游戏通常是有局限的,比如局限在棋盘或足球场内,而这个游戏涵盖了人们可能在外部做的一切事情。康德的权利论游戏受规则的支配,这些规则是二元的,它们无一疏漏地把人们可能做的所有行为分作正当的(recht)行为和不正当的(unrecht)行为,或在等价的意义上把它们分作法律上允许的举措(moves)和法律上不允许的举措。关于这个游戏的一条重要定理是,胁迫性举措是被允许的(正当的),当且仅当它们所妨碍的任何举措都是不被允许的(不正当的)。① 两个条件都是从康德的权利定义中推导出来的:不可能允许妨碍一个被允许的举措,因为在任何一个权利体现下,所有被允许的选择都是互相一致的("能够共存")。也不可能不允许妨碍一个不被允许的举措,因为任何这样的限制都将是多余的;权利排斥任何对维持互相稳当的外在自由各界域没有贡献的条件。② 这不是一条无关紧要的定理——在我所知道的伦理观中,包括康德的在内,没有一个使得对任何及一切不正当行为的妨碍都被允许——康德似乎也非常乐意看到能从如此微小的一个基础推导出如此重要的一个结果。

---

① 有必要更加细致地表述这一点。一个举措是不被允许的(不符合权利),这个事实必然意味着妨碍这个举措是被允许的——但未必意味着任何人都可以妨碍这个举措。因为有可能,如果许多人都试图妨碍一个不被允许的举措,那么这些潜在的妨碍者就会彼此妨碍。因此,一个法定秩序可能必须通过进一步的规则来限制对使用胁迫的许可,或者把这个许可限于特定的官员。

此外,一个举措是被允许的,这个事实并不意味着,使它变为不被允许必然是不被允许的。下面的情况可能是被允许的:任意某个人去占有某块尚未被占有的土地或空间,结果他人移入这块土地或空间的举措就变得不被允许,而妨碍他人那类举措则变得被允许。

② 康德在 D 节非常简练地推衍了这条定理("权利论",6:231)。有人也许会评论说,从康德的权利概念推出允许使用胁迫来遏制不被允许的行为,在这个情况下确实是比较简单明确的:如果这种胁迫意在防止越界行为(在一个人进入另一个人的界域的道路上设障),或是终止一个越界行为(把一个人从另一个人的界域中驱逐出去)。在另一种情况下则比较难于把二者这样联系起来——此时,胁迫要因一个已经完全成为历史的越界行为而惩罚一个现在乖乖地待在她自己的界域内的人。这里,有人也许会试图辩解:这样的惩罚是被允许的,因为它必然地伴生于先前被允许的一个意在遏制却没能成功的努力。

权利论游戏这个隐喻背后的基本理念很简单。玩这个游戏,就是倾向于偏爱(prefer)法律上允许的行为甚于法律上不允许的行为。给定康德的定理,这个偏爱将普及开来:我们持有这个偏爱的事实将给知情的他人一个理由去培养同样的偏爱,因为他们知道,我们不被允许地妨碍他们被允许的行为,其可能性要小于我们被允许地妨碍他们不被允许的行为。当这些游戏者的倾向巩固起来时,当更多的人被吸引到游戏中来时,互相稳当的(受约束的)外在自由各界域也就出现了。

从 C 节着手,我已在这个部分草拟了一个游戏的基本原理——我谈到它的规范,还谈到它可能会如何进展。正如已经显示的,这个游戏以如下方式关联到康德的权利定义。如果所有人的行为单单包括法律上允许的(正当的)举措,那么权利——互相稳当的外在自由各界域——就会被建立起来和维持下去。尽管如此,描述这样一个游戏——有原则地把一切外在行为都分作法律上允许的和法律上不允许的——似乎仍将是一个无意义的练习。对这个练习之要义的探寻把我们带到了康德权利论的第二个、同时也是实质性的一个部分。①

虽然我们可以把权利的普遍原则看作其核心,康德的权利论却在两个相互联系的方向上超越了这个核心。一方面,它的目的是为这条原则提供一个辩护——试图给人们一个理由以参与权利论游戏来追求权利的体现。诚然,如果我们知道他人都在提供合作,那么我们中的每个人可能也都有理由把游戏进行下去;但是我们,我们所有人作为一个群体,为什么应该玩这个游戏? 游戏的规范固然把某些行为选择界定为被允许的,而把其余的界定为不被允许的,以此指示我们玩这个游戏,但这个单纯的事实无法回答我们的问题。我们还需要一个理由来重视这些规范。另一方面,康德也打算超越能从他的权利的普遍原则中推导出来的东西,以加强这些规范。他打算这样来细述权利论游戏,以使它不仅显示出偏爱权利之得以体现(偏爱法制状态甚于自然状态),而且显示出偏爱一个特定的权利体现方式甚于其他

---

① 上文第二部分的结尾引进了这两个部分。

所有可供选择的方式。这里的第二个计划以第一个为先决条件,因为康德加强规范的试图中至少有一部分是诉诸权利论游戏的要义而得到辩护的。我将在最后两部分讨论这两个计划。

四、权利的要义(the point)

康德认为,人们有理由想望参与权利论游戏,因为他们先前就有一个想望(interest)要使人们的——至少某些人的——外在自由面迎着他人的妨碍行动有稳当性。在权利未得体现时,人们行动的试图很可能受到各种不可预料的方式的妨碍;他们会时常由于这样一些妨碍而无法完成他们想做的行为,也会时常由于害怕受到这样的妨碍而甚至不敢试图去做他们想做的行为。在权利得以体现时,人们的行为选择被约束于对他们的外在自由的稳固限制。然而,这些约束是有规律的,可预知的,为每个人划出了一个界限分明而又不受他人行动妨碍的选择域。人们的某些选择在一个有效的法定秩序的防护下有了稳当性,他们的其余选择则由法律的禁令强加了新的障碍;但是,人们的外在自由因前者而获得的增进要远远大于它因后者而遭受的减损。因此,总的来说,人们趋于从一个法制状态的存在得益。① 既然权利论游戏趋于建立和维持一个法制状态,那么,对于想望使自己和/或他人的外在自由面迎着妨碍行动而有稳当性的那些人们来说,参与这个游戏就是有意义的。

我相信,按文本来看几乎无疑,康德认为互相稳当的外在自由各界域的要义在于:其所使得可能的外在自由的增进。② 不过,他看上去竭力要把法

---

① 有一种做法可以大大地强化这个推理,即详细地说明:权利的建立如何同时会产生许多新的行为选择,例如新的社会实践或新的技术,而它们在缺乏一个有效的法定秩序的情况下是绝不会出现的。

② "自由(独立于另一个人的胁迫性选择),只要它能够与其他每个人的自由按照一条普遍的自由法则共存,是每个人凭其人性就被赋予的这个唯一的原初权利"("权利论",6:237:29—32)。"外在的权利(Recht)这个概念完全导源于人们在彼此的外部关系中的自由这一概念,而与所有人天性具有的目的(幸福的目标)毫无干系"("论通常的说法",8:289:29—33)。注意,把避免人与人之间的冲突断言为基本的原理,这不会解释康德为什么从权利中排除掉我先前称为是多余的限制。

制状态的优越性(就外在自由而言)表现为先验可知的。① 相比之下,我在上一段草草勾出的论证听起来则是相当经验的;那是因为我无法构想出一个有说服力的先验论证。例如,我们无法先验地知道:人们能够多么严重地妨碍彼此的行动;在缺乏一个有效的法定秩序时,他们的选择自由会怎样地不稳当;这样一个秩序所强加的规则会有多大的约束力;它又会保护它所允许的选择自由到如何稳当的程度。我们也无法先验地排除这种情况:能力和脆弱性在人们中间的分配极不均匀,从而各人对赞成与反对游戏的理由的权衡互不相同。如果不把这样一些经验性的复杂情况考虑进来,就无法支持康德的结论,即,想望外在自由的人们有理由参与权利论游戏。

但要得出这个结论,还蕴涵着更多的困难。只要人们想望一组他们珍视的、广泛且稳定而又免受他人行为妨碍的选择,参与权利论游戏就是有辩护的。但很难接着看出,人们为什么不也会有一个想望来扩大他们的选择域,并保护这个选择域免受其他类型的阻碍和威胁。因此,康德必须要么表明人们没有这个进一步的想望,要么表明这个进一步的想望并不提供一个这样的理由:它可能比人们愿意参与权利论游戏的理由(即,基于他们要使他们的外在自由面迎着他人的妨碍行动而有稳当性的这个想望)更重要。② 这个困难可以推广到其他可能被归于人们的想望,例如对幸福、知识、智慧、得救(salvation)和道德完善等的想望。对于任何一个这样的声称的想望,康德必须要么表明人们并不具有它,要么表明它不算提供了一个中肯的理由,要么表明它所提供的理由不对诸多理由之间的权衡造成何等重要的影响而竟至于推翻这个声言:把一切都考虑进来,人们还是有理由参与权利论

---

① 例如,再次参看"权利论"6:312:6—12 的那段话。
② 特别地,康德必须排除这样一个法定秩序被偏爱的可能:这个法定秩序,尽管它对人们的外在自由的约束超出了建立互相稳当的各界域所必需的程度,它却因为有助于(比如通过技术)消除自然的障碍和威胁或者产生更多的选择,而在总体上增进了人们的外在自由。康德看不见这个困难,因为他没有澄清他的外在自由概念,尤其没有讨论什么样的障碍和威胁要被看作减损了一个人的外在自由。康德于是没有明确地辩护就如此来论证:仿佛一个人要使自己的外在自由面迎着他人的妨碍行动有稳当性的这个想望真的穷尽了对外在自由的想望。既然已经强调过这个问题了,那么我从现在开始就要使用后面这个更加简洁的说法。

游戏。①

对这些进一步的困难,康德可能没有一个完全令人满意的答复。但我认为,他若要作出一个这样的答复,其核心思想将是:权利必须基于、且只能基于我们作为(交互影响的)行为主体必然具有的想望。只有把权利建立在这样的基础上,我们才能表明,使权利得到体现以及因此参与权利论游戏,是每个人和一切人的想望。只有被建立在这样的基础上,权利才能高于人们可能偶然归于自己和他人的那些潜在地构成挑战、导致分裂、且变化无常的想望。但是,对于康德依其选择自身行为的能力来定义的人们而言,唯一能说他们必然具有的想望就在于最充分地行使(exercise)这个能力,因此也在于这样一个选择域可被得到的程度:他们从中进行挑选的、范围广阔而且稳当的选择域。作为行为主体,我们要让我们的生活取决于我们自己的选择,而非他人通过胁迫强加给我们的选择。②

根据这样的重构,康德的形象是一个最卓越的独立不依的自由主义者。他不比罗尔斯设定更多的先决条件——以他的道德哲学和先验唯心论为先决条件;他其实反而需要更少的先决条件。他没有诉诸他那个社会的公共文化中流行的基本理念,也不坚持人们有特定的道德力量,并有相应的更高层次的想望来发展和行使这些力量;至于像他自己的社会那样的一个社会中的公民可能具有的种种善观念,他也不寻求确认实现它们所必需的通用手段;相反,他把权利的建立和维持单单建立在人们对外在自由的根本的先

---

① 从这段话我们可以看出,康德在政府问题和一个有效之法定秩序的问题上的立场非常接近于以赛亚·伯林辩护过的那个立场,却极端地有别于伯林归诸康德的东西:伯林说康德认为法律和政府应该着意于提升公民的积极自由或道德自律。对照以赛亚·伯林在《自由四论》中的"两个自由概念"一文['Two Concepts of Liberty', *Four Essays on Liberty* (Oxford: Oxford University Press, 1969)]和第 2 页注释②所援引的罗尔斯的话,来看这段例文:"但是,可悲哉,立法者竟想通过胁迫来造成一个以伦理目的为指归的政体! 因为他那样不仅会走到伦理[目的]的对立面,而且会让他的政治[目标]失去根基而变得岌岌可危"(《单纯理性限度内的宗教》,6:96:1—4)。

② 当然,这不是要给出一个令人满意的论证,而只想勾勒出康德本来可能会有理由认为可行的一个论证。特别是,并不清楚这个论证何以能够从能力推出想望,又何以能够把特殊的重要性赋予来自他人的妨碍。

验想望之上。①

可以把对权利的这个独立式论证嵌入不同的全面性观点。例如,可以把它嵌入一个康德式的道德观,即认为每个人都有责任向其他每个人提供切实的保证:因为我负有义务来帮助我周围那些人使他们的外在自由面迎着我自己的(以及他人的?)妨碍行动而有稳当性,所以我出于道德就必须贡献于权利的建立和维持。在另一个极端,也可以把它嵌入一个霍布斯式的审慎版本中:因为我的根本想望就是使我的外在自由面迎着他人的妨碍行动而有稳当性,所以我出于审慎就必须贡献于权利的建立和/或维持。在"论永久和平"的一段著名的话中(他在那里讨论权利的最佳体现),康德本人也强调后面这种嵌入的可行性:"现在,唯有共和的政体才完全适合人的权利。但它也是最难建立而又更加难于维持的一种政体,以致许多人宣称它只能在一个天使的国度里发挥作用"("论永久和平",8:366:1—4)。康德

---

① 在此,有人也许会说,康德的论证终究还是全面的,因为他断言人们实际具有的或者可能被归诸他们的其他所有的想望都无关紧要。这个指控在一个意义上是微不足道地真确的。但是,由于抹杀了政治的社会正义观念和全面的社会正义观念之间的区别,它也是自我挫败的:任何论证,如果希求诉诸人们的受社会制度影响的想望来辩护这些社会制度——社会制度还能通过什么别的途径得以辩护呢?——都要权衡数量不定的许许多多可能的想望之轻重。这个指控,如果它指责康德在本该进行抽象(abstracting)的地方进行了理想化(idealizing),那它就会变得更加重要。[关于抽象和理想化的这个区分,参看 Onora O'Neill, *Constructions of Reason* (Cambridge, MA: Cambridge University Press, 1989),第 11 章,和 *Towards Justice and Virtue* (Cambridge, MA: Cambridge University Press, 1996),第 2 章。] 与其假定其他一切想望都只有零权重,不如这样:康德理应根本不对这些想望的轻重权衡作出任何假定。但是,不清楚这样一个论证究竟何以可能支持任何实质性的结论:它遗留了一个悬而未决的问题,即,人们对诸如得救之类的想望无限地大于还是无限地小于他们对外在自由的想望(还是居于两个极端之间的某处)。然而,正如文中下一段所显示的,通过表明他的论证至少涵盖一个特定范围内的想望特性——虽然道德的人和自私的人的其他想望之间有矛盾,但是由于他们共有对自己的外在自由的一个强烈想望,他们能够集中于同一套社会安排——康德确实在某种程度上包容 O'Neill 的说法。这暗示了康德本来会有可能如何试图反驳这样一个指控:由于聚焦于人们对外在自由的想望,他接受了"不受妨碍的自我"这个理想[Michael Sandel, *Liberalism and the Limits of Justice* (Cambridge: Cambridge University Press, 1982)]。康德本来会能够争辩说:深切爱好社交的人们所具有的想望,正如那些粗犷憨厚的个人主义者所具有的想望一样,包含着对外在自由的一个基本想望。不过仍然有可能想象,对一些人来说,这个基本想望完全屈从于其他的想望,例如宗教想望。

继续写道,与此相反,即使极端自私的人们——聪明的恶人们——也会有理由建立和维持这样一个政体:

> 建立一个国家的问题……即便对于一个恶人群体,也是可以解决的(只要他们还有理智)。它是这样的:一群有理性的存在者,他们总体上为了保存自己而需要普遍的法则,但每个人私下里又倾向于使自己免于遵循此法则;他们必须这样地组织起来,并这样来安排他们的政体,以至于他们的私密态度尽管[彼此]反对,却仍以某种方式相互制约,从而这些存在者在公开行为中表现得就像他们根本没有这样的邪恶态度。("论永久和平",8:236:15—23)

我相信这段话清楚地显示,康德想独立于他的道德观来论证权利及其在共和政体中的体现。他的道德观确实很可能为其追随者提供道德的理由来支持权利,并且尤其支持一个共和政体。但它并不因此而对权利来说有特殊的地位,因为正如引文所示,下面这种情况同样真确:自私也为其不道德的追随者们提供了自私的理由来支持权利,并且尤其支持一个共和政体。

这个结论似乎与康德哲学的核心逆行:如果所有人参与权利论游戏都是基于审慎的动机,那就没有人会出于义务或者为了真正的道德原则来玩这个游戏,从而可以推测,即使权利普及开来,人类生活在这个地球上也不会有什么价值。[①] 但这并不构成理由来惋叹这个事实:权利和一个共和政体能够不需要道德动机就得到实现。恰恰相反!这个事实让建立和维持一个开明的法制状态变得更加容易,那个法制的状态接着又大大地有助于发展我们的道德气质。[②]

[①] 这里,我显然是暗指康德的一句名言:"一旦正义消失,人类生活在地球上就不再有任何价值"("权利论",6:332:1—3)。

[②] 若没有这个事实,人类很可能早已陷入了第二十二条军规的两难境地:一方面为了发展有效的道德动机而需要一个法制状态的稳当性,另一方面又需要有效的道德动机来向法制状态转变。

这个结论似乎也与《道德形而上学》"导论"的基本结构迎面相撞——"权利论"当然是那个结构中不可或缺的一部分。在"权利论"之前的导论中（"权利论"有自己的导言），此外也在别处，康德强调整部作品的统一性，声称他在为权利和伦理提供一个系统的解说——一个从权利和伦理在人类自由和绝对命令中的共同根基出发来发展它们的解说（参看"导论"，6：207，6：214，6：215：16—23，6：221—222，6：225—226）："规则论［包括"权利论"和"美德论"］的最高原则因而就是：按照一条也能够是有效的普遍法则这样的准则来行动"（"导论"，6：226：1—2）。

然而，我的结论实际上并没有受到这些段落的威胁。的确，康德不仅寻求确立他的权利论与他的哲学的其余部分的一致性，而且寻求确立它作为唯一一个在道德观中有坚固基础的权利论的独特地位。就此他意在表明，接受他的道德哲学也就必须接受他的权利论。但从这一点不能推出他还意图表明：接受他的权利论也就必须接受他的道德哲学。我们应该谨慎地避免这个错误的推论，从而也应该注意区分这两种支持方向——如果我们简单地用"依赖"或"独立"之类的术语来框定论题，我们就容易混淆这个区分。

沃尔夫冈·克斯廷（Wolfgang Kersting）对他所称的独立性论题［Unabhängigkeitsthese］的批判——他把这个论题归于尤利乌斯·埃宾豪斯（Julius Ebbinghaus），克劳斯·赖希（Klaus Reich）和格奥尔格·盖斯曼（Georg Geismann）——因为没能作出这个区分而失效了。① 克斯廷正确地把这个论题解释为断言"权利论彻底独立于先验唯心论和批判的道德哲学"。② 然而，在下一页，他谈到"一边的先验唯心论和批判的道德哲学与另

---

① Wolfgang Kersting, *Wohlgeordnete Freiheit* (Berlin: Walter de Gruyter, 1984), 37—42（下文引为 WF）。"独立性论题"的最重要的提倡者是尤利乌斯·埃宾豪斯，此人曾在许多论文中（相当好争论地）辩护过这个论题，这些论文收在他的 *Gesammelte Schriften* 第二卷 *Philosophie der Freiheit* (Bonn: Bouvier, 1988) 中，下文引为 *PdF*。克斯廷也援引了克劳斯·赖希的 *Kant and Rousseau* (Tübingen: Mohr-Siebeck, 1936)，第 17 页，以及格奥尔格·盖斯曼的 *Ethik und Herrschaftsordnung* (Tübingen: Mohr-Siebeck, 1974)，第 56 页（从第 55 页一直到第 88 页都与这个论题有关）。

② WF 第 37 页。

一边的权利论之间[sic]的独立"①;随即,为了推翻这个论题,他指出康德诉诸道德观念来辩护权利,反诘道:"如果权利论不关心自然的因果性究竟是不是人类的宿命,那么把权利当作一个道德形而上学的部分来发展又有什么意义呢?"②如果康德承诺于他的权利论和道德观之间的相互独立,那么这样做确实没有意义。但是,独立性论题不作这个断言。所以,我们能够容易地回答克斯廷的问题:康德把他的权利论作为一个道德形而上学的部分来发展是有意义的,因为他想表明它受到道德观的支持,是唯一一个契合他的道德哲学的权利论。通过表明道德形而上学让权利论成为必需,康德仅仅确立了道德形而上学对权利论的单方面依赖;他证实了权利论的失败必将导致道德形而上学的失败,道德形而上学脱离了权利论就站不住脚。而这当然不意味着权利论依赖道德形而上学(脱离了道德形而上学就站不住脚)。③

即使在做过这番澄清之后,也依旧留有一些次要的文本障碍。因此克斯廷正确地指出,康德在用感性的和智性的这些术语来区分物理上的占有

---

① *WF* 第 38 页。
② 同上。
③ 克斯廷在不同的表现形式下多次犯了这个混淆错误。另一个有趣的例子出现在一个长长的脚注中(*WF* 第 41 页注释 63),那个脚注针对埃宾豪斯提出了一个看似毁灭性的反驳。克斯廷首先引用了埃宾豪斯的一个承认:"作为确定外在自由的先验法则的权利,是作为纯粹实践理性的法则的绝对命令要求必须存在的"(*PdF* 第 242 页;克斯廷是从其他资料转引这篇论文的)。克斯廷接着引述:"试图把权利按其客观的完美性设想为依赖于内部自由的立法,从而依赖于伦理的立法,这从康德的观点来看是一个完全荒唐的论断……这个论断来自这一错误的解释:两个立法都把绝对命令作为既涵盖权利又涵盖伦理的最高道德原则来依赖于它"(*PdF* 第 243 页)。既然克斯廷把绝对命令要求权利必须存在的断言与权利依赖于绝对命令的断言相混淆,他于是就从这些引文中推论出:埃宾豪斯不得不把一个荒唐的观点归诸康德,即绝对命令也独立于康德的自由理论和自律理论。但是,还有一种更有说服力的方式来解读埃宾豪斯:在第一段话中,埃宾豪斯说绝对命令要求权利必须存在;在第二段话中,埃宾豪斯否认权利依赖于绝对命令。不同于克斯廷的理解,埃宾豪斯在那里并不是说,两个立法对绝对命令的依赖确实存在,只是已经被曲解了。毋宁说,埃宾豪斯因其错误而反对的是这个解释:以为两个立法(而不单是伦理的立法)都依赖于绝对命令。克斯廷不能够理解对埃宾豪斯的这种解读,因为他不能够理解,埃宾豪斯在说绝对命令要求权利必须存在(使权利成为必要)时,并没有在任何意义上承认了权利对绝对命令的依赖。

和法律上的占有时"使用了他的理论哲学的要素"。① 但是我估计,在必要时,这个区分可以不求助于康德的理论哲学就做出,而且实际上早在康德撰著以前就已经这样做了。从康德要把他的权利论表述为他的整个哲学的一个不可缺少的组成部分这个渴望,推不出他并不也想要让这个权利论独立不依:能被独立地表述出来。这两种表述模式是相容的,所以康德也就没有必要在它们之间作选择。

五、权利的微调(fine-tuning)

在权利未得体现时,人们有法律上的义务来合作于它的建立。考虑到权利的体现有巨多的可能性,这样的合作就涉及一个庞大的协调问题。人们必须协调来定下单一的一套描述,法律规则要按这套描述的一般类属来把特别的行为表征列为其中某类;人们必须协调来定下固定规则和生成性规则之间的分工,②并最终定下特别而完全的一套这样的固定规则和生成性规则。③ 权利论游戏若想有效地引导人们去满足他们的假定的对外在自由的想望,它就必定不仅包含对权利本身的偏爱,而且必须包含对许多可能的权利体现的偏爱所作的一个排序。对我的解释来说,这是一个重要的要点。因为看来很有可能,对外在自由的想望太不确定,以至于无法辩护对诸多可供选择的权利体现进行截然分清的排序。但这个外表是虚假的,因为辩护可以间接进行:我们对外在自由的想望辩护了一个主导性偏爱,即偏爱权利的体现甚于权利的不体现,而实现这个主导性偏爱又必须有一些足以解决协调问题的二阶偏爱。

---

① WF 第 38 页注释 57。
② 我用生成性规则表示这样一些规则:它们允许人们自愿地改变规则。例如,有些规则支配单方面的占有、契约的订立和政治决策。康德在"权利论"6:237:18—23 中简要地提到了这个区分。
③ 一套规则是完全的,当且仅当它独一无二地把所有可能的行为都分作合法的(legal)与不合法的(illegal)。我理所当然地认为,这些规则还必须满足权利的普遍原则——例如,任何行为,如果对它的妨碍是非法的,那么它就必须被算作合法的。

康德提议的二阶偏爱常常显得是相当任意的和特定的,①但如果我们把它们置于这样一个两段式辩护中,它们就变得不那么难以理喻了。那么,康德并没有从事于按照推理来把可能的规则分作正确的(correct)和不正确的(incorrect)。毋宁说,他把规则评价为更适于或者更不适于解决一个明摆着不得不解决的协调问题。既然一个权利论的任务让他感到迫切地需要设计一个突出的(salient)解决方案来引导权利的建立,他就并不觉得可以奢侈地把自己局限于寻找理性上有说服力的方案。如果无法找到任何理性上有说服力的方案,那么最突出的那个方案就得发挥作用,即便它在康德眼里只不过比与它竞争的方案更突出一些而已。

这些二阶偏爱应该占据什么样的法律地位,这是显而易见的。在权利未得体现时,这些偏爱的法律相干性就在于判定:谁正合作于建立一个有效的法定秩序,而谁没有。尽管胁迫后者是法律上允许的,胁迫前者却是法律上不允许的。在权利得以体现时,二阶偏爱不具有法律上的相干性。法律允许最高统治者维持一个劣等的权利体现,而不允许公民妨碍最高统治者那样做的努力。显然,这是康德实际上维护的立场。② 这里还有空间来至少简要地讨论一下康德的权利论中最重要的二阶偏爱——它的广泛地被持有并高于其他偏爱的、对人们之间的平等的偏爱。对于用克斯廷和罗尔斯的精神来解读康德的那些人来说,对平等的这个偏爱也许看似为他们配备了一个可以向这样一些人发动的最有力的挑战:这些人(诸如埃宾豪斯和我

---

① 一个恰当的范例就是他所偏爱的支持单方面占有土地的那些规则:"……仿佛土壤在说:如果你不能保护我,那么你也不能命令我"("权利论",6:265:4—5)。因此,对国家来说,他们在陆地上的大炮能射多远,他们就拥有多广阔的渔业领海和大陆架("权利论",6:265:5—10)。

② 例如,他一而再,再而三地坚持,臣民违抗最高统治者或被其所授权的代表是不正当的("权利论",6:320—323,6:371—372;"论通常的说法",8:299—305;"论永久和平",8:382;《沉思集》,7989,19:574—575;《沉思集》,8051,19:594)。值得强调的是,康德并未宣称违抗一个反复无常的暴君是不正当的,因为那样的暴君既不规定也不维护互相稳当的外在自由各界域(Rechtssicherheit)。但康德没有说清楚,对权力的一种使用必须怎样受法则支配才算是在建立一个法制的状态。他也没有解释,对想望自己的外在自由的人们来说,反复无常的压制和以法则为准绳的压制之间的区别为什么有如此大的重要性。

本人）眼里的康德认为他的权利论能够独立自持，而不依靠他的道德哲学和先验唯心论。出乎意外的是，据我所知尚未有人提出过这个挑战。

这个挑战可能如此进行。康德的权利论在权利得以体现时对最高权力者的指示，以及它在权利未得体现时对所有人的指示，都表明它偏爱平等的外在自由各界域；这些平等的界域最终要在一个共和政体的宪法下得到稳当性，那个宪法规定人人必须有平等的机会来参与政治，从而也必须有平等的民众统治权（popular sovereignty）。不难构想，对平等的这个偏爱可以怎样在康德道德哲学的基础上得到支持：如果一个人要求应得的外在自由和参与政治之机会超出了能够赋予其他一切人与此同等的自由和机会这个可能性，那么就是道德上不正当的。① 现在，如果独立性论题是正确的，那么康德就有必要为他的平等主义偏爱提出另一个辩护——仅仅诉诸人们对他们的外在自由的想望，而不诉诸任何可普遍化的原则。可是，文本中没有出现这样的辩护。当然依旧可以坚持，康德确实意在他的权利论能被独立地表述出来；但是这个坚持只能以如下代价来做到：指责康德偷偷摸摸地引进了平等主义偏爱——不是通过在"普遍的"一词上含糊其辞，就是通过非法地诉诸道德观而又假装没有这样做。既然独立性论题要求这样一个严厉的指责，那就应该放弃它，转而接受克斯廷所维护、罗尔斯所假定的那种更宽宏的解释。

我不能肯定我能否充分地回应这个挑战，但下面这些要点也许是个得体的开端。首先，让我特别提到：如果不得不指责康德通过模棱两可地使用"普遍的"一词进行了偷带式操作，我不会认为那是一个重大的不幸，因为就我所能见到的而言，康德在重要的第 2 节中恰恰不可否认地卷入了这个偷带式操作（"权利论"，6：246—247）。他在那里为"实践理性的法律公设"给出了两个表达式，却明显地没有注意到二者的差别。一个表达式提出，如果禁止所有的人使用一个可用的对象（"权利论"，6：246：10—17，参看 6：252：

---

① 充实这样一个梗概要困难得多，二手文献中的无数尝试已经证实了这一点。但是，让我在此就为了论证的缘故这样假定：康德有一个有希望成立的此类论证。

13—15,6:301:9—10),那将违反权利的普遍原则——将构成"外在自由的自相矛盾"("权利论",6:246:24—25)。① 另一个表达式则断言,每个人都被平等地允许,而且按照同样的原初占有(original appropriation)的条件去获得未被占有的对象("权利论",6:247:1—6)。显然,后面这个要求比前面那个更强,因为它不仅要求每一个可用的对象都必须能被某(些)人得到,而且要求每一个这样的对象都必须能被任何人以平等的条件(也就是按时间定先后)得到。只要偷带式操作这个指责(至少在涉及这段话时)是真确的,它就必须被算为不利于康德本人,同时,它如果对我的解释的可信性有任何影响的话,那它有利于我的解释。

虽如此,若能做到下面这一点,则将更加美妙:重新建构我理解到康德所致力的那项事业,以表明它是成功的,或者至少是有希望的。其实我相信,相比于康德为更具体的解决方案("二阶偏爱")提出的许多颇弱的论证——尤其是"权利论"的"第一部分:私有权"中提出的那些论证——从突出性的角度来辩护平等主义偏爱并非希望更小。康德事实上表述了一个这种类型的论证:

"任何牵涉到另一些人的权利(right)的行动,若其准则不相容于公开性,就是不正当的(unrecht)。"

这条原则应该被认为不仅仅是一条伦理的原则(属于美德论),而且也应该被认为是一条法律的原则(关系到人的权利)。因为,一条准则,如果我不可能公开地宣布它而不因此挫败我自己的意图,如果若要它成功就必须绝对地保密,如果我不可能公开地承认它而不因此不可避免地激怒所有的人来反对我的计划——那么,只是由于它威胁到一切人的那种不正义,这条准则才导致了所有人对我的这种必然且普遍的、从而也是先验的可预见的反对。("论永久和平",8:381:24—35)

---

① 这样一条普遍的禁令会是一个多余的限制的典范——这样的限制对维持互相稳当的外在自由各界域毫无贡献。

按我的理解,这段话进一步阐释了我们为建立和维持权利而合作的这个法律义务。人们的行为要想在法律上被允许,就必须预见到一个实际上可行也可达到的有效的法定秩序并对它遵守在前,而且有助于它的实现。一个行为,如果一旦完全公开就会激起广泛的反对,那么它就没能通过这个检验,从而就是法律上不允许的。一个行为,若预见一个不平等的法定秩序,则属于一种特殊的情形:这样一个行为一旦完全公开就会招致广泛的反对,而建立这样一个不平等的法定秩序的企图也会招致广泛的反对,因此是不现实的。

不过,只有当人们在力量和能力上大致相等时,这个论证才有效。否则的话,不现实的反倒是在法则之下确立人人平等的企图,因为这个交易提供给弱者和没有能力可靠地遵循规则之人的成本—收益比,与它提供给强者和有能力者的相比,更远为有利于前者。一个法定秩序,要想寻求广泛的支持,要想在有理性地追求自身利益的人们(或者聪明的恶人们)中间维持一种持久的均衡,就必须更加平等地分配对参与这个秩序的激励,必须使这个秩序为参与它的人们所提供的益处与他们的参与成本以及对它的贡献大致上成比例。这样一个秩序,如果它要支配想把他们自己的外在自由的稳当性和深广度增到最大限度的理性的人们,那么它就必须把更大的外在自由界域分配给强者和有能力者。这些想法导向如下的反驳:即便公开性论证确实不诉诸一个(道德的)可普遍化原则就证实了对平等的二阶偏爱,这里所偏爱的却是错的、非康德式的那种平等。

可是,这真的是对非康德式平等的偏爱吗?想想康德怎样把平等主义偏爱联系于他所一再地赞成的妇女的法定次等地位(例如,"论通常的说法",8:292:4,8:295:15;"权利论",6:314:29):

> 因此,如果有人问,法律是否违反了配偶的平等来这样说男人对女人的关系:他应该做你的主人(他的角色是发布命令,她的角色则是服从),那么[答案是],只要这种主人身份的唯一根据是男人在促进家庭共同利益的能力方面具有自然的优越性,就不能认为这违反了一对夫

妻的自然平等。("权利论",6:279:16—25)

这样,看来康德本人(至少在此处)拥护的这个平等主义偏爱相当类似于我概括的独立于道德观的论证而被证实的那种偏爱——令人沮丧的是,它却相当不同于我们本来指望从康德的道德观中推导出来的那种偏爱。于是,有理由信任我对康德的解释——康德认为权利论,包括它的二阶偏爱在内,能够成功地得到独立的表述。

我的解读在此也许又会被说成是不宽宏的,因为它让康德背负一个按我们现行的标准以及按康德本人(若被正确地理解)的标准都是在道德上令人讨厌的政治理论。我的回答是,虽然可能有一些更宽宏的误解,我的解读实际上却是我们可得到的最宽宏的解读。康德显然确实对妇女和较低等级的社会成员持有非平等主义的观点——这些观点出现得太频繁也表达得太分明,以至于不可能被当作笔误来打发掉。按照我的解读,这些观点可以根据康德的一个目标来被解释,并在某种程度上被原谅:这就是他要发展一个独立不依的自由主义的目标——康德很可能基于和罗尔斯同样的理由而认为这个目标具有道德的重要性。我认为这样解读是最宽宏的,尽管它把我导向了这个结论:康德要为一个自由主义作出明细的规定,这个自由主义是康德主义式的道德的人们和聪明的恶人们双方都能拥护的,但他的这个试图最终失败了。

(作者系美国哥伦比亚大学哲学系教授)

政治的概念与政治自由主义

● 谭 安 奎

通过分析理论界对政治自由主义的批评,我们可以发现,政治的概念这一问题处于政治自由主义的理论起点上,同时它也关涉到政治自由主义重叠共识的目标。一种指向规范性秩序的狭义政治概念可以为政治自由主义提供起点上的辩护,它也是政治自由主义所依赖的隐蔽的前提。一种超越既定规范的斗争性政治概念则使得政治自由主义可以容纳某些形式的临时协定,而且对于这种完备性自由主义从理论上造成了遮蔽的政治现象,政治自由主义具备潜在的解释力。在政治自由主义中,所谓正当之于善的优先性,只能是政治学说相对于完备性学说的优先性,而这也是政治中立性的基本精神所在。

罗尔斯从《正义论》转向《政治自由主义》,被许多人批评为一种实用主义的理论退却,亦即为了自由民主社会的稳定而走向传统诉求,并在理性多元论的背景下让政治哲学无涉于完备性的宗教、道德或形而上学学说,从而求得一种理性的重叠共识。

我们认为,对于稳定性的考虑其实在《正义论》中就已经存在,因而并不构成罗尔斯理论转向的充足根据。究其根源,罗尔斯的理论转向主要是基于两个方面的考虑,一是理论自身的融贯性及自由民主社会的稳定性。在《正义论》中,罗尔斯对原初状态作了康德式的解释:"原初状态可以被视为对康德的自主性与绝对命令的程序性解释。指导目的王国的原则是那些会在这一状态中被选择的原则,对这一境况的描述使我们能够解释在什么意义上按这些原则行动表达了我们作为自由而平等的理性人的本质。"①言下之意,原初状态代表着一种康德式的人的形而上学理想。但是,罗尔斯在理论界的批评下认识到,自由制度的实践必然带来多元论,这种关于人的形而上学学说不可能被人们普遍接受,因而人们认可作为公平的正义的动机就失去了保证。这样一来,《正义论》中的良序社会的设想就显得极不可靠,因为"由任何完备性学说——无论是宗教的还是世俗的——良好组织起来的自由民主社会肯定是一种贬义上的乌托邦。实现它无论如何都会要求国家权力的压制性运用"。②第二个方面的考虑是对自由民主社会及自由主义精神本质的新认识,这从他的如下判断中可以看出来:"政治自由主义为何没有在早得多的时候被创制出来,这是一个极大的疑惑:在政治生活中理性多元论的事实之下,它似乎是描述自由主义观念的一种如此自然的方式。"③虽然这一判断是否可靠是值得怀疑的(我们在后面将指出政治自由主义究竟在何种情况下才有可能),但它至少是我们不能简单地用"实用主义"来批评或拒斥政治自由主义的一个根据。

澄清罗尔斯理论转向的基本背景之后,本文的剩余部分试图以政治的概念为分析视角,并以价值多元论与道德判断的某些基本特性为基础,为政治自由主义作一个理论上的辩护,并提出对其某些核心立场的理解。为此,我们将会考察自由主义的政治概念、它在价值多元论的前提下所面临的困境以及理论家(主要是施米特)对自由主义政治概念的批评。在这一过程中,我们一方面去回答对政治自由主义的主要理论批评,并论证政治自由主义较之以传统的完备性自由主义对政治生活具有更大的解释力;另一方面我们也力图表明政治自由主义为此所必须作出的若干理论补充与调

---

① John Rawls, *A Theory of Justice*, Cambridge Mass: Harvard University Press, 1971, p. 256. 亦可参见中译本《正义论》,何怀宏等译,北京:中国社会科学出版社,1988年版,第247页。以下简称"中译本"。

② John Rawls, *Justice as Fairness: A Restatement*, ed. by Erin Kelly, Cambridge Mass: Harvard University Press, 2001, p. 187. 关于"多元论"这一概念及其在罗尔斯理论中的模糊之处,我们将在后文中予以澄清。

③ John Rawls, *Political Liberalism*, New York: Columbia University Press, 2nd, 1996, p. 374, note1.

整。

一、为什么以政治的概念为分析视角

政治自由主义的本意在于，鉴于西方自由民主社会中存在的理性多元论的事实，没有任何一种特殊的完备性学说可以为政治正义提供公共正当性证明的基础，因此需要走向一种正义的政治观念。它有三个特征，一是适用于特殊的主题，即社会的基本结构和根本正义问题；二是对它的接受不预设任何完备性的宗教、道德与形而上学学说；三是它以隐含于民主社会的政治文化传统中的某些直觉性政治观念为前提。政治自由主义试图在这个基础上建构起一套正义原则，这种原则在竞争性的善观念及支持它们的完备性学说之间保持中立，从而可以获得相互冲突但合乎理性的完备性学说的重叠共识的支持。罗尔斯曾明确地指出，理性多元论是自由民主社会中的一个恒久的事实，除非权力的压制性运用，民主社会中的公民不可能就一种完备性学说达成一致，因此才有了政治自由主义的必要。

《政治自由主义》问世以来，受到许多具有实质意义的理论批判。我们可以把这些批判作一个类型化的处理。第一类是起点上的，即政治自由主义一开始就对某些价值作出了一种规范性的承诺，从而它试图无涉于特定的善观念并达到政治中立性就是不可能的。确实，罗尔斯在谈到理性多元论时曾明确地认为，"只有国家权力的压制性运用才能维持对一种完备性的宗教、哲学或道德学说的持久的共同认可。"[①]他一再表示，对宽容的唯一替代就是国家权力的压制性运用。显然，这种观点与洛克当年为宗教宽容所作的辩护大不相同，它并不认为强制不能达到对某种信念的共同认同，相反却认为强制可以做到这一点。由此就带来一个问题：既然可以通过强制达到对一种完备性学说的共同接受，那么政治自由主义排除权力的压制性运用就成了一种有

[①] John Rawls, "The Domain of the Political and Overlapping Consensus", in his *Collected Papers*, ed. by Samuel Freeman, Cambridge Mass: Harvard University Press, 1999, p.474.

争议的价值承诺,而这与政治自由主义的基本精神可能是相悖的。比如,著名理论家拉兹在批评政治自由主义时就认为,"它承认基于共识的——也就是不过分诉诸暴力而获得的——社会统一和稳定是足够重要的有价值的目标,这使得它们成为一种面向我们社会的正义理论的基础,且仅靠它们就足够了。没有这种假定,就没有理由视这一理论为一种正义理论,而不是一种社会稳定理论"。① 拉兹以此作为根据之一,认为政治自由主义还是以某种真理诉求为基础的,而这是它的形而上学基础之所在。无独有偶,桑德尔也认为,"即使宽容有道德与政治上的重要性,对一种既定实践的宽容的论证必须把该实践的道德地位,还有避免社会冲突之善、让人们自己决定等等考虑在内"。② 这一批评显然指向了自由主义所倡导的正当之于善的优先性。而对正当的优先性的强调是政治自由主义的一个重要方面,所以如果这一批评是成立的,那么政治自由主义从起点上就违背了自己的追求。

相应地,我们可以把第二类批评视为目标上的,它指向重叠共识的可能性。之所以说这个问题是目标上的,是因为政治自由主义的最终目标就在于,它所建构的作为公平的正义,或其他相近的正义原则,必须成为各完备性学说之间重叠共识的焦点,而不是成为一种各方之间的临时协定。这也是稳定性的依靠之一。但理论界似乎对在自由民主社会中形成这种重叠共识的可能性表示出极大的怀疑。如加尔斯通就尖锐地指出,政治自由主义以人们形成和修正自己的善观念的能力为基础,并将此视为最高的人类利益,重叠共识是建立在这一假定之上的。但是,"我怀疑,宗教原教旨主义者们是否会视形成和修正一种善观念的能力为一种善,更不用说是最高阶的人类利益。他们可能宣称,最好的人类生活要求一种获得外在善(上帝的真理)而不是为自己形成一种善观念的能力,并在一旦

---

① Joseph Raz, "Facing Diversity: The Case of Epistemic Abstinence", *Philosophy and Public Affairs*, Vol. 19, No. 1(Winter, 1990), p. 14.

② Michael J. Sandel, "Review of Political Liberalism", in *Liberalism: Critical Concepts in Political Theory*, Vol. III. ed. by G. W. Smith, New York: Routeledge, 2002, p. 481.

获得(received)那一真理后就牢牢抓住它而不是修正它"。① 同样顺着这种设想,有人认为,原教旨主义者只会把所谓的共识当作临时协定来接受。此时,政治自由主义要么承认自己的正义原则是一种临时协定,要么声称它所倡导的宽容原则是正当的(而这就意味着声称道德真理,从而是在从事形而上学),"没有中间性的'第三条道路'"。② 根据这种批判,与《正义论》一样,《政治自由主义》的重叠共识理想仍然是一个乌托邦,而且这个乌托邦设想因为放弃了对真理与形而上学的依靠而显得根本不像哲学,因为在这样的批评者看来,从事哲学无论如何是一种对真理的探索活动。

上述两个方面的批评可以说是指向了政治自由主义的首尾两端。把这两端联结起来的,正是一些与政治自由主义及其批评相关的重要的理论与方法问题,如诉诸自己的政治文化传统是否太过实用主义和保守、在没有形而上学的前提下是否可以从事政治哲学、正当是否可能优先于善等。当然,我们的这种分类更多地是为了论证的方便而作出的一个简化处理,因为连结这两端的问题本身也可以包含在这两端之中。但这并不影响实质的理论分析,因为这种区分只是形式的,它指向的是理论所涉及的范围而不是理论本身。

上述关于对政治自由主义批评的分类是为了为本文分析角度的选择提供一个基础。从第一类批评来看,政治自由主义在起点上有着某种规范性的价值承诺,这是无可争辩的事实。因此,问题就在于,作为公平的正义如果还要能够声称自己是政治的而不是形而上学的,就必须回答这样一个问题:这种规范性承诺是不是可以容纳在某种政治概念之中?众所周知,政治自由主义是建立在一定的道德基础之上的,其所追求的政治中立性也立基于某些道德原则。但仅仅靠这一点(姑且假定它是合理的)却不能消除理论上的疑虑,因为更为重要的是,如何保证政治自由主义据以为基础的

---

① William A. Galston, "Pluralism and Social Unity", *Ethics*, Vol. 99, No. 4 (Jul., 1989), p. 714.

② Jean Hampton, "Should Political Philosophy be Done Without Metaphysics?" *Ethics*, Vol. 99, No. 4 (Jul., 1989), p. 804.

道德不是一种完备性的道德学说的结果？即便像罗尔斯那样把自由、平等这些道德特征赋予公民而不是一般意义上的人，它也并不能说明自身就一定是政治的。因为我们完全可以追问：为什么政治一定与自由、平等的"公民"而不是与处于等级体系中的"臣民"相关呢？我们也可以设想，有些人出于某种道德理由而鼓吹一种所谓"自然的"等级制，并以此来指导政治安排。此时，如果这样的人指责民主政治本身是不道德的，那么政治自由主义与这种观点的争论就必然是一种道德争论，而且是完备性道德学说意义上的争论。政治自由主义显然不能回避或拒绝这样的辩论，因为作为一种正义理论，它不能不保证自己是合乎道德的。因此，作为公平的正义要保证自己是政治的，它必须追溯到政治的概念本身，看它能否容纳它据以为基础的规范性价值承诺。换言之，只有当罗尔斯能够认为，这些承诺是政治本身的题中应有之义，他才能保证作为公平的正义一开始就是政治的。虽然对于什么是政治，可能仍然存在分歧，但既然作为一个概念，它绝不能是个人主观臆断的产物，至少也应该是约定俗成的结果。如此看来，对某种政治概念的必要预设其实是处于政治自由主义的起点上的。这是我们选择以政治概念为分析角度的第一个理由。

但即使政治自由主义能够找到这样一个基点，这种政治概念也一定是规范性的，即它指向的是具有特定规范内容的社会秩序，而且它只能应对上面所说的起点上的批判，而对于目标上的批判，问题仍然没有解决。目标上的批评的关键在于，临时协定似乎是不可避免的，政治哲学及其正义原则应该追求真理，哪怕这种真理并不得到事实上的普遍承认。[①] 罗尔斯提出了一种理性标准，但他并没有否定在自由民主社会中非理性学说的存在，这似乎也为政治自由主义的批评者提供了一个关于重叠共识之不可能性

---

① 这里涉及对真理这一概念的理解。在罗尔斯那里，作为公平的正义虽然符合理性的标准，是一种重叠共识的内容，但它不声称自己是一种真确的正义观念。原因在于，罗尔斯认为，"对许多人而言，真确的，或有良好宗教和形而上学根据的东西超越于理性的东西"(John Rawls, *Political Liberalism*, p. 153)。

的佐证。这实际上意味着人们对规范(包括政治自由主义可能依靠的那种政治概念中的规范,从而也就是这种政治概念本身)不可能达到共识。这就可能出现斗争,而不是规范性的竞争或合作。而我们知道,即使一种规范性的政治概念是可能的,把超越具体规范的斗争视为政治的本质,这也是一种极有影响的传统,它甚至也包含在人们的日常思维之中。因此,当有学者批评罗尔斯的政治哲学是以"消除政治理念"和"政治缺席"[①]为前提的时候,这一点也就毫不奇怪了。有学者认为,政治学的概念,包括政治这一概念本身,都属于"本质上聚讼纷纭的概念",因为"我们现在所能理解的普遍理性准则不足以明确地解决这些争论"。[②] 这样一来,作为公平的正义就可能堕入临时协定,从而失去自己的政治自由主义品格,而政治自由主义也就会尴尬地面对一种截然对立的政治概念。此时,对于政治自由主义是否可能、是否合理,就再次离不开对于政治概念的分析了。政治的概念与政治自由主义能否达到自己的目标直接相关,这是我们选择政治的概念作为分析视角的又一条理由。

我们已经初步提示了可能存在两类有着根本区别的政治概念,一种是作为规范性秩序的狭义政治概念(我们在此并不是在与描述性相对的意义上来谈论规范性,而是说某种政治概念指向的是一种社会秩序,而它自身就包含着某些规范性的价值承诺,因此我们有时会简单地称之为规范性政治概念。之所以说这种政治概念是狭义的,主要是因为任何政治秩序都会有自己的规范性标准作为其合法性的基础,但我们所说的这种政治概念中的规范性内容却具有特定的指向,这一点我们在具体谈论这一政治概念时会作出说明);另一种是超越既定规范的斗争性政治概念(它意味着处于政治关系中的双方没有共同认可的规范基础,他们无法共容于一种规

---

① Chantal Mouffe, *The Return of Political*, London: Verso, 1993, p.51.
② William E. Connolly, *The Terms of Political Discourse*, 2nd, Oxford: Martin Robertson & Company Ltd, 1983, p.225。作者使用了"essentially contestable concepts"与"essentially contested concepts"两种不同的表达,但含义没有差别。据作者自己说明,这一提法源于 W. B. Grallie 的同名论文。

范性秩序之下,因而进行斗争,并且这种斗争的性质不能简单地用任何一方所持的规范性标准来评价。我们在行文中有时会将其简称为斗争性政治概念)。下面我们需要一个必要的迂回,也就是说,我们不是直接提出这两种政治概念,而是从道德哲学的角度为这两种可能性甚至必然性提供一个基础。后文将会表明,除了两类政治概念之外,与政治自由主义相关的一些重要问题,如对政治文化传统的诉求、是否应当或可能不诉之于形而上学、正当的优先性、临时协定是否不可避免等,都直接或间接与此相关。

二、两种政治概念的基础:道德判断的内部性及其价值多元论的依据

如果存在一种普遍的道德而且它得到人们的普遍遵守,那么政治似乎不再有必要,这是乌托邦主义赖以确立的一个重要思想基础。似乎没有任何一种乌托邦思想是建立在人性恶的预设之上的。这也就意味着,这种道德不仅具有普遍的规范性,而且还有普遍的动机基础,它可以驱动每一个人按照它去行动,从而社会的基本秩序和正义可以以这种道德得到维持。

然而,正是在把规范性与驱动性统一起来这一问题上,道德理论,尤其是正义理论本身面临着迄今为止远没有解决的难题。一个传统的理论争论在于,如果认为主观动机、情感先于行为的正当性,那么道德规范的约束力就失去了保障;相反,如果认为行为的正当性独立于主体内在的情感和动机,那么驱动性就没有了基础。这一难题在休谟的学说中得到了典型的表达。根据休谟的怀疑论,行为的德不在对象的关系之上,而是依赖于人们的情感。在我能根据行为的美德或正当性而行动之前,我需要一种关于何种行为是有德的或正当的先在信息,而这显示了道德感的必要,它将使我们能择出使行为正当的美德动机。并且,道德感所要核准的动机必须是责任动机之外的动机。这给我们留下了难题:如果要保留是动机并行为在本质上正当这一论点,那么,它显然是对正当性的关切之外的动机;而另一方面,如果要保留美德行

为的首要动机是责任的动机,我们必须有一种方式去确认或界定不依赖于其动机的正当行为。

在休谟看来,"我们并没有遵守公道法则的任何真实的或普遍的动机,除了那种遵守的公道和功德自身以外;但是因为任何行为如不能起于某种独立的动机,就不能成为公道的或有功德的,所以这里就有一种明显的诡辩和循环推理。因此,我们除非承认,自然确立了一种诡辩,并使诡辩成为必然的和不可避免的,那么我们就必须承认,正义和非正义的感觉不是由自然得来的,而是人为地(虽然是必然地)由教育和人类的协议发生的"。① 休谟是通过人为性,即把正义当作人为美德来走出这一循环的,理论上的循环最终需要自然的力量来破除,道德的规范性与驱动性的统一是在人类生活实践的基础上达成的。

有人认为,康德的道德哲学通过分析一个"好人"的动机开始,在此基础上推演出可普遍化的道德原则,从而解决了这一难题。② 但这一结论似乎并不可靠,因为"好人"之"好"在这里已经是一个道德概念,它的基础又何在呢? 而且,康德的可普遍化推理是从"我"开始的,而正如威廉姆斯所指出的那样,实践慎思在任何情况下都是第一人称的,而且第一人称不能引申出或自然地代之以任何人,因此,不可能通过反思达到不偏倚的和平等的立场,也不能由此"获得正义的动机",③ 它仅仅能达到"如果我是你"④这样的视点。所以,康德的道德理论最终还是没有逃脱休谟所说的那种悖论。

休谟是从人类一般的角度得出结论的,因为在他那里,正义只是指一种作为人类的社会生活得以进行的基本道德条件,它用于补救由人

---

① 〔英〕休谟:《人性论》(下册),关文运译,北京:商务印书馆,1980年版,第523页。

② 参见 Christine M. Korsgaard, "Kant's Analysis of Obligation: The Argument of *Groundwork* 1", in *Kant's Groundwork of the Metaphysics of Morals*, ed. by Paul Guyer, Maryland: Rowman & Littlefield Publishers, Inc, 1998, pp.51—79。正是她在此文中将上述理论难题称作"休谟难题",并认为康德解决了这一难题。

③ Bernard Williams, *Ethics and the Limits of Philosophy*, Cambridge Mass: Harvard University Press, 1985, p.69.

④ ibid. p.61.

类心灵的某些性质和外界对象的情况结合起来所产生的不便。这就是他关于正义环境的著名论述,即人心的自私与有限的慷慨,外物的容易转移及相对匮乏。由于这种正义的环境乃是人类社会的一般处境,所以我们可以由此得出一种普遍主义的基本人类道德,这种道德的适用性不会受政治安排的差异性的影响。但是,从过去到现在,人类生活在不同的政治安排之下得以展开,因此在与具体政治制度相关联的意义上又存在不同的政治正义观念,尤其是关于分配正义的观念。那么根据上面的结论,这样的正义观念的具体规定性必然对于特定群体的特定实践具有极大的依赖性。只有这样才能保证这种正义观念的规范性要求与人们的主观动机大体上能够统一起来。在事关正义等人为美德的问题上,当我们说一个人应当做某事的时候,我们实际上暗示着这个人可以为我们所持有的相关道德考虑所驱动,而这种动机显然与特定群体的教育与其他实践传统有关(由于休谟反对原始契约理论,因此他所说的协议也只能从生活实践与习俗的角度去理解)。这种"某人应当做某事"的判断被哈曼称为"内部判断",它有两个特征:"首先,它们意味着行动者有能够驱动他的理由去做某件事情。其次,说话者(即判断者——引者注)认可并设想听众也认可那些理由。"①对道德判断的这种理解意味着,就人为美德尤其是政治正义而言,有些群体中的人们可能会处于我们的内部判断之外,他们不能为我们的道德考虑所驱动去做我们认为应当做的事情。当然,对于这样的内部判断,我们不能将其理解为行动者在每一个具体的行动中都实际上为那种道德考虑所驱动,但至少经过反思之后,他可以做到这一点。比如,两个同样做了某件被认为是道德上错误的事情的人,如果一个人经过反思或在别人的指责下感到内疚,那么我们就可以对他进行"内部判断"。此外,有两个问题需要进一步强调,一是

---

① Gilbert Harman, "Moral Relativism Defended", *Philosophical Review*, LXXXIV(1975), p. 11。他将这一观点视为道德相对主义,但我们将以价值多元论为之提供一个基础,而价值多元论却是承认客观价值的。关于价值多元论与价值的客观性之间的关联,下文中将会提到的伯林的观点可以向我们表明这一点。

哈曼所说的内部判断指向所有关于"应当"的判断,而我们在此更具体地将其指向政治正义尤其是分配正义的情况;二是,哈曼所说的内部判断主要是一种严格的逻辑论点,①而我们在此则用群体在实践中形成的道德的规范性与驱动性的统一来为这种逻辑形式注入实质的内容。

但即使在一个地域性的群体之内,仍然可能存在着亚群体或个人处于占主导地位的内部判断之外的情况。因此我们所说的内部性显然不能理解为一个单纯的地域概念,它更多的是一个与道德心理相关的概念。在同一种政治生活形式之下,可能会有积极的政治反对派,这一点本身就是一个最好的证明。这同样是为什么政治自由主义的批评者有时会搬出原教旨主义来做例证的原因所在,而且罗尔斯在设定理性多元论的事实时,也并没有否认非理性学说在自由民主社会的存在,只是他对这一点所可能带来的理论冲击没有足够重视。认识到这一点对于我们讨论重叠共识的问题具有重要的意义。

道德判断的这种内部性完全是一种历史的与主观的偶然吗?我们认为,这种情况之所以出现,是有其客观的价值基础的,这种基础就是价值多元论。根据伯林的经典解释,多元论的含义在于,"存在诸多客观且的、终极的价值,其中一些价值与其他的价值互不相容,它们由不同时代的不同社会所持有,或由同一社会的不同群体,由整体的阶级或教会或种族,或由它们内部的特殊个体所持有,其中的任何一种都可能发现自己处于不能结合,然而却具有同等终极性和客观性的目的的冲突性要求之中。"②根据多元论的本质,不同的价值是不可通约的,而且没有任何可靠的理由在不同的选择之间作权威性的价值排序,因为它们具有同等的终极性和客观性,这正是多元论不同于相对主义之处。我们由此可以看到,价

---

① 哈曼认为,正如评价某东西很"大"只有相对于某类可供比较大小的族类才有意义一样,从逻辑上讲,说某人做某事是错误的,这种评价也只有相对于某种隐含的协议或共同的理解才有意义,道德的相对性正是这样体现出来的。因此他把其相对主义称为一种严格的逻辑论点。

② Isaiah Berlin, *The Crooked Timber of Humanity*, ed. by Henry Hardy, New York: Alfred A. Knope, Inc, 1991, pp. 79—80.

值多元论所说的价值的客观性，乃是关乎价值的本性，而不是指向人们所持有的具体的价值观念或善观念，因为后者恰恰被认为是因人而异的，因而具有较大的主观性。根据价值多元论，我们可以说，价值观念与善观念的主观性与多样性正是不同的个人、群体在诸多客观价值之间进行选择和排序的结果。多元论的事实导致我们必须面对选择，而且是悲剧性的选择，因为正如伯林自己所说，一件东西是什么就是什么：自由就是自由，不是平等、公平、正义，不是文化，也不是人类的幸福或平静的良心，它们之间是不可通约的。而且群体与个人都是价值的主体，都是价值的选择者与承载者。显然，这里所说的价值多元论与罗尔斯的理性多元论是不同的，因为价值多元论是一种关于价值的本质与根源的形而上学学说，而理性多元论只是自由民主社会中人们持有相互冲突的善观念及完备性学说的一个事实。一个价值一元论者，只要他是理性的，他仍然可以被政治自由主义所包容。虽然理性多元论之所以出现，可能是因为有价值多元论这一客观基础，但罗尔斯的政治自由主义只需、也只能停留于理性多元论的事实，而不能明确承认价值多元论，否则就会改变其政治自由主义的政治性质。①

任何一种道德规范都意味着对某些价值的追求，或对价值追求的约束，因此它必然包含着价值排序。虽然这种排序可能是把某种更少实质性的价值（如自主性）放在首位，但它既然作为一种价值，就必然与其他价值存在竞争。这样一来，任何一种道德规范在本质上都会与价值多元论之间出现内在的紧张，因此就可能出现这样一种情况：一个群体可能没有去做另一些群体认为应当做的事情的动力，同样，群体中的一些人也可能没有去做另一些人所认为应当做的事情的动力，但他们所追求的东西仍然可能具有客观价值。我们从这里可以看出，正如同价值多元论因为承认的是客观价

---

① 罗尔斯自己对这一问题比较模糊，这主要表现在他对伯林的多元论的某种程度的认可（参见 John Rawls, *Political Liberalism*, p. 303, note 19），另一位政治自由主义的倡导者则明确地认识到这一点，参见 Charles Larmore, *The Morals of Modernity*, Cambridge: Cambridge University Press, 1996, pp. 153—154。

值因而不是相对主义一样,我们所说的道德判断的内部性因为是以价值多元论为基础的,因而也不是与主观好恶相联系的那种相对主义。正因为任何道德"应当"都意味着不可能得到普遍同意的价值排序,因此也就没有任何一种道德尤其是政治道德可以保证让每一个人有主观动机去遵守。在我们所说的政治正义问题上,不同群体或群体中不同的人们可能会持有不同的"应当"标准。而如果一些人经过反思也仍然不去遵守我们所坚持的正义原则,我们该如何去评价他们?伯林提供了一种极具象征性的方案,他认为,除了生理特征之外,也有特定的道德特征同样深刻地进入了我们设想为人性的东西之中。如果我们碰到一个人,他看不到为什么他不应该为了减轻小手指头上的痛苦而破坏整个世界,或在刑及无辜、背叛朋友、折磨儿童的行为中看不到任何伤害,"那么我们发现,我们根本无法与这种人争论,因为我们感到惊骇,更因为我们认为他们在某种意义上是非人性的——我们称他们为道德白痴"。①

我们在此关心的首先不是伯林所举的具体事例,而是这种评价中所体现的一种道德思维的方式。显然,伯林之所以称之为道德白痴,我们可以理解为,这些人没有一种主观动机去做那些我们认为是"人性的"行为或去批判那些"非人性的"行为,他们根本不为这些道德考虑所动。根据道德判断的内部性这一本质,问题此时已超出了任何单一的道德体系所能容纳的范围,从一定意义上讲,它揭示了道德判断的极限与边界。我们由此可能进入到另一个领域,在这个领域中,道德诉求即使有意义,也完全掩盖了事物的本质。此时,对立的人们之间如果必须要建立某种统一的政治与法律秩序,他们由此将会面对的,可能只能是斗争,而且这种斗争的性质无法用道德判断来解释。这种斗争意味着没有共同认可的规范基础,而我们在后文中将会看到,这种斗争正好被自由主义的某些批评者视为真正的政治。伯林的问题在于,他此时仍然坚持一种道德化的思维并使用一种道德化的语言,这一点

---

① Isaiah Berlin, *The Crooked Timber of Humanity*, p. 204.

其实是传统自由主义思维方式的一个缩影。

到此为止,我们从道德判断的内部性及其价值多元论的根据中,可以初步引申出与本文主题相关的两点具有政治意义的结论:特定群体在自身之内基于道德共识确立一种规范性的政治概念是可能的;没有共同的规范基础、因而超越于特定道德评价的斗争性政治必然存在,而这意味着在自由民主社会中,最佳的稳定也难以排除某种妥协或临时协定。显然,这些结论对于政治自由主义而言,既有有利的一面,也有严峻的理论挑战。

三、作为规范性秩序的狭义政治概念、传统诉求与正义观念的政治性

我们在这一部分将表明,罗尔斯有一种可以依赖并且他自己也实际持有的规范性政治概念,政治自由主义凭此可以应对我们一开头所说的针对它的起点上的批判。而且,在道德判断的内部性与价值多元论的背景下,这种规范性的政治概念及其政治安排必须立基于文化传统之上,而一种自由主义正义原则可以在相对成熟的自由民主社会中只以其政治性质表现自身。

本来,从价值多元论的前提出发,我们只能得出韦伯那样的"诸神竞争"的结论。但正如我们上面所指出的,自由主义却又在自主性的基础上倡导一种普遍的道德,并认为人类社会的政治安排应该立于这种基本的道德原则,从而让政治受到这种道德的强有力的约束。从这个意义上讲,自由主义的政治概念是一种规范性的概念。

近代以来的主流政治观显然建立在公民之间的平等与自由之上,而如果仅仅从"什么是政治"这一角度来看,这种政治观其实在亚里士多德那里就可以找到源头。在亚里士多德看来,政治家不同于一般的家庭主人,"政治家所治理的人是自由人;主人所管辖的则为奴隶。家务管理由一个君主式的家长掌握,各家家长以君臣形式统率其附从的家属;至于政治家所执掌的则为平

等的自由人之间所付托的权威"。①亚里士多德显然并不认为人与人之间都是平等的,而且不平等本身乃是正当的。但是,在他看来,政治却只能是平等的自由人之间的事情。他无疑是肯定奴隶制的,但他所说的奴隶制乃是指向所谓"自然的奴隶",即没有理性的人,而有理性是成为公民的条件。一切通过单纯的强力压迫与剥夺所造成的奴隶制并不在亚里士多德所辩护的奴隶制之内。因此,他对政治的理解虽然极大地限制了政治主体的范围,但同时也为我们提供了一种规范性政治概念的典范。此外,他还反对柏拉图式的共产主义,反对在政治中进行压制性的单一化:"一个尽量趋向整体化(划一)的城邦最后一定不成其为一个城邦。城邦的本质就是许多分子的集合,倘使以'单一'为归趋,即它将先成为一个家庭,继而成为一个个人;就单一论,则显然家庭胜于城邦,个人又胜于家庭。这样的划一化既然就是城邦的本质的消亡,那么,即使这是可能的,我们也不应该求其实现。"②从亚氏的观点中可以看出,政治首先应当是平等的自由人之间的活动,其次,政治应该有对"多"的包容,即使达到"一"是可能的,也应包容"多",这至少可以理解为对暴力的排除。

这种政治观代表着西方的一种政治传统,它在共和主义思想中尤其显示出强大的活力,而这种传统的某些方面也体现在自由主义的政治观当中。区别首先在于,自由主义把它从一元论的假定之中解放出来,政治活动不再是公民个人完善与幸福的最重要的部分,也不是人的本质实现的最高形式。这种政治概念的主要的特点就是,解决人类社会秩序的方式是多种多样的,而政治只是其中的一种可能性,它是不依非法的暴力治理分化社会的一种方式。如此来理解的政治,其中是没有专制者的位置的。③ 这就是我们将这种政治概念说成是"作为规范性秩序的狭义政治概念"的原

---

① 〔古希腊〕亚里士多德:《政治学》,第 19 页;商务印书馆 1965 年版(下同)。
② 同上书,第 45 页。
③ 美国政治学者肯尼斯·米诺格在其《当代学术入门:政治学》中,以"政治中为什么没有专制者的位置"为第一章的标题,这就是一个典型的例证。该书由龚人译,沈阳:辽宁教育出版社,1998年版。

因,因为它一方面指向规范性秩序,同时,这种秩序的规范性标准却又是特定的(一种专制的政治社会显然也有自己的规范性标准作为其合法性基础)。这种解决社会秩序的方式在自由主义思想中既是政治的,显然也是道德的。在洛克那里,政治安排被看作是"自然法"的延伸和体现。而在密尔那里,尽量少的权威主义干预被视为可以最大限度地促进个人天赋和能力的发展。

在自由主义的政治观念中,政治制度的安排与政治活动的展开都是建立在道德的基础上的。在这个道德基础上,人们就社会正义问题是否经过妥协达成一种权宜之计,或是形成一种理性共识,这是一个更进一步的问题。妥协在自由民主社会也被视为是一种重要的政治美德,因为愿意妥协至少就意味着排除暴力的使用。

这种规范性的政治概念最典型地体现在康德的政治理论之中。他明确提出,"真正的政治不先向道德宣誓效忠,就会寸步难行"、"一切政治都必须在权利的面前屈膝",①而且这需要"道德的政治家"。②他因此甚至反对政治中的权宜之计,这从他在国际政治中反对均势理论可以看出来。在他眼中,均势"就好像斯威夫特的那所房子一样,它由一位建筑师根据全部的平衡定律建造得那么完美,以至于当只不过是一只麻雀栖息在那上面的时候,它马上就倒塌了"。③言下之意,只有政治纯粹变为道德的,它才是可靠的。

正因为自由主义的政治概念是一个高度道德化的概念,因此理论家才能够这样说:"自由国家的道德共识不是某种神秘地优先于或高于政治的东西:它是政治活动(文明化活动)自身。"④在这个意义上,政治就成了一个能够得到自我辩护的自主的领域:"政治伦理不是某种低级的伦理活动,而是一种自我包容并可以充分辩护的伦理生活层面。"⑤

---

① 〔德〕康德:《永久和平论》,载其《历史理性批判文集》,何兆武译,北京:商务印书馆,1990年版,第139页。
② 同上书,第132页。
③ 〔德〕康德:《论通常的说法:这在理论上可能是正确的,但在实践上是行不通的》,载其《历史理性批判文集》,第209页。"斯威夫特的房子"可能取材于小说,不详。
④ Bernard Crick: *In Defense of Politics*, 2nd, England: Penguin Books Ltd, 1982, p.24.
⑤ ibid. p.140.

在这里,辩护,或者正当性证明,意味着提供某种道德的理由和根据。因此,所谓政治的独立性与自主性,就不是在独立于或超越于道德的意义上而言的,它恰恰是建立在特定的道德基础上的。它的独立性与自主性恰恰源于它包含着某些道德原则于其中。据此,如果有某些个人或群体不同意这种政治,自由主义者们仍然会毫不犹豫地以对方"不道德"而拒斥他们。

现在我们可以说,政治自由主义有了应对起点上的批判的根据,因为不诉诸暴力、避免暴力冲突而达到社会统一与稳定,这本来是政治的题中应有之义,政治自由主义的这种规范性价值承诺并没有超出政治之外。在这里,政治可以简单地界定为自由而平等的公民之间的交往、合作与竞争。罗尔斯自己虽然从未直接讨论政治的概念,但他对正义概念却多有论述。正义概念主要用来说明正义观念的作用,其本质在于不在人们之间作任意区分,并在不同的利益要求之间作恰当的平衡。而在他看来,"正义概念的特色在于,它把每一个人当作平等的主权者来对待,仿佛本来如此,并要求从平等自由的特定原初状态而来的一致承认"。① 根据正义的概念,"国家被看作是公民的联合体,去规制他们对其最深刻的利益的追求和最严肃的义务的实现,按平等自由的原初状态中的每一个人可以接受的方式去型塑他们的关系"。② 其实,正义作为一个概念,本来有着更宽泛的包容性,它理当在不同的正义观念之间保持中立。但至少柏拉图式的或者法西斯式的正义观念与国家观念在此却被罗尔斯的正义概念排除了。可以说,对正义、国家的理解表明,在罗尔斯的理论中,他虽未言明但却自觉地处在一种规范性的政治概念传统之中,而这构成了其理论构思的一个隐蔽的前提。当他把其契约论建立在道德的基础之上时,他更加强化了其政治概念的规范性。

在特定的道德基础上,自由主义政治概念当然可以容纳影响权力格局的各种竞争。罗尔斯的政治自由主义极少涉及这些问题,但由于

---

① John Rawls, "Constitutional Liberty and the Concepts of Justice", in his *Collected Papers*, p. 94.
② ibid, p. 90.

它关涉的是社会基本结构与根本正义问题,因此对于作为公平的正义的定位,我们只能像罗尔斯自己所认为的那样,认为它表达了在有利的条件下"使民主得以可能的"的价值。① 也就是说,他所论述的东西还不能等同于民主政治本身,而只是它存在的条件。

在论证了罗尔斯可以凭借一种规范性政治概念来面对起点上的批评之后,我们接着需要讨论与此相关的几个问题。第一个问题是,一种规范性的政治概念是否离不开对文化传统的依赖,如果是,罗尔斯是否找到了这样一种可以依靠的传统?

自由主义政治是建立在对平等和自主性等价值的承诺之上的,而从多元论的立场来看,这种承诺本身虽然可以导致一种具有普遍规范力量的规则体系,尤其是个人的权利体系,但它是否能得到人们的普遍诚服,亦即是否能够具有普遍的驱动力量,则显然是难以设想的。另一些人完全可能诉之于其他"具有同等终极性和客观性的价值",并建立起不同的"应当"标准,以及相应的政治体系。诚如格雷所说,"价值多元论不能以任何一般的,更不用说普遍的方式使自由主义成为必需,或为之提供基础。特定社会中善观念或世界观的多样性的历史事实可能是在那一社会中采用自由主义制度的良好理由。但是,如果价值多元论是真确的,那么,真正人类幸福的形式的范围就会明显大于能被容纳于自由主义生活形式之内的东西。仅仅作为一个逻辑问题,我们就可以妥当地说,价值多元论并不能命定一种被视为一种声称普遍权威的理论或原则体系的自由主义"。②

虽然说自由主义不能从多元论的事实中推导出来,但是,"在相关的背景赞成宽容、个人自主性和文化多样性的地方,我们会有一种对自由主义的论证"。③ 因为可能有一些"产生理由的背景(reason-gen-

---

① John Rawls, *Political Liberalism*, p. 156.
② John Gray, *Enlightenment's Wake: Politics and Culture at the Close of the Modern Age*, London: Routledge, 1995. p. 133.
③ George Crowder, "From Value Pluralism to Liberalism", in *Liberalism: Critical Concepts in Political Theory*, Vol. IV, p. 51.

erating context)"提供了排列价值的理由,而且"这不会是个人生活的背景,而是一个特定社会或文明的生活、它的历史经验、地理与经济条件、文化承诺的背景",①在这样的情况下,自由主义的政治选择就与价值多元论相容。用我们上面的术语来讲,这种传统的存在就划定了一个"内部判断"的范围,在这个范围内,道德的规范性与驱动性能够得到统一。这说明,自由主义可以在特定的社会中体现为人们的群体认同的基础。从本文的分析角度来看,一种规范性的政治概念及相应的政治安排只能建立在某种传统的道德与价值共识之上。

政治自由主义的道德基础集中体现于"理性"标准,也就是说,理性多元论的事实之中本身就包含着规范性的因素。一种合乎理性的学说是一种能够以合乎理性的方式去肯定的学说,但什么是合乎理性的标准?罗尔斯有两种表达,一是"准备提出作为合作之公平条款的原则和标准,并在确信他人会遵守的情况下去自愿地遵守它们",②二是"能够基于所有人都能接受的条款与他人合作"。③这其中的道德内容是显而易见的。罗尔斯能把这种道德要求中的规范性与驱动性统一起来吗?

哲学家奥尼尔敏锐地看到,罗尔斯上述两种对理性标准的表达是不同的类型,第一个是动机型的,第二个是模态型的。模态是一个逻辑学术语,指事物或认识的必然性和可能性等这类性质。一种模态型的道德显然强调的是规范性的力量,如康德所理解的义务就是一种实践"必然性"。罗尔斯对理性的这两种表达其实正好显现出道德所要求的驱动性与规范性这两个因素,但他对二者如何协调和统一却并未直接说明。在奥尼尔看来,"罗尔斯的公共理性观念以其公民共享一种政治认同的自足而民主的社会观念为前提,这一事实解释了为何他不需太多地关注公共理性的动机观念与模态观念之间的鸿沟。在一个封闭的民主社会中,理性的公民只要有可能,确实会愿意寻求并遵守为着其根本生活安排的共享的原则和标准,这一点无甚惊奇。那或多或少正是作为一个民主

---

① ibid. p. 44.
② John Rawls, *Political Liberalism*, p. 49.
③ ibid. p. 50.

社会的公民的含义所在"。① 如果我们不设定理性的背景是一个民主的公民的封闭社会,对于以确信他人会同意我们提出的原则和标准为条件的理性观念,我们可能会有疑虑。从局外人的角度看,他人的同意可能被认为是反映了与他们的理性极为不同的问题。他人的拒绝同意可能被认为是反映了认同的多样性,或者真实利益之间的冲突,而不是他们不合乎理性。因此,我们可以说,罗尔斯通过把一种道德判断范围作明确的自我约束,从而为自由主义的规范性政治概念找到了它所需要的道德土壤。我们在前面已经看到,在价值多元论的背景下,对一种道德规范与生活方式的认同其实是需要一个共同体的实践与历史基础的。

至此,我们又可以说,罗尔斯诉诸民主社会的政治文化传统是可能的,因为在价值多元论的背景下,它可以构成道德上"内部判断"的基础。

第二个问题是,对传统的诉求怎样才能表明它只是政治的,而不是形而上学的。我们的上述论证仍然是关于道德与道德判断的本质的形而上学观点,而这是罗尔斯所不能依赖的。政治自由主义只能把理性多元论当作事实来接受,而且,理性作为一种有道德含义的规范性标准,它必须限于政治范围之内,而不是源于一种完备性道德学说,也并不声称自己体现了客观的道德秩序。因为后者并不是民主政治文化中所包含的共同直觉信念。罗尔斯明确地提到,"合乎理性(being reasonable)并不是一种认识论的观念(虽然它有认识论的因素)。毋宁说,它是民主的公民资格的政治理想的一部分,包含着公共理性的观念。这一理想的内容包含着理性的自由平等的公民在其理性的完备性观念方面能相互要求的东西"。② 简言之,理性是政治的,它涉及的是平等自由的公民之间可以相互要求的东西。而这一点可以在自由民主的政治文化中抽象出来,因此它不必依赖一种完备性的道德学说,也不必声称自己是一种真确的观念。

---

① Onora O'Neill, "Political Liberalism and Public Reason", *The Philosophical Review*, Vol. 106, No. 3(Jul., 1997), p. 421.

② John Rawls, *Political Liberalism*, p. 62.

在这里，对一种政治性的理性标准的基本共识在政治文化的基础上既是可能的，也是充分的。

我们可以进一步通过评估先前提到的罗尔斯的一个判断——政治自由主义应该在早得多的时候就被创制出来，以此来说明政治自由主义正义原则的政治性质。罗尔斯的这一判断其实是一种过于乐观的估计，而且可能导致其自身理论上的不融贯。因为政治自由主义的正义原则是建构起来的，当无知之幕被拉开的时候，它要保证正义原则成为重叠共识的焦点，就必须设定理性多元论，而不是一般的多元论。从上面对理性的分析可以看出，理性多元论是有道德含义的，而一般多元论却可能包含一些疯狂的、侵略性的学说于其中。[1] 建构起来的正义原则要成为重叠共识而不是临时协定，并以此保证社会的稳定性，它要求公民必须是充分自律的，而不是像原初状态中的各方那样，在被限制的信息条件之下只是从被代表者的利益最大化的合理性角度去选择。用罗尔斯的话来说就是，"虽然原初状态作为整体同时代表着两种道德能力，因此代表着充分的人的观念，但作为社会中人的合理自律的代表的各方则只代表合理的（道德能力）：各方同意那些他们相信对被代表者从其善观念和形成、修正与合理追求这一观念的能力——只要他们知道这些东西的话——来看是最好的原则。理性的（道德能力）或人的正义感的能力——在此即是尊重社会合作的公平条款的能力——则是由各方在原初状态中所服从的各种限制以及施于其同意的条件来代表的。当由各方采用的正义原则由社会中的公民肯定并依之而行动时，那么公民就是以充分的自律性在行动"。[2] 关键的区别在于，如果社会中只是一般多元论，原初状态中各方选择的原则并不会有什么不同，但此后公民们却不能形成相应的正义感去支

---

[1] 关于"理性多元论的事实"与"多元论的简单事实"之间的区分，可参见 Joshua Cohen, "Moral Pluralism and Political Consensus", in *The Idea of Democracy*, ed. by David Copp, Jean Hampton and John E. Roemer, Cambridge: Cambridge University Press, 1993, pp. 270—291. 他的这一区分启发了罗尔斯对理性多元论与一般多元论的区分。

[2] John Rawls, *Political Liberalism*, p. 305.

持这种原则。这对于政治自由主义来说无疑是不可取的。因此,对于理性标准的广泛接受,这是政治自由主义的一个前提。宗教战争结束后,各教派开始只是形成一种临时协定式的妥协,并没有对宽容达成道德上的共识,因此它还只是一种不稳定的状态。政治自由主义的批评者有时会提出美国南北战争前夕林肯与道格拉斯的争论,以此说明林肯在当时必须就奴隶制在道德上是错误的作出表态,因而政治自由主义在这里是不可能的。虽然政治自由主义是建立在道德基础之上的,但此时关于奴隶制的争论首先涉及的不是公民之间的问题,而是奴隶究竟算不算作"人"的问题,因此这种争论必然以一种完备性道德学说的方式表现出来。因此,我们可以认为,政治自由主义确实只能在相对成熟的自由主义社会中才有可能。在这种社会中,对奴隶制这样的问题早已在道德与政治中得到解决,自由主义才有可能只在政治的范围内运作。否则,南北战争的发生本身就足以说明政治自由主义所寻求的稳定性是建立在沙滩上的。政治自由主义是自由主义制度实践的一个成果,它没有能力为自由主义本身的优越性作任何辩护。

第三个问题是,基于政治文化传统的政治哲学必然是在政治与道德上保守的吗?也许有人会认为,这种把自由主义区域化、历史化与背景化的观点,可能体现了一种极端保守的道德观点与政治观点,它似乎使得特定群体对道德的反思不再可能,而且它似乎意味着"存在的即是合理的"这样一种判断。其实不然。首先,从传统内部来看,体现在人们的日常判断中的正义与道德观念可能是不连贯的,这就需要一种对它的提炼和组织。罗尔斯所说的反思平衡,做的正是这样一项工作。有人认为,反思平衡本身可能也是保守的,但罗尔斯认为,有两样东西防止了这种保守倾向,一是,一个人并不把人们所考虑的更特殊的判断,比如那些关于特殊行为和制度的判断当作穷尽了他们道德观念的相关信息,我们要试图发现人们如何将其调和成一个融贯的体系,因此,"在一般性的任何层次上都没有原则上可以免于修正的判断";二是,我们所要求的是宽泛的而不是狭隘的反思平衡,"我们探究的是,当人们有机会考虑其他可能的观念和评估它们的支持根据时,他们会承认并接受其后果的原则。把这一过程发挥到极至就是,一个人寻求的是观念或多元的观念,它们能经受对所有可行的观念和支持它们的理性论证的合理考量"。①

其次,即使我们持有上述区域化的观点,人们经过反思是否接受新的价值与价值观念,这个问题仍然是开放的。我们可以发现,如果新的价值与道德观念能够被原来的群体逐渐容纳,一个社会当然可以实现渐进式的变革。因此一种政治哲学本身也可以是批判性的,只要倡导者认为传统的观念应该得到批判和改进。但一个值得提出的事实是,对政治自由主义的批判一般还是建立在自由主义的基本价值之上的。此外,明显也有另一种情况,即新的价值与道德观念与原有观念势不两立,从而走向了暴力革命。这后一种现象恰好说明,两种道德观念的对立超出了道德范围,它们互相对对方的信奉者们没有说服力与驱动性,这种对立因而转向了下文将会谈到的政治性的斗争。

四、超越既定规范的斗争性政治概念、重叠共识与临时协定

上文中已简单提到,多元论本身并不必然逻辑地走向自由主义。我们似乎可以发现,一方面,多元论被认为是一个事实,但另一方面,任何一种规范性的要求,包括自由主义的普遍道德,都不能直接从多元论的事实中推导出来。这说明,规范性是不能够还原的,比如还原为认识论的问题。也正是因为它不能还原为对一种事实的认识,所以才会出现这样一种情况,即不同的规范性主张之间的冲突不可能有一个可以普遍接受的解决之道。这样,这种冲突就表现出绝对性的一面。这种绝对性使得当冲突出现时,一方以"不道德"作为理由批判对方显得不合时宜,因为道德判断的前提正是把对方看作"内部人"。我们从前面提到的伯林关于"道德白痴"的判断中可以看出,道德判断在这里走进了死胡同,它走到了自己的

---

① John Rawls, "The Independence of Moral Theory", in his *Collected Papers*, p. 289.

边界上。此时,如果停留于以"不道德"来批判对方,就会显得没有意义,更为重要的是,它没有把握住这种对立的本质。因此,自由主义道德化的政治概念确实回避了一个超道德的斗争领域,这正是施米特批评自由主义最甚的地方。之所以说自由主义遮蔽了超道德的斗争领域,首先正是从理论认识和思维方式上而言的。

虽然我们已经得出结论,认为在特定的历史背景下,人们可以构筑一个道德上的"内部判断"的范围,并在此基础上可以推演出一种作为规范性秩序的狭义政治概念及相应的政治安排,但是,既然承认了价值多元论的条件,我们就不能断言在一个群体内部,绝不会有"内部判断"不管用的情况。因为"内部判断"是一个观念性的分析工具,而不是一个简单的地域概念。因此在自由民主社会内部可能有原教旨主义者,这也不足为怪。此时,由于双方没有基本的道德共识,政治自由主义显然不可能实现其重叠共识的目标。这是不是否定政治自由主义的充分理由呢?

我们在下文中将通过分析施米特对自由主义的经典批判,来揭示自由主义的规范性政治概念及其所包含的道德化思维的缺失,然后论述政治自由主义较之以传统的完备性自由主义在应对这一批评上的理论优势,并尝试在政治自由主义的范围内对重叠共识与临时协定的关系作出新的定位。

与自由主义道德化的政治概念针锋相对,施米特提出了一种决断论的、以敌友划分为中心的政治概念。在他看来,自由主义的典型难题在于,它"试图站在经济学的立场上把敌人变成竞争对手,又从知识的角度把敌人变成论争对手。在经济学领域,没有敌人,只有竞争对手,在彻底的道德和伦理领域则或许只有论争对手"。[①] 我们前面曾提到,自由主义的规范性政治概念并不否认各种竞争,但之所以说是竞争,而不是敌我斗争,正在于有一种共同的道德基础。而施米特显然更关注没有道德共识的状态,用他自己的话来说,就是相对于规范状态的"非常状态"。非常状态的首要特征就是不受限制的权威,它意味着终止整个现有秩序。显然,在这种状态下,国家仍然

---

① 〔德〕卡尔·施米特:《政治的概念》,载其《政治的概念》,刘宗坤等译,上海:上海人民出版社,2003年版,第143页。

存在,而法律则黯然隐退。由于"法理学中的非常状态类似于神学中的奇迹",①从而,非常状态是与政治神学联系在一起的。他明确地讲道:"非常状态比规范状态更令人感兴趣。规范证明不了什么,而非常状态却能证明一切:它不仅确认规范,而且确认规范的存在,因为规范只能来自非常状态。"②似乎非常状态相对于规范状态更具有优先性,因为"如果必须首先引发某种状态,以使各种规范能够在其中生效,那么非常状态便处于绝对形态之中"。③言下之意,规范状态总是由某种非常状态,即高于法律之外的权威引起的,否则规范状态无以确立,因而非常状态更有意义。之所以说非常状态处于绝对形态之中,这一点可以与下面会讲到的政治的基础地位相关联来理解。

他认为,政治必须以自身的最终划分为基础,而一切具有特殊政治意义的活动均可诉诸这种划分。我们可以设想一下,这样的最终划分在道德领域是善与恶,在审美领域是美与丑,在经济领域则是利与害,相应地,"所有政治活动和政治动机所能归结成的具体政治性划分便是朋友与敌人的划分"。④ 这种划分是有独立的价值的,"无论在何种情况下,它都具有独立性,此处的独立性并非指一个截然不同的新领域,而是指它既无法建立在其他任何一个对立面或不同对立面的组合之上,也无法诉诸其他对立面"。⑤ 怎样理解政治既具有独立性,却又不是一个截然不同的新领域?我们不妨从前文中运用多元论所作的分析来思考他的这一结论。⑥ 正因为

---

① 〔德〕卡尔·施米特:《政治的神学:主权学说四论》,载其《政治的概念》,第31页。
② 同上,第14页。
③ 同上,第12页。
④ 〔德〕卡尔·施米特:《政治的概念》,载其《政治的概念》,第138页。
⑤ 同上。
⑥ 这种思考的角度应该是合理的和可行的,因为根据施特劳斯对施米特的解释,施米特也是以多元论、价值冲突为前提的:"一个肯定政治本身的人尊重所有希望战斗的人;他完全像自由主义一样宽容——但他们的意图却正好相反:自由主义者尊重并宽容一切'诚实'的信念,只是他们仅仅认为法律秩序与和平神圣不可侵犯,而一个肯定政治本身的人则尊重并宽容一切'严肃'的信念,即定位于战争之现实可能性的一切决断。因此,肯定政治本身被证明是处于对立一极的自由主义。"(施特劳斯:《〈政治的概念〉评注》,载刘小枫选编:《施米特与政治法学》,上海:上海三联书店,2002年版,第23页)因此他说施米特的批判仍然"停留在自由主义划定的水平上"(同上,第24页)。

多元论的事实,道德判断实际上必然只能是内部判断,因此当人们的道德判断出现冲突,而且经过反思仍达不到一致的时候,那么此时冲突就超出了道德范围。在施米特看来,这个新领域就是政治,是敌友划分和敌我斗争。从道德、审美等方面的冲突上升到政治冲突,这其中有一个根本的飞跃,有一个质的变化。因此,政治可能与道德、审美等领域有关,但却绝不能用道德判断或审美判断来评价或解决。用施米特的话来说就是,"任何宗教、道德、经济、种族(ethnische)或其他领域的对立,当其尖锐到足以有效地把人类按照敌友划分成阵营时,便转化成了政治对立"。① 此时,说对方是不道德的或丑陋的,显然已经没有意义,特定道德判断的作用力已经走到了尽头。如果我们站在一个更高的视点来看,就可得出这样的结论:"政治敌人不一定非要在道德方面是邪恶的,或在审美方面是丑陋的;他也不一定非要以经济竞争者的面目出现,甚至与政治敌人拥有商业来往会更加有利。"② 从我们所关注的政治与道德之间关系的角度来看,之所以说政治敌人不一定

在道德上是邪恶的,我们可以理解为,何谓道德邪恶这样的判断在敌我双方存在着尖锐的冲突,无法达到共同立场,因此这样的评价用在这里不适宜。在施米特那里,由于敌我斗争是一种无法消除的可能性,政治因此恰恰是一种基础性的东西,是人类走不出的自然状态。

我们已经可以初步看到,在自由主义的政治概念中,道德内在于其中。而在施米特的政治概念中,道德则似乎成了政治之上的一种"巫魅",应当予以祛除,因为政治就是一种带来规范状态的决断,是一种超越既定规范的斗争。

施米特想把各种决断完全道德中立化,这一点显然是走了极端。决断本身必然具有规范性的价值承诺与内容,否则任何决断与选择其实都是不可能的。即便从施米特的政治概念来看,我们也只能说,当且仅当一种决断所诉诸的某种规范性内容得不到某些人的认可,它才可能转化成政治斗争,我们也才可以把这些不认可而又不愿妥协的人称

---

① 〔德〕卡尔·施米特:《政治的概念》,载其《政治的概念》,第153页。
② 同上,第139页。

为政治上的敌人。他认为,"非常状态最为清楚地揭示了国家权威的本质。决断在这里与法律规范分道扬镳,若用一个悖论来表示就是,权威证明了无需在法律的基础上制定法律"。① 但没有既定的法律规范作基础,并不意味着没有任何规范性承诺,因为没有一种价值上的承诺,新的法律规范也无从制订。由于施米特是从群体的角度来论述政治的,我们更有理由认为,一个群体的价值追求与生活方式就是他所说的政治决断的规范基础。如果不承认任何政治决断的规范性背景,那么它只能是一种赤裸裸的政治存在主义。因此,严格地讲,在政治中并没有什么神学般的"奇迹"发生。施米特的政治神学判断最多在法理学的意义上可以成立,而从伦理学的意义上根本上是不可能的。

因此,自由主义政治概念首先作为一种建构群体生活方式与身份认同的道德求索,显然仍然具有不可替代的价值,至于这是不是可以叫做政治,则似乎只是一个语言问题了,我们完全可以同时接受两种形态的政治的存在。

我们可以认为,施米特与自由主义在政治概念上的极大反差首先根源于双方对于政治所欲解决的问题的范围,或说政治所适用的社会状态的理解有着根本的对立。前者指向非常状态,自由主义显然立足于文明化的、规范性的状态。然而,自由主义的政治概念由于是一个道德化的概念,因此它忽视了超出道德范围的冲突的可能,或者说,它总是用一种道德化的语言和思维去看待超道德的问题。施特劳斯在分析施米特的政治概念时曾指出,施米特继承了霍布斯式的自然状态观念,然而,"事实上,施米特对自然状态的界定与霍布斯有着根本的差别。在霍布斯看来,自然状态是个人之间的战争状态;而在施米特看来,自然状态则是群体(尤其是国家)之间的战争状态。对霍布斯而言,在自然状态中,每个人都是其他人的敌人;而对施米特而言,所有的政治活动都定位于朋友和敌人的划分。这种差别植根于霍布斯自然状态定义的论战意图:既然自然状态是一切人对一切人的战争状态,那

---

① 〔德〕卡尔·施米特:《政治的神学:主权学说四论》,载其《政治的概念》,第12页。

么它就可望激发人们摆脱自然状态。施米特则以政治状态反对这种对自然状态或对政治的否定"。①因此对于道德化的政治概念而言,问题就在于,人类究竟是否已经走出,或能够走出这种"自然状态"?如果我们必然会面对这种状态,那么自由主义的道德化思维如何去解释它?

我们在前面已经分析指出,多元论是一个认识论的事实,我们无法从多元论中推出任何一种可供所有人接受的道德规范与生活方式。因而分歧必然存在,而这种分歧本身由于有着相冲突的然而却同时是客观的价值基础,它是不可能用道德本身来解决的,它只能是施米特意义上的政治性的东西。从这个意义上讲,人类永远无法完全走出霍布斯和施米特式的自然状态。即便在相对成熟的自由民主社会中,我们所能期待的,最多也只能是一个理性多元论与一般多元论并存的状态,只不过理性多元论占据着主导地位而已。所以,自由主义确实需要一种应对这种政治的理论资源,甚至需要一种新的评价性语言,而不是停留于道德化的思维里面。在自由主义的内部,还有这种可能性吗?我们是否能够维持一种自由主义式的宽容社会,而同时又把自由主义从对斗争性政治的遮蔽中解救出来?

下文想表明,政治自由主义能够在自身之内容纳某种形式的临时协定,而且它还拥有解释敌我斗争的政治概念的理论资源。

毫无疑问,承认在自由民主社会可能有一些非理性学说存在,这种情况让理性的重叠共识变得让人怀疑。虽然正如我们在前面所说,在封闭的自由民主社会中,罗尔斯所提出的动机型与模态型的理性标准在原则上可以统一起来,但这仍然不是否定非理性学说在这种社会中存在的可能性的充分条件。极少关注非理性学说的存在对其理论的冲击,这反映出罗尔斯为了理论建构之需而表现出的理想主义心态。事实上,罗尔斯在政治自由主义中之所以要设想理性多元论而非一般多元论的事实,也有其为达到理论上的融贯性的考虑。因为如果只是

---

① 〔美〕列奥·施特劳斯:《〈政治的概念〉评注》,载刘小枫选编:《施米特与政治法学》,第8页。

一般性的多元论,那么虽然在原初状态中各方的选择并不会因此而不同,但一旦"无知之幕"拉开,人们是否会形成一种为政治自由主义所需要的正义感,就成了问题,而这无疑会影响到罗尔斯孜孜以求的稳定性。而且,其稳定性是建立在道德基础上的,而不仅仅是实用的考虑,设定理性多元论就在于表明,"在架构政治观念以让它能在第二阶段赢得理性的完备性学说的支持时,我们并没有全然调整那一观念去适应世界中的非理性强力,而是适应自由人类理性的不可避免的结果"。[1] 依据同样的理由,在现实中,如果面对非理性学说的存在,它们必然被重叠共识所排除:为什么要让理性的重叠共识去迁就和服从非理性的强力呢! 如果我们承认这种可能性,政治自由主义者似乎可以说,重叠共识是合乎理性的完备性学说之间的事情,非理性的学说(设想他们无力改变现状)对这种重叠共识的认可与服从,则可能只是他们的一种权宜之计,而这并不损害政治自由主义的合理性。如此一来,在政治自由主义内部,就出现了这样一种情形:重叠共识的主体,即各种理性的完备性学说,与非理性学说之间形成了一种临时协定。临时协定的问题在于它的不稳定性,这正是前面所引用的康德的"麻雀"论所要说明的道理,也是罗尔斯的顾虑所在。但既然非理性的学说必然存在,那么对于一个由政治自由主义所规制的自由民主社会,它的稳定性只能取决于理性多元论相对于非理性学说的优势。虽然我们从道德上可能不希望这种力量对比发生扭转,但从政治上讲,谁又能给予绝对的保证呢? 我们能相信历史终结于此的预言吗?

我们实际上已经触及到另一个问题,即政治自由主义相对于传统完备性自由主义在解释斗争性政治方面的理论优势。虽然政治自由主义继承和认可了一种规范性的政治概念,但是,这其中所包含的规范性道德,即理性标准,却又是限定在政治范围内的。罗尔斯局限于一个低限的、政治性的理性标准的主要目的,乃是保证正义原则的建构有一个可以广为接受的基点。但正是因

---

[1] John Rawls, *Political Liberalism*, p. 37.

为政治自由主义把理性作为一种政治理想,所以,当有人拒绝这种基本的理性标准,从而进行道德上的"内部判断"不再可能的时候,政治自由主义就可以不再局限于从道德上去评价他们。罗尔斯本人对此比较模糊。他曾举例说,如果有人认为教会之外无拯救,因此保障宗教自由的宪政制度是不能接受的,政治自由主义对此的恰当回答是说"那一结论是非理性的",①而不是说它是不真确的。这种模糊性的根源恰恰在于理性与非理性既是政治的,又是道德的。虽然罗尔斯本人由于对理性在民主的公共政治文化中的普及程度充满乐观,并小心谨慎地沉浸于重叠共识的建构,从而极少考虑拒绝这种理性标准的情况的可能,但罗蒂对政治自由主义作了一个有意义的延伸性的解读。如果政治自由主义者面对尼采或Loyola,自然会面对两难:"拒绝争论人应该像什么样子似乎表示出对和解和宽容精神的藐视,而这种精神对民主是根本性的。但对人应该成为自由派而不是狂热分子这一论断如何争论而又不至于被拽回到人性理论和哲学,却又不太清楚。"②此时,罗蒂

认为,我们不得不把他们说成疯子,"我们不是因为尼采和Loyola对某些'根本的'主题持有不一般的观点而得出结论说他们是疯子,毋宁说,我们只在经过广泛的交换政治观点的尝试使得我们认识到我们达不到共识之后,才作出这种结论"。③而且,他强调,"这种结论限于政治"。④

我们看到,虽然建构政治自由主义的本意在于为分化的自由民主社会寻找一种基本的共识,并在此基础上谋求自由民主社会的长治久安,但恰恰因为作为公平的正义的政治性质,使得对于不接受它(或与之相近的某种类似的正义原则。罗尔斯在《政治自由主义》中显然更关注政治哲学的方法论问题,而不是其得出的实质性正义原则的绝对

---

① John Rawls, "The Domain of the Political and Overlapping Consensus", in his *Collected Papers*, p. 483.
② Richard Rorty, "The Priority of Democracy to Philosophy", in his *Objectivity, Relativism, and Truth: Philosophical Papers*, Vol. 1, Cambridge: Cambridge University Press, 1991, p. 190.
③ ibid. p. 191.
④ ibid. p. 191, note 42.

性)并试图挑战它的人,自由主义有了从政治而非道德上去称谓这种"敌人"的观念基础。我们看到,两种根本对立的政治概念在各自的边界上相遇了。

从伯林的"道德白痴"到罗蒂的"政治疯子",这一术语上的变化本身具有重要的理论意义,因为前者显然是一种纯粹的道德思维,而后者则理解到对立与冲突可能具有的超道德的含义,而我们在前面已经说明,这一点正是人类社会,包括一个国家内部可能会面对的永久事实,自由主义必须具备对这种现象的解释力。政治多元论者墨菲在批评罗尔斯时说:"在政治学中,'理性的'与'非理性的'这种区分本身就已经划定了一个边界,它具有一种政治特征并始终是某种既定霸权的表现。"①事实上,我们现在可以看出,政治自由主义的理论逻辑本身并不必然否定这一点。在针对自由主义的批评中,一个重要的方面就是说它掩盖了对斗争性的政治的认识。现在,政治自由主义有了应对这一批评的理论资源,它在自己的政治原则的范围内对超道德的政治起到了"解蔽"(借用荀子的语言)的作用。如此一来,自由主义就有了包容两类政治形态的理论能力,即一方面有共同体内实现认同的道德基础,并在此基础上展开规范性的政治活动,另一方面,它又可以承认"统治"的事实,即超道德的敌人的存在。反观那些从目标上批评政治自由主义的人,他们显然仍然停留于伯林在称谓"道德疯子"时的那种思维层次。因为他们仍然试图用一种真确的道德去批评原教旨主义者,并认为罗尔斯放弃了哲学家的这种知识与道义上的责任,从而他们就没有从思维上认识到这种斗争的性质所在。

五、政治自由主义中正当之于善的优先性

我们已经从政治的概念这一角度出发,回答了对于政治自由主义两端上的批评以及与它们各自相关的一些问题。但政治自由主义还有两个重要的并互相关联的主张,上述任何一端的批评都足以对它们构

---

① Chantal Mouffe, *The Return of Political*, p. 143.

成挑战,因此我们在分别应对这两端的批评之后,利用我们前面所作的分析将它们提出来进行专门讨论。这两个主张就是正当之于善的优先性和政治中立性。在《正义论》中,罗尔斯明确地提出,"在作为公平的正义中,正当对于善的优先性成为这一观念的中心特征"。[1]这是一个在政治自由主义中继续得到坚持的观点。这种优先性的含义显然是指向义务论伦理学的根本原则,而不是他所说的两个正义原则之间的词典式序列问题。然而,既然我们已经承认政治自由主义一开始就有着某种规范性的价值承诺,而其最终的正义原则又不可能在所有学说之间形成共识,似乎它所包含的正当之于善的优先性与政治中立性这两个主张就不攻自破了。

在价值多元论的背景下,不同的个人、不同的群体可能选择不同的价值,而任何一种道德要求,实际上都是把某些价值看作更为重要的东西。如此一来,正当对于善的优先性就成了一种不可能的诉求。因为它的含义正在于不脱离正当来定义善,这无疑是把某些价值当作并不是真正的善。在《正义论》中,罗尔斯将此表述为:"正当的优先性部分是通过主张需要违犯正义的利益没有价值来得到理解的。由于一开始就没有价值,它们就不可能压倒正义的要求。"[2]但这一结论在《政治自由主义》中似乎有一种转变。因为罗尔斯此时认为,在多元论的背景下,自由主义允诺,通过坚持正当之于善的优先性,为不同的生活形式留下充分的社会空间。但他更为明确地认识到了这其中所包含的价值上的损失:"应该继续明确地拒斥这样一种观念,……即在正义的宪政制度中,只有无价值的生活形式从中没落","充分空间的观念是隐喻性的。"[3]这种观点似乎更忠实于价值多元论。

正如我们在前面所说,价值多元论本身并不命定自由主义的道德与政治形式,伯林之所以从多元论中得出乌托邦之不可能性与自由主义的必要性,恰恰因为在他看来,

---

[1] John Rawls, *A Theory of Justice*, pp. 31—32,参见中译本,第 28 页。
[2] ibid, p. 31. 参见中译本,第 28 页。
[3] John Rawls, *Political Liberalism*, p. 198.

"所有罪恶中之为最甚者,就是为了某种普罗克汝斯忒斯式的方式——它有某种不顾及人的抱负的客观权威——让人们被迫违反他们的意志,从而贬低人们的人格或伤害他们的自尊"。[1] 他把这种罪恶视为是对自主性的侵犯。但从价值多元论的角度来看,自主性只是多元价值中的一种,显然难以保证人们的普遍认同,因此把自主性排列到如此之高的地位本身无疑是有争议的。即便自主性的最有力倡导者们也不否认,它并不是一种会得到普遍认可的价值。但事实上,自主性一直被视为自由主义的核心价值,在康德、密尔那里莫不如此,所谓正当优先于善其实不过是在这个基础上才可以得到理解。

这似乎是一种悖论:以一种善观念为前提而推导出正当之于善的优先性。不过,这一悖论并不像表面上显示的那样严重。其中的根源就在于,自主性或自由虽然本身都是一种价值,一种善,但它们都是二阶的(second-order)、形式的价值,而不是一阶的、实质的价值。从而,对自主性或自由的承诺使得自由主义具有很大的包容性,以此为基础可以建立一个宽容的社会。

值得注意的是,对正当之于善的优先性,在自由主义理论内部还有另一种理解,那就是从"道德责任独立于行动者自己的善"这一角度来理解。据此,功利主义也就是正当优先于善的典型体现者,因为"正如它要求我们应当去做的那样,善是通过不偏不倚地考虑所有相关个人的总体善来界定的,无论我们自己的利益是什么。因此追求这种善的责任无条件地约束着我们"。[2] 这相当于认为,正当的优先性只不过是它不在行动者中间作区分,这正如帕菲特在评论后果主义伦理学的时候所说,"既然后果主义给所有的行动者以共同的道德目标,我将称之为行动者中立的(agent-neutral)(理论)",而许多其他理论不采用这种形式,这些理论给不同的行动者不同的目标,它们是"行动者相

---

[1] Isaiah Berlin, *The Crooked Timber of Humanity*, p. 199. 普罗克汝斯忒斯是希腊神话中的巨人,他将俘虏拔长或截肢以使他们与床齐长。

[2] Charles Larmore, *The Morals of Modernity*, Cambridge: Cambridge University Press, 1996, p. 23.

关的(agent-relative)"。① 但我们认为,这种理解并不能表达自由主义强调正当优先于善的良苦用心。因为正如罗尔斯所强调的,正当优先于善的一个重要方面还在于,不能用总体的善来规定正当,而功利主义通过合成所有的欲望体系,把个人的选择原则适用于社会,从而"使得正义所保障的权利受制于社会利益的计算"。② 因此,正当优先于善的原则在自由主义理论中首先是用来保障个人权利的重要原则,因此如果仅仅停留于"行动者中立"的层次,完全可能违背自由主义的初衷。正当之于善的优先性的根本似乎在于,正当的原则不能以任何实质性的善为根据。相对而言,总体的善是实质性的,而自主性则是一种二阶的善。

虽然我们认为正当的优先性可以建立在自主性这种二阶善观念的基础上,但这对于政治自由主义没有帮助,因为后者不能依赖于这样一种完备性的道德学说。显然,在政治自由主义中,由于它是以自由平等的公民观念为前提的,因此,"当作为公平的正义在良序社会中充分实现时,充分自主性的价值也同样得到实现。以这种方式看,作为公平的正义确实与康德和密尔的自由主义相似;但与它们相反,充分自主性的价值在这里由正义的政治观念,而不是由完备性道德学说所明确"。③ 换言之,公民被认为能够形成、修正自己的善观念,而且能形成某种正义感,这两个条件本来相当于传统以来的自主性观念的两个基本方面,但在政治自由主义中,它是建立在公民观念而非哲学意义上的人的观念之上的,因此不是完备性学说的体现。根据我们前面的分析,我们也可以说,这种自主性之所以能够实现,乃是因为它潜在地包含在政治自由主义所赖以建立的规范性政治概念之中。

从完备性道德学说的层次上摆脱了对自主性的依赖,这似乎意味着政治自由主义具备了把正当之于善的优先性推进到底的理论力量。

---

① Derek Parfit, *Reasons and Persons*, Oxford: Oxford University Press, 1986, p. 27.

② John Rawls, *A Theory of Justice*, p. 30. 参见中译本,第 27 页。

③ John Rawls, "Justice as Fairness: Political not Metaphysical", in his *Collected Papers*, p. 410.

但一个进一步的问题在于,政治自由主义又空前地引入了一系列的善观念,除了基本善,还有作为合理性的善、可允许的完备性善观念和政治社会之善。这就再一次使得正当的优先性成为疑问。对此,我们只能从罗尔斯对这些善观念所给出的限制上去理解:"所包含的善观念必须是政治观念,亦即,它们必须属于一种理性的正义之政治观念,以便我们可以假定:a. 它们由或能够由被视为自由而平等的公民们所共享;以及 b. 它们不预设任何特殊的充分(或部分)完备性的学说。"①这里的意图非常明显,那就是仍然让善观念在政治的范围内去运作。由此,基本善是一个在公民之间进行人际比较的公共尺度,它保证公民之间对什么东西是有利的、什么东西是可以正当地相互要求的这类问题有一个共享的理解。而合理性的善恰恰正是为了帮助拟订一个基本善的清单。可允许的善观念则意味着政治设计要为公民的善观念的追求留下一个尽量充分的空间,而政治社会之善则是公民们共享的政治目的。这样理解的善观念确实仍然停留在政治的范围内,而且是停留在政治自由主义所依赖的那种规范性政治概念范围之内。唯一的疑问可能在于,罗尔斯在这里似乎承认了善观念(即便说它们是政治的)在实践推理上较之以正当具有优先性,因为没有合理性的善,连基本善都不可能制订出来,而没有可允许的善观念,也无需考虑正当问题。正如罗尔斯自己所说,如果没有合理性的善,"政治正义的问题根本不会出现"。② 这似乎是对正当的优先性的一个否定。但是,善观念在实践推理上的优先性并不意味着正当直接以某种善观念为依据而被推导出来,也就是说,并不是因为要追求某种善因而就直接决定了相应的正当。而后者才是正当之于善的优先性所要表达的意义所在。因为毫无疑问,任何正当都源于协调利益冲突的考虑,因而把利益冲突作为一个前提来考虑并不必然损害正当的优先性。

那么,罗尔斯在政治自由主义

---

① John Rawls, *Political Liberalism*, p. 176.

② John Rawls, "The Priority of Right and Ideas of the Good", in his *Collected Papers*, p. 452.

中坚持正当之于善的优先性是合理的吗？我们知道，就一般而论的正当与善来说，它们恰恰都是完备性道德学说中的概念，因此，政治自由主义就不应该再坚持正当之于善的优先性这个义务论原则，因为它实质上已不可能再持有这样一种属于完备性道德学说的标准了。对于善与正当何者更为优先这样的一般性论点，它应该保持沉默，如此才符合政治自由主义的理念，否则，后果主义者们在政治自由主义中就找不到罗尔斯为他们留下的位置了。从效果上讲，政治自由主义因为摆脱了对自主性的传统依赖，从而把正当之于善的优先性论点推进到了一个更深的层次。但是从精神实质上看，政治自由主义其实把这一传统论点转换成了政治正义观念对于完备性善观念（或学说）的优先性。政治自由主义只能坚持后一种优先性论点，否则就会自我挫败。在提出了上述一系列善观念之后，罗尔斯一方面仍然坚持认为正当优先于善是作为公平的正义中的一个中心观念，同时又作了如下自圆其说的解释："正当与善是互补的：没有一种正义观念能全然运用一个或另一个，而是必须将二者以一种明确的方式结合起来。正当的优先性并不否认这一点。"[①]从我们上面的分析来看，这种对正当优先性论点的辩解其实完全没有必要，相反，这一论点本身在政治自由主义中应当付之阙如。

如果上述分析能够成立，那么对于政治中立性的论点就容易解决了。政治中立性的一般含义在于，国家不应该奖赏或处罚特殊的好生活观念，而是应该提供一个中立的框架，使得不同的和潜在地互相冲突的善观念能在其中得到追求。中立性有时候被当作自由主义的基本思想，但在最近三十多年来的自由主义思想中表现得尤其突出，而且反映出某些全新的特征。事实上，这种发展暗示了两个不同层次的中立性观念，其背后又隐含着自由主义对政治合法性追求的演进。简单说来，正如自由主义在坚持自由或自主性这样的二阶价值的前提下可以做到正当之于善的相对优先性一样，它同时也就做到了在一阶善观

[①] John Rawls, *Political Liberalism*, p. 173.

念上的中立。基于人们善观念的分歧与多元性,这在过去一直被当作自由主义的政治合法性标准。

但是,人们的善观念往往与某种完备性学说相关联,它也并不总是意味着个人利益的满足。而传统的自由主义由于是一种完备性的学说,而且往往具有某种个人主义的倾向,这一点随着自由民主社会中合乎理性的完备性学说的多元分歧的逐渐明朗而遭到持续的批评。正如罗尔斯所说:"历史地看,自由主义思想的一个共同主题是,国家绝对不应支持任何完备性学说及其关联性的善观念。但它没能做到这一点,而是事实上武断地偏惠于一种或另一种形式的个人主义,这同样是自由主义批评者的一个共同主题。"①当然,罗尔斯的这一解释本身似乎赋予了传统自由主义思想一种对完备性学说保持中立的理论自觉,这其实并不符合自由主义思想史的实际。不过,随着合乎理性的完备性学说的多元化的发展,自由主义的合法性就面临着新的考验,它要求一个"对政治中立性的中立的辩护"。②也就是说,自由主义需要从一个中立的立场出发为自己对一阶善观念的中立寻找根据。显然,这种中立性本身是一个道德立场,但根据新的要求,这种道德立场不能是源于完备性的道德学说,它只能是源于一种政治观念。在政治自由主义中,正如正当之于善的优先性其实是政治观念之于完备性善观念(或学说)的优先性一样,政治中立性也只在于政治观念只在政治的范围内运作,它不依赖于独特的完备性学说,不因为任何一种善观念的内在优越性而支持它。根据自由主义的规范性政治概念,如果一种完备性学说本身是非理性的,它不可能是正义原则的重叠共识的主体,因而反对它也就不构成对政治中立性标准的违反。③

(作者系北京大学哲学系
博士研究生)

---

① ibid. p.190.
② Charles Larmore, *Patterns of Moral Complexity*, Cambridge: Cambridge University Press, 1987, p.53.
③ 笔者在写作本文之前曾与何怀宏教授讨论了一些相关问题,徐向东博士阅读了文章初稿并提出了诸多宝贵意见,在此谨对他们表示衷心感谢。当然,对于本文的观点与论证,我当文责自负。

证明与计算：契约论的两种方法
——罗尔斯与布坎南的政治哲学比较

● 李风华

> 在当代契约论作家中，布坎南和罗尔斯是比较突出的两位。本文通过对二人的理论逻辑的比较，指出契约论存在两种基本的方法，它们实质上代表着当代契约论的两个基本潮流。

一、引言

某个人群应怎样行动才能取得对整个人群来说最优的结果？这一问题是公共理性分析的基本问题，也是政治哲学的一个基本问题。

存在两种分析角度。一个是从其中的单个行动者出发，他们各自根据自己的偏好而自主采取行动。个人之间相互作用，最终达致一种结果。这种结果可能符合所有人或大多数人的偏好，也可能出乎所有人的意料。这种分析是以每个参与人有效的行动集合出发，以说明公共理性形成的具体过程。另一个角度是从联合行动的结果出发，集中讨论整个人群而不是哪个参与人能做什么。这种分析角度与上一种的区别在于，它不考虑参与人群内部作用的具体细节。其分析有助于帮助我们理解公共理性所需的各个条件和制度。前一种分析即博弈论中的非合作博弈(noncooperative game),后一种即合作博弈(cooperative game)。① 对于非合作博弈的方法来说,问题在于博弈的参与人能否达成帕累托最优的协议;而对于合作博弈的方法来说,问题在于博弈的参与人将达成一种什么样的协议以及在什么条件下达成该协议。

政治学中的契约论基本上可以归于合作博弈这一范式。在近代思想史上,它曾占据过相当重要的地位。由于种种原因,它在19世纪中被各种方法所替代,直到20世纪六七十年代,契约论方得以复兴。契约论在政治思想史上有着独特的地位和作用,尤其表现在对于政治合法性的探讨上,而当代契约论则在各个方面都深化和扩展了原有的传统,极大地丰富了哲学、法学、经济学和政治学等社会科学。

詹姆斯·布坎南和约翰·罗尔斯是当代契约论的突出代表,他们以不同的方式发展了契约论。他们所关注的主题并不完全一致,罗尔斯集中关注于社会正义问题,是当代政治哲学最优秀的学者之一;而布坎南是公共财政的研究专家,并以此获得诺贝尔经济学奖。但二人的论述所关涉的问题极其广泛,其基本的方法又都属于契约论的传统。作为同时代的学人,两人彼此对对方的著作都相当熟悉,在各自的著作中有不少地方提及对方。本文的任务是将他们二人契约论的逻辑过程进行梳理、比较,分析各自建构公共理性的方法。我们得出的结论是,当代契约论存在两种相反背的基本方法,并分别称之为证明的契约论方法和计算的契约论方法。

二、公共理性的历史前提

对于契约论来说,探讨公共理性的一个重要的问题就是,它在什么条件下可以存在,亦即公共理性的历史前提。由于理论往往可以视作现实的某

---

① 马丁·J.奥斯本和阿里尔·鲁宾斯坦:《博弈论教程》,魏玉根译,北京:中国社会科学出版社,2000年版,第227—228页。

种反映,这一问题所要解答的是理论与历史社会的关联,它一方面是理论对当代社会的描述与解释,另一方面也是理论对自身存在理由的证明。在这个问题上,布坎南和罗尔斯的看法、角度有别,但实质上是一致的。

布坎南指出,在集体选择的问题上,可以有两种理解,一种把集体决策的单位作一种有机的理解,比如存在一个有机的国家(organic state),其价值独立于生活于其中的成员;另一种是作个人主义的理解。他认为,对集体性的这种有机的理解在本质上是与西方政治哲学的传统相对立的。如果我们想针对现代西方民主国家建立一种集体选择的理论的话,就不能采用这些前提和预设。既然我们需要理解当代西方民主社会,我们就必须对它采取一种个人主义的理解方式。[①] 布坎南认为,在立宪问题上的理性计算只有在个人主义的现代西方社会才有可能。他在 1975 年《自由的限度》一书中指出,他和戈登·图洛克在《同意的计算》中所描述的立宪民主的政治结构,具有许多美国国父们设想的政体的特征。[②]

布氏的论述是比较粗略的,而罗尔斯在这一问题上提出了一系列深刻的命题与思想,可以视为当代契约论对自身理论所处社会历史环境的具有代表性的反思。布坎南承认,自己的理论的分析背景与罗尔斯的论述存在密切的关联[③]。虽然布坎南并未使用罗尔斯的概念作为理论工具,但事实上他基本接受了罗尔斯对社会历史环境的分析。

罗尔斯认为,当代政治社会处于一种理性多元主义的现实(the fact of reasonable pluralism)之中,这决定了正义的环境并不是一个社区(community)。社区是由一群享有共同的统合性或部分统合性教义(comprehensive doctrine)的人组成,其特征在于人们对于善有着共同的理解。而当代政治社会中的人们持着不同的统合性的哲学、宗教、道德或美学观念,显示着巨

---

① James M. Buchanan and Gordon Tullock, *The Calculus Of Consent*: *Logical Foundations of Constitutional Democracy* (Ann Arbor: The University of Michigan Press,1965), pp. 10—15.

② James M. Buchanan, *The Limits of Liberty*: *Between Anarchy And Leviathan* (Chicago and London: The University of Chicago Press, 1975), p. 6.

③ Buchanan, 1975, p. 181.

大的、不可调和的差异。① 人们彼此之间存在分歧，但这并不意味着它不合理。这种理性多元主义的现实并不是一种转瞬即逝的历史现象，它是必然的，并成为民主社会中的政治文化上的永久事实(permanent fact)。② 为什么会出现这种合理的分歧(reasonable disagreement)呢？

罗尔斯并没有采纳通常的解释，即认为人们的判断受其利益的影响，或者人们往往是非理性的。他之所以不采纳这些解释，并不是它们没有道理，而是想给理性多元主义的现实一个更深刻的基础。罗尔斯认为，即使每个人都是理智的，其处境都是处在理想的条件下，合理分歧仍然是不可避免的。因为在人们的政治生活中，存在许多障碍，以致于无法形成正确的判断和推理③：(1)人们用以支持某一论断的证据往往相互冲突、极其复杂，因此很难评估；(2)即使我们考虑到所有的因素，但对其各个因素的权重仍有不同的看法，而这将导致不同的判断；(3)在某种程度上，所有概念都是模棱两可的，这意味着理智的人们的判断和解释上会产生差别；(4)我们在证据的评估和价值的评估上往往受自身总体经验的影响，显然人们的总体经验总是千差万别的；(5)通常情况下，对一问题不同方面存在多种不同的规范性考虑，因此很难作出总体评价。罗尔斯把所以导致理性多元主义的根源称之为评判的重负(the burdens of judgment)。由于这些因素，人们很难指望通过自由而公开的讨论来达成一致结论。这一点使得罗尔斯与哈贝马斯形成对立，后者认为，在理想的语境中，人们可以通过交往和对话达成最终的一致意见。

在这种深刻的理性多元主义的现实之中，在政治社会里，要想人们都持某一种统合性教义是不可能的，除非用国家力量来压迫民众。④ 这种压迫不可避免地包含粗暴和残忍，并导致宗教、哲学和科学的堕落。欧洲中世纪

---

① John Rawls, *Justice as Fairness: A Restatement*, (Cambridge, Mass.: Harvard University Press. 2001), p. 3.
② Rawls, 2001, pp. 33—34.
③ John Rawls, *Political Liberalism* (New York: Columbia University Press. 1996), pp. 54—58; Rawls, 2001, pp. 35—36.
④ Rawls, 1996, p. 37; Rawls, 2001, p. 34.

的宗教压迫便是证明。罗尔斯甚至认为,即使一个社会将康德或密尔的学说——罗尔斯的理论可视为康德和密尔的发展——作为联系的基础的话,也不例外,哪怕这种理论倡导宽容和良心自由。德雷本认为,罗尔斯的这一观点在哲学史上是首次提出,是一个彻底的激进观点。[①]

人们既然在许多问题上无法达成一致意见,这是否意味着我们就必须持一种哲学怀疑主义的立场,并且对宗教问题等不闻不问呢?罗尔斯并不希望如此。[②] 罗尔斯认为,在政治领域(political domain)里,我们不能持怀疑主义的立场,而必须就基本政治问题达成一致同意。因为政治领域的最大特点是,政治问题,尤其是宪政实质(constitutional essentials)上的意见冲突并不能让人们各行其是,它必须得到解决。政治领域不同于社会内部的协会和自愿群体,在后者中,人们有了不一致意见,至少可以随时退出,但是政治社会却很难退出。在观念不一致的情况下,我们就必须向那些持不同意见的人证明自己的观点的正确。这种证明实质上是公民之间的相互裁定,而不是某个立法者的裁决。罗尔斯称作公共证明(public justification)。公共证明其根本的特点在于它依赖人们自愿的支持。为什么人们会支持一种公共证明的结论呢,不是存在评判的重负吗?罗尔斯认为,公共证明所以成立,是因为公共证明里公共理性(public reason)的存在。

三、理性与合理性

在布坎南和罗尔斯的理论体系中,其行动的主体都是个人,个人是契约论的当然出发点。布坎南曾明确指出,他的方法是方法论个人主义(individualism as of method of analysis)。[③] 罗尔斯虽反对将他称之为个人主

---

① 布尔顿·德雷本:《论罗尔斯》,载哈佛燕京学社、三联书社主编:《儒家与自由主义》(北京:生活、读书、新知三联书店,2001年版),商戈令译,第132页。
② 约翰·罗尔斯:《正义论》(北京:中国社会科学出版社,1988年版),何怀宏等译,第201—206页。
③ Buchanan and Tullock, 1965, p. 315.

义①,但在其原初状态中,其选择正义原则的主体就是个人。布坎南指出,罗尔斯在论述其两个正义原则时,并不是从任何外部伦理原则推导出来,而是基于个人的选择,因此,罗尔斯的方法也是个人主义的②。

布坎南将其理论中的个人设定为理性的(rational)。理性人的含义在于:订约人能否合乎逻辑地排列他们的目标;他们尽量采取达到其目标的最有效的方法,并选择最可能实现目标的方案;此外,在其他情况相同的情况下,选择更多而不是更少地完成。他明确表示,其理论对人性的假定是一种经济人,这种人与种种非私利的动机,如伙伴般的友情、兄弟情谊、同情心、基督式的爱、康德式的绝对命令、公共利益不相容③。布坎南认为,就人是理性的而言,个人是自私自利,还是利他主义,这都无关紧要。这样,契约中就不存在道德因素,其中的契约人既不是道德的,也不是不道德的。布坎南所以如此,显然是为了将理论简化,避免在订立契约的过程中引入道德风险和机会主义等问题。

在许多经济学文献中,搭便车等行动一直是集体行动或公共理性形成的根本障碍。而博弈论也指出个人有隐瞒自己的动机的倾向,致使合作无法形成。公共选择会不会也出现这种情况呢?如果有,应该如何解决呢?布坎南认为,以投票为形式的偏好表达过程,本质上与市场上个人的偏好表达是一致的,个人没有动机隐瞒自己的偏好。他在公共财政的研究中指出,"在集体决策活动或对税收的私人市场反应中,他将不会试图掩盖或隐藏他对公共商品或服务的真正偏好"④。

但是这纯粹理性的人们能否订立一个相互间可以接受的契约呢?或者说,即使这一契约对他们来说彼此能够接受,但对于其他人来说能否接受呢?罗尔斯对此持怀疑态度。他认为,纯粹理性除了个人愿意获得更多而

---

① 罗尔斯,1988年,第571页。
② Buchanan, 1975, p. 175.
③ 詹姆斯·布坎南:《财产与自由》(北京:中国社会科学出版社,2002年版),韩旭译,第80页。
④ 詹姆斯·布坎南:《民主财政论》(北京:商务印书馆,1999年版),穆怀朋译,第42页。

不是更少这一基本的含义之外,还包括嫉妒和鄙弃他人的倾向、对风险和不确定性的厌恶以及控制他人并实施影响的强烈意志。而这是罗尔斯所不愿意看到的①。囚徒困境表明,纯粹理性的两个人的博弈很有可能是一个非合作的结果。更让罗尔斯不安的是,即使纯粹理性的人们如同布坎南所设计的那样,取得了一致同意,但是他们的合约仍然可能是不正义的。

为此,罗尔斯在人性假定上作出了重大的修正,即契约人既是理性的,更是合理的(reasonable)②。其中合理性这一规定是他的独创之处,理性的规定性也有着不同的内容。这一人性假定对其理论有着奠基性的作用。

首先我们来看看他对理性的界定。罗尔斯在理性的基本定义上与经济学家所运用的并无什么区别③。但是与布坎南中的理性并不具体指涉何种偏好和目的不同,罗尔斯在理性的运用时更强调了理性的基本内容。罗尔斯提出了基本善(primary goods)这一概念。基本善是对公民恰当发展和发挥其道德能力,追求他们明确的各自的善的观念来说是必要的社会条件和手段。罗尔斯认为基本善有下列五种:(1)基本权利和自由,如思想自由和良心自由等;(2)移居自由和职业选择自由;(3)赋有权威和职责的职位上的权力和特权;(4)收入和财富;(5)自尊的社会基础④。基本善这一概念的提出,表明罗尔斯与布坎南对理性有着不同的理解。用赖克的话来说,布坎南所采用的是一种程序理性(procedural rationality),而罗尔斯则采取了一种实质理性(substantial rationality)的含义⑤。

---

① Rawls, 2001, p. 87.

② 按:关于 rational 和 reasonable,在汉语里大致有两种译法,两种译名恰恰相反。一般说来,哲学界将 rational 译成合理的,reasonable 译成理性的(如何怀宏译《正义论》,万俊人译《政治自由主义》,姚大志译《作为公平的正义:正义新论》);而经济学界则将 rational 译成理性的,reasonable 译成合理的。考虑到人们使用理性人这一概念时通常遵从经济学界的用法以及词典的习惯,本文姑从后者,不过在 reasonable pluralism 则从哲学界通译。

③ Rawls, 2001, p. 87.

④ Rawls, 2001, pp. 57—58.

⑤ William H. Riker, "Political Science And Rational Choice", in James E. Alt and Kenneth A. Shepsles (eds.) *Perspective on Positive Political Economy* (New York: Cambridge University Press, 1990), pp. 173—174.

就合理性而言,罗尔斯认为,具有合理性的人乐意提出为所有人都视为公平合作的条款的原则,并且当其他人提出这类条款时会乐于接受。合理的人具有道德感和道德能力,在其他人也尊重这些原则的情况下,自己也会尊重它们,即使这样做会有损自己的利益。纯粹理性的人会利用种种有利的情形来获取种种不公平的利益,但合理的人并不会这样做[1]。

理性与合理性之间又是什么样的关系呢?罗尔斯认为,这两者分别代表两个不同的和独立的基本概念,它们之所以不同,是因为它们之间不存在谁派生谁的问题。罗尔斯借用康德的概念,把合理性等同于康德的绝对命令,而把理性则等同于假言命令。当两者发生冲突时,合理性对理性具有优先性,它使后者处于从属地位[2]。从其所包含的信念来看,合理性对理性的优先表达了权利的优先性这一观念,而从推理过程来看,合理性的优先性的证明还要求这样一种推理装置的设计,既能够恰当地表达出合理性的优先性,同时也包括理性的作用这样一种推理条件。这种推理条件在罗尔斯那里就是原初状态(original position),而在布坎南那里则是自然分配(natural distribution)。

四、自然分配与原初状态

自然分配与原初状态都是一种推理条件或者说推理装置,是设计者所限定的对契约人选择的初始条件以及外在限制。在古典契约论中,这些条件表现为自然状态(the state of nature),自然状态的不同决定了最终的契约结果将是千差万别。如霍布斯的自然状态是"一切人对一切人的战争",这决定了霍布斯式的契约是一种专制式的君主制度;而洛克的自然状态则是一种人们比较幸福的状态,其中生命权、自由权和财产权已经确立,循此而订立的合约则是一种古典自由主义的政治契约。

---

[1] Rawls, 2001, pp. 6—7.
[2] Rawls, 2001, pp. 82—83.

布坎南认为,社会契约是作为交易的结果而达成的一个协议,在达成协议前,首先必须得确立交易的初始状态。这种初始状态,在布坎南的理论中,表现为一种自然形成的社会环境,布坎南把它称之为自然分配,并建立了一个模型来描述它。① 在一个没有规则的世界里,人们可以通过掠夺性的或生产性的活动来增加他们的利益。面对稀缺的物品时,人们实际上处于彼此冲突的境地。为了使其效用最大化,他们以最佳的比例分配用于生产和掠夺的时间。他们对其他人的选择作出最适宜的反应;在其他方面他们则互不相干。结果每个人都进行了一定程度的生产和掠夺,以致个人的活动对除自己以外的所有人的选择都是一个最佳的反应。这个结果就是纳什均衡。纳什均衡反映了一系列个人的理性选择。布坎南将这一纳什均衡解释为自然分配,又称之为自然均衡(natural equilibrium)。②

布坎南指出,自然分配中并不存在平等。人们是千差万别的,他们在体力、勇气、想像力、技巧、理解力、偏好、对他人的态度、个人的生活方式、处理社会关系的能力、世界观以及控制他人的水平等等都不相同。这一关于个人差异的陈述的基本有效性是不容否认的。因为"我们所处的是一个个人的社会,而不是平等的社会"③。它是根据人们的实力自然形成的均衡,自然分配有利于更强的、效率更高的和技巧更娴熟的人,因为他们易于获得资源,这对于那些境况很不错的人来说,这将会导致谈判能力的增强。此外,自然分配尚不存在严格意义上的财产权。因为财产权是契约的产物,在这种环境中,只是存在某种类似财产权的事物。

但是自然分配是无效率的,因为资源由于掠夺和防御而被浪费。如果在自然分配的基础上,每个人都尊重他人的权利,不再投资于掠夺和防御等浪费性活动,那么,每个人都将获益,实现了帕雷托改进。④ 契约人在自然分配的基础上订立契约,确定各自的权利以及各种宪政安排,从而也确立了

---

① Buchanan, 1975, pp. 55—64.
② Buchanan, 1975, pp. 23—25; p. 58.
③ Buchanan, 1975, p. 11.
④ Buchanan, 1975, pp. 58—59.

财产权。在这种宪政安排下,每个人的利益都获得了改进。布坎南将宪政安排与具体的立法以及实施区别开来,宪政安排是契约的结果,其内容是关于政治交易的规则。在宪政层面上,制订政治游戏的规则时,必须获得契约人的一致同意。具体的立法以及实施则直接关系到具体的利益,由于具体利益总是有冲突的,因此在具体的立法以及实施并不需要获得所有契约人的同意。

但是,要想每个人都对某种宪政安排达成一致意见,似乎是不可能的。无论是在历史还是在当代,从未出现过社会中所有人都一致支持的宪政安排。布坎南认为,要想取得一致同意,在订立宪政契约时,并不可以让契约人自由地进行讨价还价,而必须对它作出限制。如果每个契约人以及其他人对自己在社会中所处的位置获得了完全的信息,那么很难指望所有人会接受某个协议。在这种情况下,任何宪政安排都是不可能的。为此,他指出,契约人在对宪政安排进行订约时,必须让每个人对自己在社会中所处的具体位置一无所知。这时他在制订普遍规则时,他无法准确预测自己将属于哪个群体,因此,他将假定,他时而属于这个群体,时而属于那个群体。当每个人都这样想时,他们就能在规则制订上取得一致的结果。① 因为,这时契约人就要考虑如果他处在劣势的社会位置上,这一规则对他来说也是可以接受的。当每个人都这么思考时,他们最终将能达成一致意见,订立共同契约。这样,在自然分配的基础上,加上宪政交易时的无知,便成了布坎南契约论中的推理条件。

布坎南在宪政设计上,安排让契约人对自己的情况一无所知,这是他的创见。相比较卢梭的契约论中立法者必须考虑所有一切因素这一观点来说,是契约论的一大进步。但布坎南在这一问题上的论述是模糊的,并且在其著作中也未特别地重视。而在罗尔斯看来,这种社会环境的契约装置仍然是不够的,因为它仍然有可能导致某种在罗尔斯看来无法接受的结果。为此,罗尔斯提出了原初状态这一概念,作为其契约的推理条件。这一概念

---

① James M. Buchanan and Gordon Tullock, 1965, pp. 77—78.

一方面继续了布坎南在"无知"上的创见,同时又与布坎南的思想有着非常大的差异。

原初状态的设计目的是模拟人们所持的公平信念,并将公平协议的观念应用到社会基本结构上[①]。但是要做到这一点存在困难,因为个人所具有的财富、知识和地位的差异,使得契约人在订立契约时具有种种谈判优势或者劣势。具有优势者完全可能利用这一点为自己谋取有失公平的利益,而处于劣势者则为他人所剥削。此外,现在社会基本结构的特征和环境也往往影响或扭曲了人们达成协议的内容。因此,有必要消除契约人的不公平的谈判优势(bargaining advantages)。罗尔斯所用以消除谈判优势的办法就是设立无知之幕(the veil of ignorance)。

在无知之幕的掩盖下,代表者(既代表人们来订约的契约人)并不知道他们所代表的人们的社会地位和他们所持的统合性教义;他们也不知道其种族、性别以及力量和潜力之类的自然天赋[②]。当然,契约人也不能什么也不知道,否则他们将无法进行推理。罗尔斯限定他们知道社会的一般事实(这是由社会理论提供的人们普遍接受的事实)和环境,亦即正义的一般环境[③]。

无知之幕是罗尔斯在推理条件问题上所拈出的一个概念。这一概念的重要性不仅在于它是契约结果的前提,更在于它对于契约装置的分析作用和启发作用。从中我们可以清楚地看出,罗尔斯的公共理性所需要的各种条件是什么。它有助于我们加深对公共理性推导过程的理解,也激发了许多饶有兴趣的问题:罗尔斯的无知之幕是否太厚?一般知识中是否有某种阻碍协议达成的可能?它们与社会现实的相关程度如何?……等等。

要把握布坎南的社会环境与罗尔斯的原初状态之间的区别与联系,我们可以用一个比喻来表达。设想有位设计者制订游戏规则时,他想让自己的规则能够让别人愿意参与进来。这一规则就必须是公平的。在一般人的

---

① Rawls, 2001, p. 15.
② Rawls, 1996, pp. 24—25.
③ Rawls, 2001, p. 87.

观念中,游戏里面的参与人所处的位置有优势和劣势之分,但是如果游戏中的位置对于每个参与人来说都是机会均等的,甚至设计者本人也并不知道他将处于何种位置,那么,这种游戏装置便是公平的,是可以接受的。如果某个人在游戏中处于一种不利的地位,那么他只能怨运气不好,而不能归罪于整个制度。但在罗尔斯看来,这并不是真正的公平观念。真正的公平不仅仅要求这一游戏里面所体现的机会公平,而且要求游戏里的具体的得失、位置的优劣等实质内容上也是公平的。游戏的设计者能够让其他参与者任意指定自己应处于游戏中的任一位置,这样的话,游戏的设计者就不会对最后的游戏结果设计出过分大的差别,即使他处于游戏中的劣势位置,这种劣势位置也是可以接受的。用这一比喻来看布坎南和罗尔斯,布坎南所持的公平观念相当于前一种,而罗尔斯的公平观念相当于后一种,它更严格,对游戏装置的设计也更为精致。

五、政治交易与反思平衡

在契约人的动机以及契约条件确立以后,接下来就看契约人如何达成协议了。在契约方式上,布坎南提出了政治交易这一概念,而罗尔斯用的是反思平衡的方法。

布坎南认为,政治生活中的人与经济生活中的人一样,都是理性的人。他们参与政治,也是为了自己的效用最大化。布坎南用经济学方法来分析集体决策中的契约人的利益计算。他从个人在集体行动中所担负的成本着手。个人在集体行动中承担两个成本,一为决策成本(decision-making costs),即组织集体行动中,个人所付出的直接成本;一为外部成本(external costs),为集体决策中由于他人的参加而造成的以自己所承担的成本。这两种成本合起来为相互依赖成本(interdependence costs)。一般而言,相互依赖成本的大小与集体决策的规则相关联。在要求一致同意的规则下,外部成本为零,而决策成本则可能相当大;如果是只要一个人同意就可以采取集体行动,则决策成本非常小,而外部成本相当大。个人在集体决策时,会根据外部成本和决策成本的总和即相互依赖成本的大小进行决策。相互依赖成本越小,则集体决策就越有效率。①

而相互依赖成本的大小往往与决策的领域和对象相关。在市场领域里,每一个人在交易时必须与另一方达成一致同意,否则交易无法进行。这种一致同意促进了效率,改进了人们的福利。但在政治领域中,指望所有人对公共产品的需求和产出都持一致意见,似乎是不可能的。由于各种利益相互冲突,如果满足了一些人的利益,则另一些人势必承担这一决策的外部成本。许多民主理论家认为,在政治领域里一致同意是不可能的,民主的实质只是满足大多数人的利益,它实行的是多数决策规则。但布坎南认为,多数决策很有可能导致多数人剥削少数人,这也是不合理的。真正合理的规则必须是一致同意规则(rule of unanimity)。

那么应如何达成一致同意呢？布坎南提出了政治交易这一概念。他认为,政治活动与经济活动一样,本质上也是交易。但政治交易与经济交易不一样,它是一个集体选择的事情,其具体做法就是：在一个单一的议案中,一方投票人想使有利于自己的议案通过时,他为了让另一方也能接受,便给对方进行一种补偿,布坎南把这种补偿称之为边际支付(side payment)。如果存在有多个议案的情况,由于投票人的偏好强度不一,他们彼此之间可以通过互投赞成票的办法达成一致同意。所谓一致同意规则,其实就是通过补偿而达成协议的方式。②

布坎南提出这种观点时,可谓惊世骇俗。政治生活中原有的贿赂、选票交易等等行为一直是人们所谴责的对象。他则对这些现象进行了全新的诠释,并给予了一种效率意义上和伦理意义上的支持。这一观点的影响是巨大的,在改变人们对于政治的认识上具有革命意义。

布坎南的契约中,参与人是纯粹的经济理性的个人,他们之间的利益可以交易,由此决定了政治领域里交易的可能性和合理性。但在罗尔斯看来,

---

① Buchanan and Tullock, 1965, pp.43—46.
② Buchanan and Tullock, 1965, p.91.

政治领域里的契约人绝非是纯粹经济理性的,他们更是合理性的。而且在公共领域里很多问题也无法进行交易,每个人都持某种统合性的教义,他们对善的理解千差万别,彼此之间无法通约。那么他们如何在政治问题上取得一致意见呢?罗尔斯采用了一种名为反思平衡的论证过程。

罗尔斯指出,我们的各种判断往往存在多种一般性的层次(at all levels of generality),包括具体行动上的判断、社会政策和制度上的判断以及最终达到非常一般的信念。当单个人进行反思平衡时,他试图将自己各种层次上的判断保持一致。反思的平衡就是自己的道德原则(principle)和判断(judgement)的来回往复的校对和修正过程。如果原则与我们所认可的判断不一致,那么或者认为我们的判断是不合适的,从而修正我们的判断,或者人们要改变我们所要采取的原则。这里存在一个修正过程(revision),由于这种修正只是在单个人的正义观念之下做出的,它的修正必然并不多,罗尔斯把它称之为狭窄的反思平衡(narrow reflective equilibrium)。这个过程的结果是,我们使我们自己的各个层次上的道德判断相互支持和协调,整个道德观念获得了一致性。但是狭窄的反思平衡是不够的,因为个人的判断往往是带有偏见的,即使个人的道德原则与道德判断相符合,它也难以提供一个对他人来说可以接受的正义观念。

下一步是一种广泛的反思平衡(wide reflective equilibrium),即他把自己本人所认同的正义的判断与从其他正义观念(这主要是从社会的哲学传统中寻找)的正义的判断相比较,并权衡各种观念的力量与理由,以作最大限度的修改并仍然保持着一种正义判断的内在连贯性,最终达到一种为所有人都能接受的一种政治正义观。从理想的意义上看,反思的平衡要求,提出所有可能的正义的描述,并将个人的判断及其全部的哲学依据与其相适应。但由于事实上做不到把所有正义判断都描述出来,因此,对于罗尔斯来说,广泛反思的平衡所能做的是,第一步,研究和考察我们通过道德哲学史所得知的以及自己的正义观;第二步,将作为公平的正义观的原则和论据与别的一些熟悉观点相比较。如果公平的正义是更可取的话,这样作为公平的正义就使我们更接近于哲学的理想。

至于作为公平的正义的原则,则是从一种假设的原初状态中由理性的人们进行选择的结果。也就是订立契约的结果。当然最初提出作为公平的正义时,并不能保证它必然与我们的深思熟虑的判断相一致。在这种情况下,我们必须在原则和判断之间进行来回往复地校对和修正。有时改正契约环境的条件,有时又撤销我们的判断以符合原则。我们总是在这些原则和判断之间前后往复,最终达到原则与判断之间的平衡。① 罗尔斯把这一过程称之为反思的平衡,"它是一种平衡,因为我们的原则和判断最后达到了和谐;它又是反思的,因为我们知道我们的判断符合什么样的原则和是在什么前提下符合的"②。

布坎南的政治交易是一种典型的讨价还价理论。讨价还价理论所对付的主要问题就是利益的分配。一般而言,讨价还价中的参与人就达成某种协议而言具有共同的利益,因为有某种协议要比没有协议要好;另一方面,他们就达成何种协议又存在利益冲突。在这样一种模式中,参与人的谈判力量对最后的分配起着决定性的作用,而正义并没有存身之处③。就其模式的应用性而言,它在许多方面都具有广泛的解释力,其最大的成功之处,是对民主政治生活中广泛存在的互投赞成票作了突出的解释。但是这一模式也有其局限之处,如果讨价还价的参与人无法在伦理上接受这样一种边际支付,则政治交易仍然是无法实现;另一方面,如果参与人中的某一方没有足够的钱来实施边际支付,则仍然可能会出现多数压迫少数的情况。

而罗尔斯的反思平衡本质上与上述讨价还价模式有别,它是一种理性讨论(rational discussion)的方法。理性讨论可以说是一种特别的讨价还价,它不允许存在参与人的策略性表达等机会主义行为,另外与参与人的地位、财富、技巧、自然天赋等相关的谈判力量也被屏蔽掉。它所唯一要考虑的因素是"更好的论证的力量"(power from the better argument)。它与讨价还价模式

---

① 罗尔斯,1988年,第15—19、38—49页;Rawls, 2001, pp.29—32。
② 罗尔斯,1988年,第18页。
③ Jon Elster, *The Cement of Society: A Study of Social Order* (Cambridge: Cambridge University Press, 1989), pp.50—51.

的另一区别是,它还考虑一些没有谈判力量的人的利益,比如残障者和后代。在讨价还价模式中,由于残障者和后代并未对当前的社会有所贡献,他们没有任何谈判力量来保护自己。而理性讨论模式则通过一种合理的论据来证明一种正义的制度,从而保证没有任何谈判力量的代表者的利益。

六、结论

通过对两人的考察,我们的结论是,他们都是契约论建构主义。两人的理论结构中都试图以参与人缔约的形式,通过共同协议来达成一种政府或宪政制度的基本框架。两者最大的共同之处就在于对同意这个基本要素的强调,但是对这一要素的强调并不能掩盖两种理论之间存在的重大差别。

布坎南将经济学应用到公共理性的研究中去,其最大的功绩是在契约论中引入计算的成分。在布坎南那里,计算(calculus)是一个极为关键的词语,在他看来,民主的根本问题,在于个人的偏好如何表达并形成一种合理的公共选择。在这一选择中,个人(或社会利益集团)对成本与收益的计算是天经地义的事,能否获得最大收益的表达方式就成为衡量新制度的根本标准。因此在契约中引入计算不但是可能的,而且也是必然的。这种可计算性,使得公共选择的政治哲学开始日益关注制度设计、公共政策方面的问题,其优点在于:1. 精确性;2. 不同的制度进行细微比较。

然而在罗尔斯看来,将制度建立在这种计算的基础上是极为危险的。罗尔斯并不否认在订约过程中有某种利益计算的成分,但是正义制度的根本基础并不是计算,而是自由和平等人们之间的相互尊重。他认为,"如果我们把社会利益的计算视为与基本权利和自由永远相关的话,那么,基本自由的地位和内容将无法确定。这将使基本自由随特定时间和地位的变迁的环境而发生变化的做法,很容易引起政治争论,增加了公共生活的不确定性和敌意"[①]。在自由和平等的人们之间的相互尊重的基础上建构的正义观

———
① Rawls, 2001, p. 115.

念和正义制度,其基本的方法就是证明。罗尔斯认为,宪政自由民主社会中有一个思想的传统,这个传统即"一个社会的基本制度以及对这些制度的已被接受的诠释形式",它"可视为一种非明确地共同拥护的观念与原则的源泉"①。政治哲学的任务就在于揭示和发现这个传统,将"非明确地共同拥护的观念与原则的源泉"明确化并取得逻辑的前后一致性。而这就是一种证明的契约论方法,它与计算的契约论形成相互关联,而又相互对立。

这两者的方法各有千秋,计算方法对于契约条件的反思并没有证明方法的深入,后者所提出的问题完全超出了经济学的视域,从而使契约论有更多的历史感,对现实条件的把握也更深刻。而证明方法则在成本收益的分析、运用数学模型方面更胜一筹。从而其应用性也更强,能够针对现实的问题提出对策建议,这一点却是证明的契约论所无法做到的。从当代契约论的发展历程来看,诺齐克、范因伯格(Joel Feinberg)、高斯(Gerald F. Gaus)主要采用的是一种证明方法;而哈桑依(John Harsanyi)、高西尔(David Gauthier)和宾莫尔(K. Binmore)则走的是计算的路子,从而形成两个基本不同的潮流。总的看来,这两种契约论的方法都不应忽视。而如何把这两种方法有机结合起来,并运用到现实问题中去,则是契约论发展中应当实现的目标。

(作者系北京大学政府管理学院博士研究生)

---

① Rawls, 1996, p. 14.

苏格拉底与亚里士多德论意志软弱*

● 卢华萍

通过结合苏格拉底和亚里士多德对伦理生活的理解,我试图消除他们在意志软弱问题上的表面张力。苏格拉底否认把意志软弱现象解释为快乐/痛苦的感觉胜过了知识。他的最终目的是捍卫知识在伦理生活中的引导地位。为此,他首先把知识概念(苏格拉底知识)和普罗塔哥拉式的审慎判断严格地区分开来,把前者界定为对人的伦理生活进行反思的那个"点";其次,他把知识所引导的对象定位成作为一个整体的伦理生活,而不是具体的伦理行为。亚里士多德从激情的角度对意志软弱现象所作的说明并不成功。但是,他可以从欲望的角度给出一个更合理的说明,并且借此指出人的伦理生活的必要性和可能性都是由人的理性和欲望共同构成的;意志软弱的现象只是尖锐地表现了这一点。这样,苏格拉底和亚里士多德都可以承认,现象(包括意志软弱)在伦理生活中有不可忽略的意义;这是一切伦理思考和伦理努力需要坚持的一个要点。

是不是有可能,一个人在行动中会违背他所作出的最好的、同时又在他的践履能力范围内的判断?如果答案是肯定的,那么这又何以可能?这个问题对常人而言并不陌生。但是,首先把它放在"意志软弱"的名下进行哲学讨论的是苏格拉底和亚里士多德。表面上看起来,苏格拉底似乎宣称一个人在行动中不可能明知故意地违背自己的更好判断,因为真正的知识总是可靠地导向相应的行动,这之间绝无断裂。作为对比,亚里士多德则争辩说,日常识别到的意志软弱不仅完全可以理喻,而且也对伦理思考具有不可忽略的重要性,因此理应得到严肃的哲学探究。

然而,这样来描画苏格拉底和亚里士多德的讨论,可能过于肤浅了。而如果我们就此推论说,两位先哲在"意志软弱"论题上势不两立,那我们则更是受了

---

* 非常值得注意的是,当亚里士多德谈论 akrasia 现象时,这个概念对他而言意味相

误导。我的猜测是,对两位先哲本人而言,在他们的显明论证即他们明确声言的论证中,可能还隐含着另外某些更为深刻的考虑;可能正是在这个更深刻的层次上,他们在表面上相互反对的辩论背后能够握手言和。这样的猜测给了我一个新鲜的动力来验证这个见解:苏格拉底和亚里士多德表面上对意志软弱作为一种现象的可能性持有相反的论点,然而,当我们试图公正、合理且融贯地理解他们各自为这些论点提出的论证时,我们发现也许有必要把这些论证进一步和他们对伦理生活之可能性的理解联系起来——而正是通过把意志软弱论题在某种意义上处理成伦理生活的可能性问题,我们看出他们在意志软弱论题上其实也有可能共享一种理解,或者能够彼此同情,或者至少绝不针锋相对。基于我自己对《普罗塔哥拉》①中的苏格拉底和《尼各马科伦理学》②中的亚里士多德的解读,我将在下文尝试着发展和辩护这个见解。

当广泛,"意志软弱"(weakness of will)和"缺乏自制"(incontinence)这两种通行的译法也许都无法精确地涵盖和把握他的全部本意。首先,后来的亚里士多德研究者们从未就下面这类问题达成过一致意见:亚里士多德本人究竟有没有一个明确的"意志"概念来对应我们现在的理解;或者,换种方式,我们是否能够从他的伦理学作品中按照他的应有之意来合理地重构出一个这样的概念,却又不因此而损及他的整个伦理学体系的一贯性;甚至,鉴于论证的经济性原则,我们究竟是否非得引入一个"意志"概念才能有意义地理解亚里士多德对 akrasia 的处理(关于围绕这些问题展开的争论,参看且比照这两部著作:Anthony Kenny, *Aristotle's Theory of the Will*, New Haven: Yale University Press, 1979 和 Justin Gosling, *Weakness of the Will*, London: Routledge, 1990, 163—166, 169—170)。此外,亚里士多德本人在《尼各马科伦理学》中区分了两种类型的 akrasia——一种是鲁莽(rashness),也就是直接受感觉和情感的牵引,而不作任何意义上的实践推理;另一种大略地相当于现代版本的"意志软弱",这种情形中的行动者确实经由深思熟虑(deliberation)作出了他所能作出的最好判断,但在实际的行动中,他还是因"强烈的情感"的影响而违背了这个最好的判断(1105b18—28)。尽管后来的——尤其是中世纪以来的——哲学家把相当大的重要性分配给了后一种类型的 akrasia,本文的分析却将表明,前一种类型对亚里士多德而言也占据不可忽略的权重,尤其当我们把这种类型和他的伦理教育思想联系起来考察时。正是主要基于这两方面的观察,我宁愿使用 akrasia 来贯串本文的讨论,尽管我注意到苏格拉底本人从来没有使用过这个词。但是,为了行文的流畅,我仍然权且沿用"意志软弱"——只是在这里提醒读者不要依此作狭窄的联想。

① 本文对苏格拉底的引用全部来自 *Protagoras*, Plato, tr. S. Lombardo & K. Bell。
② 本文对亚里士多德的引用全部来自 *Nicomachean Ethics*, Aristotle, tr. T. Irwin。

不过，在开始正式的论证之前，允许我首先澄清一个要点。在反驳意志软弱的可能性时，苏格拉底径直瞄准的靶子理应是对意志软弱现象的日常解释，而不是那种现象本身。① 苏格拉底拒绝像日常解释那样，把意志软弱的现象归结为快乐之类的东西战胜和支配了知识。这样的话，苏格拉底对日常解释的反驳很可能还蕴涵甚至必定要求一个正面的努力，以澄清和维护知识的引导地位。苏格拉底的这个隐含的意图是我要通过本文的论证逐步挑明的一个方面。但是，为了基于其自身的合理性来尽量不偏不倚地阐释和辩明这个意图，我首先反而要帮助苏格拉底的对手以最好的姿态站出来。相应地，我要做的第一步工作是借力于普罗塔哥拉意义上的审慎判断（prudential judgment）来为日常的知识观念润色，帮助它在一定限度内显出它自己的最大合理性。但是，即使经过了这样的竭力修正，日常知识观念仍然会在意志软弱的情形中被挫败。这将让我们折回苏格拉底本人的一个极端策略，即把知识概念和一切判断区分开来；结果，我们将得到苏格拉底知识（Socratic Knowledge）。这个区分表明：一旦涉及伦理生活，一切判断，即便是我们所能作出的最好判断，都要受制于我们作为现象性存在的那些条件，从而我们应该对我们所获得的任何"知识"始终保持反思性的关注。相应地，苏格拉底知识的本质就在于标示出一个点，正是在这一个点上，我们能够注意、承认、进而反思这些判断的限度，并且由此获得改进它们的动力和出发点。

这种解读开放了一条途径来容许苏格拉底承认，日常观察到的意志软弱现象确实具有某种可能性。这时候的苏格拉底能够说，在意志软弱的情形中发生的是判断（而绝不是知识）在引导行动一事上失败了，或者显出了软弱。然而，对这一种失败和软弱的识别和承认反而促使苏格拉底去寻求一种确实能够可靠地引导伦理生活的知识。仅仅就这个知识概念而论，苏格拉底说：在意志软弱的情形中，知识绝没有被挫败。

---

① Gerasimos Santas 在 "Plato's *Protagoras* and Explanations of Weakness"（*The Philosophical Review*，Vol. 75，Issue 1，Jan. 1966，3—33）中也这样认为。

如果这是苏格拉底关于意志软弱确实要说的东西,那么亚里士多德在《尼各马科伦理学》中对苏格拉底的反驳就是有问题的。在我看来,亚里士多德的这个反驳恰恰显示他误解了,或者说过于肤浅地理解了苏格拉底对意志软弱的辩驳。此外,虽然亚里士多德论证的出发点是要维护日常的见解,他的策略却将被证明是不合常识的。尽管如此,这个显而易见的失败反倒让我好奇地想要探究一下,①亚里士多德在他的论证中可能还隐含了什么。在尝试挖掘这个可能隐含的本意时,我发现了一种更合理地根据欲望的影响来理解意志软弱的方式。亚里士多德相信,我们的多数欲望自有其特殊的渊源。②存在着某些欲望,它们在我们对世界的反应中已然占据了如此重要的分量,以致它们可能跟我们的种种情境建立了一些强有力的关联。因此,如果的确是欲望产生了意志软弱的可能性,那么所涉及的欲望可能首先正是在这种意义上发挥作用的。

　　在我看来,对苏格拉底和对亚里士多德的含蓄考虑的这些深究并不相互分离;相反,它们被同一个论题牵系在一起——伦理生活的限度和可能性。显然,苏格拉底和亚里士多德对意志软弱的讨论分别从不同的方向接

---

① 在这一点上,我以同等的态度对待苏格拉底和亚里士多德:我相信,如果我们今天认为可以轻易地对他们各自的论证提出反驳,那么我们自己很可能冒了误解他们的危险;我相信,两位先哲中的每一位在思想上都有其自身的"圆融性",只是我们必须通过解释,甚至通过一定意义上的重构,来帮助他们把这种圆融凸现出来。

② 值得注意的是,亚里士多德在这里心想的理应是"渊源(derivations)"而不是"理由(reasons)"。照我的理解,一个渊源客观地描述了事情首先何以出现,而一个理由——就其经由思考而被"想"出来而言——则是"理性的"。戴维森(Davidson)认为,"意志软弱"没有"逻辑上的困难";因为,如果一个人经过深思熟虑后作出一个好的判断,即他"最好做 B 而不是做 A",但他同时也"有一个理由"做 A,那么,假定他想做 A 的那个理由是条件性的(conditional)或者"关系性的(relational)",而让他判断"最好做 B"的理由则是"非条件性的",这里就不存在逻辑的冲突(第 39 页)。把这个分析运用到我们的例子中:一个人可能按照某个欲望来行动,同时却又充分地意识到理性相对地提出的禁令——这里不存在逻辑的矛盾。不过,在亚里士多德提供的吃甜食的案例中,在引导行动方面有时候可能胜过理性的那种欲望也许是有"渊源"的,但从来都无法前后一贯地具有"理由"。因为,在如下的意义上,这样一个欲望所能采取的合法形式总是条件性的:一个人能够按照某个欲望来行动,当且仅当不存在来自任何一般信念的禁令,而且行动本身在他的能力范围之内。从逻辑的观点来看,一个这种类型的欲望绝不可能胜过理性,因为"按照这个欲望来行动"的"关系性理由"总是必然意味着理性的介入。

近了这个论题。但是,在最终的意义上,它们之间并没有决定性的对立。不管怎样,我们不能忽略两位先哲共同给我们留下的一个线索:如果权当日常识别到的意志软弱现象为我们思考人的伦理生活提供了一个特殊的契机和视角,那么我们应该能够不限于对"意志软弱"持悲观的见解,而是借此进一步获取对我们的伦理处境的深刻理解。

一

在《普罗塔哥拉》中,关于意志软弱的讨论出现在一个更宽泛的话题之下,即,什么是善(goodness),或者善本身。苏格拉底从这个问题着手:是否,一件令人快乐的事情仅仅因为令人快乐,所以是善的,一件令人痛苦的事情则仅仅因为令人痛苦,所以是恶的。普罗塔哥拉立即觉出了这个问题的复杂性:要想得出一个合适的答案,一个人最好不要把自己局限于他现在已有的思想资源,而首先应该提升到一个全局性的观点,这就是说,他得把他的整个生活和整个一生都考虑进来(351d1—5)。

也许可以把普罗塔哥拉的策略性回答理解为,一旦涉及"善的"与"恶的"、"令人快乐的"与"令人痛苦的"这些概念,以及它们之间错综交合的关系时,判断就必须在对一个人生活的全景式透视的背景下作出。但我们也知道,不管一个人企图把自己的全面性观点推伸得多么广阔,以便涵盖他的"整个"生活,他却是基于已经积淀在他内部的那些经验、观念、信念和想象来进行这种推伸的。换句话说,一个人对自己的未来的设想、预期和见解等,可能根本上还是有赖于这个人目前的资源。若是这样,那么从普罗塔哥拉的策略中还能筛得出多少智慧来?然而,另一方面,假定我们的伦理思考根本不可能简简单单地抛弃它对审慎的一贯坚持,那么苏格拉底何以可能倡导一种伦理的生活却又不简单粗暴地打发掉审慎?这样,苏格拉底在解决意志软弱问题时将面对的真正的挑战就是:他得仍旧容许普罗塔哥拉式审慎在伦理生活中发挥某个角色,只是他同时必须小心而又严格地为那个角色划定限界。所以,如果苏格拉底执意要用他自己的知识概念来辩驳有关意志软弱的日常解释,那么苏格拉底知识就必须能够有力地回应我们在此关切的这个挑战。

关于意志软弱的日常解释,苏格拉底真正要反对的地方在于它对知识的描述。既然如此,我们最好就从那个描述着手。人们常常说,就其引导行动的能力而言,知识是软弱的。一个人也许具有知识,但支配他的不是知识而是欲望,欲念,以及诸如爱和害怕之类的其他激情(passions)。更糟糕的是,人们说知识像个奴隶一样被这些陌生的力量拖来拽去(352b2—c1)。正是在意志软弱的情形中,人们最经常地见证到知识的这种软弱性:许多人,尽管他们知道,关于如何行动,他们已经作出了最好的判断,并且(知道)那样的判断也在他们的践履能力范围之内,但在实际行动中他们还是背叛了这个知识。对这样的现象,日常的解释直截了当:知识被快乐或者上面提到的其他某些力量占了先(352d3—e2)。

这个解释自有其道理。为了弄清这个道理,我们需要注意到隐含在对意志软弱的日常描述中的某些区分。可以测知,人们日常谈到知识,指的是关于什么是善什么是恶①的判断。一般而言,某件事,当它带来的快乐大于痛苦时,它是善的;当它带来的痛苦大于快乐时,它是恶的。但是,我们还可以进一步区分目前的快乐/痛苦与长远的快乐/痛苦。显然,普罗塔哥拉式审慎与这个进一步的区分紧密相关。这可以通过两个常见的案例展现出来。许多人基于他们自己的生活经验而判断一件事为恶,所参照的并不仅仅是它所带来的即时的快乐或痛苦,而是它在预期中将造成的某些痛苦(353d1—8)。比如,油炸食品被判断为恶的,因为一个人预料它长远看来终将弄糟他的健康,尽管他没有必要因此而否认它在当下为他带来的好的口感。还有,许多人虽然感到某件事带来了即时的痛苦,却仍然出于别的理由而认可其价值。比如,一个人认为一个手术是值得的——因为他预期它终将给他带来健康——尽管代价只能是当前一段时期必须忍受如此多的痛苦和不便(354a2—b4)。在前一个案例中,即时的快乐没有仅仅作为快乐而被

---

① 我在这里谈论的"善"和"恶",分别粗略地对应于英文的"good"和"bad"。

否定:这种快乐之所以不被评价为善,是因为人们预期它长远地看将造成占据支配性分量(与快乐的分量相比)的痛苦。同样,后一个案例中的即时的痛苦就其自身而言也无权要求一个人来承担和忍受:支持人们来承受这种痛苦的是对某些长远的快乐的预期。

假定,意志软弱的日常解释所谈论的知识就是这种普罗塔哥拉意义上的审慎判断。那么,就此而论,日常观察到的知识的软弱可能部分地缘于普罗塔哥拉式审慎的脆弱性。那种脆弱性进而又可以被追究到现象的相对性。快乐和痛苦是对特定现象的经验,不管这些经验是真实的还是想象中的,是当下的还是预期中的,是迅即的还是延续的,等等。在这样的关系中,现象的相对性预先决定了这些经验缺乏足够的可靠性来充当判断的基础和根据。正像同一个物体从不同的距离来看会让人感觉到不同的大小,同样,诸如"战争带来痛苦"这个判断,若由亲历过战争的老兵说出来,相比于由一个激进却未谙世事的年轻人来宣称,其蕴含的深刻性和真诚度也要大得多。那个年轻人若要足够严肃地看待这个判断,严肃到让它成为抵制切身卷入任何战争的首要的理由,就必须以特定的方式来想象人们在距他遥遥的地方感到的痛苦,以致那些痛苦仿佛融入了他自己的切近的情感(immediate feelings);否则的话,我们没有理由指望他首先和主要地参照他人的痛苦来作出个人的决定。类似地,要让一个人鉴于油炸食品将会造成的特定痛苦来决定不吃它们,这个人就必须以某种方式感觉到那些被预期的痛苦。例如,相比于一个体弱如风烛的老人,一个身强力壮的年轻人可能更加难于抗拒美味的油炸食品的诱惑——未必只是因为那位老人更加明智或者更加坚毅,而很有可能也是因为,相比于这位年轻人,老人以一种更切近的方式感觉到了油炸食品将会产生的痛苦。

在根据现象的相对性做过这番诊断之后,普罗塔哥拉式审慎几乎根本就不可能免于脆弱性。因为,本质上而言,任何普罗塔哥拉意义上的审慎判断都至多是种种快乐和痛苦间的一个明智的权衡。这样的话,知识的软弱就是根本性的:知识会辜负它引导行动的角色,说到底是因为它自己本来就缺乏一个真正稳固的基础。然而,换个角度看,相对性诊断可能也指示了一个恰当的方向来理解伦理生活。按照这种理解,伦理生活不是独立于或分离于日常生活的另一种生活,而是以一种伦理的方式来过我们的日常生活。如果日常生活不得不在一个现象的世界中度过,而相对性又是我们的现象性存在的一个本质特征,那么,为了以一种伦理的方式来过我们的日常生活,我们为什么要取消这种相对性呢——我们又何以能够一贯地取消它呢?此外,如果人终究是有理性的存在者,那么,他在面对相对性时就不该是完全消极的。不管怎样,完全可以设想:正是对相对性的这种识别和承认,激励我们经常以反思性的眼光审视任何已经获得的知识。而且,鉴于人的条件几乎没有任何固定的界限,亦即,鉴于新的限制总是紧跟着已经被克服掉的限制而来,我们应该谦虚地承认:我们有能力过的伦理生活也许至多受到我们的条件允许我们获得的最好知识的引导。这意味着,对伦理生活本身的界定也要以我们的条件为背景,或者建立在我们对这些条件的理解之上。这为伦理思考开辟了新的空间:应当对伦理生活本身进行反思。结果,普罗塔哥拉式的知识无疑有能力为伦理生活提供一个基础,只是这个基础的稳定性是有限的,绝不意味着在任何意义上都永恒不变——作为伦理反思的结果,总是会有一些变化和改进发生在这个基础中。

借助对相对性诊断的这一正面解读,我们可以再一次改进日常的知识观念,让它指称在一个人的现象性条件限度内的最好的普罗塔哥拉式判断。这样一类知识仍然无法避免日常解释对它在引导行动方面的软弱性的责备。事实上,只要我们还用判断来定义知识,知识就很难在任何意义上合理地避免这个责备。毕竟,一般而言,判断区别于行动。意志软弱只是以极端的方式凸显了这个区别,甚至于它仿佛变成了一个不得不借助他力来架通的沟壑。在这一点上,为了维护知识的引导地位,我们很容易想到的一个策略就是转嫁提供支持的负担。我们在判断和行动之间识别到的区别产生了一种可能性,即,知识本身并不同时产生出任何相应的资源来确保它对行动的引导得以兑现。那么,不妨引进一个第三要素,比如"意志"(will),来支持那种兑现。这样的话,当知识对行动的引导没有被兑现时,该受责备的就不是知识,而是本该为这种兑现提供支持的那个要素了。这样,一个新的版本的解说也许会提出:在意志软弱中被揭示出的不是知识过于软弱以致无力引导行动,而是被引入的那个要素过于软弱而没能支持这种引导的兑现。可惜,这大概不是一个有前途的策略。首先,如果知识不得不依赖另外某个东西来成全它对行动的引导,那么它恰恰因为这个依赖而仍然可以说是软弱的。即使这个策略保存了知识对行动的引导地位,我们还是觉得迫切地需要根据论证的经济性原则来抛弃这个策略。因为,由于引进了一个新的要素,这个策略实际上不必要地增加了意志软弱论题的复杂性。它留下了更多需要加以解释的东西,诸如:知识、行动和被引进的要素之间存在什么样的复杂关系,那个要素将用什么样的方式来沟通知识和行动,以及它事实上又为什么可能达不成沟通,等等。①

这些日常见解和理论努力,不管它们的意图是质疑、还是辩解甚或在一定程度上维持知识的引导地位,在某种意义上统统可以被收归于苏格拉底的一个双刃计划;只是这个计划相当曲折地隐藏在苏格拉底对意志软弱的讨论中,需要我们抓住最关键的线索,谨慎地揭示出来。当然,苏格拉底反驳对意志软弱的日常解释;但是另一方面,这个反驳也充当他的一部分策略,目的是为知识概念②作为伦理生活的指针这个地位作辩护。在我们到此为止已经草草完成的第一步工作中,我们从关于知识的日常描述着手,尽

---

① 这是我本意上不愿把 akrasia 译作"意志软弱"的又一个理由。"意志"本该属于这个策略所引进的"第三个要素"。这样的解说不可能有效地打发掉日常观察到的知识之软弱,而且也不会是苏格拉底的选择。

② 注意,我现在开始使用"知识概念"(conception of knowledge),以示区别于前面谈到日常解说时所用的"知识观念"(idea of knowledge)。当我说"知识观念"时,我用它(不严格地)指称人们具体地、有内容地拥有的知识(主要由判断构成),也包括人们对这类知识的"定义"。而按照我将在下文展开的理解,当我说"知识概念"时,我大致用它表示一个没有任何内容的"点";这个点可以为伦理反思提供一个相对而言最彻底、最根本、也最"抽象"、最"超脱"的观点(point of view),而伦理反思的内容当然部分地包括上述的"知识观念"。

这个区分在此之前并不明确。我只是笼统地谈到"知识"。不过读者仍然可以看出,那些"知识"有时对应现在的"知识观念",有时又对应"知识概念"。至于"苏格拉底知识",它可能同时涵盖二者。这可以从下文的分析中看出来。但是,考虑到论证的简洁性,我在正文中不会刻意强调这些术语的特殊用法。

最大可能改进了这个描述所指涉的知识观念。尽管我们显然看到,这些改进无一能够真正成功地维护知识的引导地位,我们所做的这些工作却并非全无成果。因为,通过这些努力,我们至少已经明白苏格拉底将贡献出的知识概念不可能是什么,并且猜测到了他理解意志软弱的这样两条相互承接的可能思路:借助一定的语汇和概念,确实可以合理地表述意志软弱现象的可能性;同时,寻求理解意志软弱现象,这在更深的层次上可能也蕴含了对伦理生活之究竟可能性的某种理解。从现在开始,苏格拉底将用他自己的独特方式向我们表明,这两条思路是如何可能的。为了做到这一点,他需要发展出一个苏格拉底式的知识概念。在相当重要的意义上,这个概念将有别于我们此前考察的那个知识观念。另外,我们必须预先记住,当苏格拉底直面意志软弱现象来为知识概念在伦理生活中的引导地位作辩护时,他并不着意证明或者确立知识概念的这个地位——对苏格拉底而言,知识概念就是伦理生活的指针。苏格拉底的论辩主要是想表明:究竟是何种知识概念,在意志软弱现象所提出的挑战面前,能够成功地保持它的引导地位。

苏格拉底首先需要澄清有关的概念和语汇。他指出,在意志软弱的日常解说中,其实并不存在对"善"与"恶"这两个概念的实质性指涉(354e8—355c1)。一个人把快乐多于痛苦的状态判断为善的,而把痛苦多于快乐的状态判断为恶的。这时候,一个人谈论"善"与"恶",仅仅是用它们来方便地代表对快乐和痛苦的计算结果。就算这样一些计算已经把最复杂、最多样、最广泛的快乐和痛苦都考虑进来了,根本而言,"善"与"恶"在此也不代表更多的东西。这意味着,日常的善恶判断可以被正当地化约为对一些快乐和一些痛苦进行计算得出的结果。若是这样,那么发生在意志软弱现象中的事情其实不过就是某些快乐/痛苦超过了另一些快乐/痛苦。

苏格拉底理应不会否认,这样描述的意志软弱作为一种现象是可能的。至多,他会说,单单快乐/痛苦这一对概念就足以把握意志软弱这样的现象了——甚至出于清楚性和简单性的考虑,单单使用这一对概念来把握这个现象,反而更好。更重要的是,由于已经限定了恰当的概念和语汇来谈论意志软弱的可能性,苏格拉底现在甚至能够从意志软弱的现象中挖掘出更深刻的意味。看来,一切意志软弱的情形其实都显示了快乐和痛苦的不同感觉之间的一场斗争。诚然,我们大多数人都同意,必须把长远的快乐和痛苦严肃地考虑进来。但是,如果我们仅仅依赖我们的感觉来把握这些长远的要素,那么,那样的考虑根本不会带来任何实质上的区别。因为,主要由于时间的隔阂、空间的距离或者经验的肤浅之类的障碍,我们在对快乐和痛苦进行实际的权衡和计算时常常在一定程度和一定意义上取决于更加切近的感觉;①或者,毋宁说,任何所谓的长远的快乐和痛苦,就一个人对它们的经验要凭借他自身当下的资源而言,本质上仍然是一种当下的感觉。

这些是现象地经验到或者想象到的快乐和痛苦感觉。但是,使得意志软弱成为可能的也许不是快乐和痛苦本身,而是人们经验它们的方式。经验的现象性一面也不应该以伦理生活之类的名义来被否定掉。更精确地说,苏格拉底在这儿看到的症结是,人们单单从现象性的一面来经验快乐和痛苦。往更深处考虑,这可能又进一步暗示了人们的一种生活状态:那是一种隶从于现象的存在状态,在这样的状态中,一个人拘囿于变动不居的经验,持久地滞留和踌躇在经验性的世界中,却又不理解这样的世界(356d3—5)。这种状态极端地配不上人之作为人的地位(358d1)。

伦理生活可能正好代表一种与此相反的状态;不过,即使这样,两种生活状态仍然共享一样东西。究其根本,每一种状态都是一个人过日常生活的一种方式,一个人的现象性存在则至少是那种日常生活中不可或缺的一个方面。如果苏格拉底知识宣称要引导的正好就是这种意义上的伦理生活,那么苏格拉底就是在处理一个非常有挑战性的任务。因为,苏格拉底的知识概念若想贯穿一个人的现象性存在,引导一个人用伦理的方式来过他的生活,它就必须至少对那个现象性方面作出一个合理的表态,给出一个合理的说法。

前面已经暗示过,为了理解苏格拉底知识究竟是什么,一个有用的步骤

---

① 类似的观点,参看 Wiggins 提出的衡量欲望的力量的三个尺度,即欲望的活泼性,它们吸引想像力的强度,以及它们的迫切性程度。

是首先弄清它不是什么。这一步也在苏格拉底本人的策略之中。我们已经通过把知识定义为审慎的判断,来挽救知识作为行动的指针的地位。这种尝试的最终失败让我们看到,苏格拉底知识理应(至少)不完全是判断,它也理应(至少)不直接引导行动。此外,作为最谨慎、最粗略的正面猜测,我们从这种失败中又探出了两条线索,以勾勒出苏格拉底知识究竟是什么:一条线索是,我们用来定义知识的东西必须在一个重要的意义上有别于判断,或者还必须包括除了判断以外的其他要素;另一条线索是,知识引导行动的方式可能是非直接的,或者是非因果性的。

苏格拉底需要拧合这两条线索,最终指向他自己的知识概念。苏格拉底知识引导伦理生活。诚然,一种伦理生活需要在行动中得到表达。但是,伦理生活不能因此而被单纯地化约为伦理的行动。实际上,我们已经注意到,在我们对意志软弱的讨论中,伦理生活主要是作为一种状态出现的,它正好对立于我们从意志软弱现象中揭示出的那种状态。另一方面,即使我们没有十分的把握说苏格拉底知识根本不是判断,我们却可以肯定它不仅仅是判断。① 正如我们已经注意到的,即便是一个人能够得到的最好的判断,也无法避免现象的相对性,从而必须经常得到反思。但是,进行这样的反思要求我们具备相应的资源。假定苏格拉底知识的核心恰好在于提供这样一类资源。那么,尽管知识也可能涉及判断,它最重要的意义却是代表一个观点——从这个观点,一个人能够作出恰当的判断,反思已经作出的判断,并进行相应的改进。这解释了苏格拉底为什么也把知识称作"权衡的艺术"(357d6—7)。因为,就此而论,拥有知识——拥有苏格拉底式知识概

---

① 这符合我在前面第94页注释②提到的一个观点,即"苏格拉底知识"可能同时涵盖我所区分和界定的"知识观念"和"知识概念"。因为,在最强的意义上,这两类"知识"可以分别代表完整的伦理生活所需要的不同的、最好相互伴随但又不可彼此替代或彼此僭越的东西——亦即,一个人在条件允许下能够作出的最好的审慎判断,和一个人借以反思这些判断甚至反思这些条件的观点。但是,我最好更加谨慎地说,即使"苏格拉底知识"具有如此大的包容性,它给予两类"知识"的权重却并不平等:"知识概念"代表它的本质,是苏格拉底之所以能够借它来辩驳意志软弱的关键;至于"知识观念",只有在以"知识概念"作为参照点和鹄的时,才对伦理生活有正面的意义,也才有可能被包括进"苏格拉底知识"中。

念——首先就是摆脱现象的权威,也就是看透现象,推翻它们对我们的统治,并揭示它们背后的真理(356d6—e3)。在这种情形下,即使我们已经在有限的条件下作出了最好的判断,我们也不轻易地自诩已经完全得到了知识。至多,这些判断是通向苏格拉底式知识概念之路上的一些脚步。或者,在一种意义上,知识概念指引着判断的演进。这不是说,知识是这条演进之路上的一个固定的终点。毋宁说,知识就像地平线:我们总是有望抵达它,但其实,它总跟我们保持着一段诱人的距离。这是一个事实,主要是因为我们的条件意味着无定界的限制。一旦我们迟疑地不愿称任何已经得到的判断为"知识",我们大概就已经领会了这些限制,同时也开放了一些可能性来改进我们的判断。

正是在这个更深层的意义上,知识能够成为伦理生活的可靠指针。这个知识的地位不可能被快乐之类的东西动摇。在意志软弱现象中被挫败的是一个判断——而任何一个判断,至多也不过是密切地临近知识的一步。按照这样的解读,判断总是有可能辜负它们引导行动的角色,不管这些判断可能得到过多么精到的修正。意志软弱的现象已经相当清楚地显示了这种可能性。但是,一旦我们超出对意志软弱现象的表面性观察,深入追究其根源,我们就会发现这种全新的伦理思考方式:以苏格拉底知识作为参照,对在意志软弱现象中受到挑战的判断进行开放的反思。

这些就是理应蕴含在苏格拉底对意志软弱现象的讨论中的深刻考虑。按照这个解读,苏格拉底的思路是这样的:他把普罗塔哥拉式审慎在意志软弱现象中表现出的失败部分地归结于那种审慎自身固有的脆弱性,部分地归结于人们在过他们的日常生活时隶从于现象的状态。在任何意义上,苏格拉底知识都让最精到的普罗塔哥拉式审慎也相形见绌,黯然失色。然而,这不意味着彻底地抛弃那样的审慎。相反,基于对伦理生活的理解,苏格拉底理应把普罗塔哥拉式判断作为策略性的行动指针接受下来——只是,同时,他需要提醒人们注意这些判断的限度。进一步说,苏格拉底知识的本意不是要取代审慎的判断来引导行动,而是主要充当一个反思之点来引导作为一个整体的伦理生活。这样做,苏格拉底就能宣扬一种伦理生活却又不至于肤浅地否认日常对审慎的坚持。实际上,苏格拉底一直在教导人们正确而恰当地坚持那样的审慎。这样,苏格拉底成功地回应了我们早先评论普罗塔哥拉式审慎时指出的那个挑战。

有人也许会辩驳说,我附会了太多的东西给苏格拉底,把太多的东西读进了他的心思,他本人却似乎从未对伦理生活的现象性一面表示过如此大的耐心和包容。但是,就我的阅读来看,苏格拉底也从未决定性地否定过那个方面。所以,我宁愿给苏格拉底一个无罪推定(benefit of doubt)。这个宽松的阅读让我看到,正是由于隐含着对伦理生活的深刻理解,苏格拉底对意志软弱现象的显明辩驳才显示得出最大的合理性。如果我的这个解读是有效的,那么,任何要在意志软弱论题上反对苏格拉底的人就得与他进行更加透彻、也更加困难的探讨。不管怎样,我现在可以说,我的策略符合苏格拉底可能持有的这个心意:他苛刻地挑剔日常的伦理思考,归根结底是为了人们好;他发展出那样的苏格拉底式知识概念,是因为他深深地理解到,伦理生活部分地是由人的条件来界定的,从而它的一切进展和改善也需要以人的条件作为基础。① 不妨说,当苏格拉底从概念上把知识区别于最好的判断时,这个知识也变得更加有助于人们理解和追求伦理生活。

二

亚里士多德也是从关于意志软弱现象的日常观察和日常信念着手的。他对这些信念的态度代表他对一般而言的日常信念的这个设想:他主张,一

---

① 在结束对苏格拉底的辩论的分析时,我们看来也更加清楚地领会了"伦理生活的可能性"究竟指什么。它说的大概是这样一种可能性:伦理生活作为一种生活方式,虽以人的有条件的存在为起点和基础,但同时又可以通过突破这些条件本身的限度,也通过反思这些限度及其可突破性,而得到(不断的)进展和改善。换句话说,苏格拉底在这里不必确凿地为我们刻画伦理生活究竟是什么;而是,伦理生活仿佛代表了人跟自己的现象性存在的一个张力:人在这里要摆脱现象的支配,但又永远不可能彻底否定掉自己的现象性存在;相反,他最好去理解后者,等等。当然,这个进一步的工作将由亚里士多德来完成。

旦涉及人的伦理生活，人们总是共享某些信念；即使为所有这类信念提供哲学的支持是件过于理想而无法实现的事情，我们至少也应该维护其中的大多数信念，尤其是最最重要的那一些；如果我们已经通过考察，驳斥了对这些信念的所有关键的反对意见，那么，我们就可以赋予它们以恰当的优先性(1145b3—8)。

亚里士多德解说意志软弱现象，直接的目的是反驳苏格拉底的解说。亚里士多德认为，苏格拉底否定意志软弱作为现象的可能性。既然已经注意到苏格拉底的论证极大地依赖于一个知识概念，亚里士多德的策略首先就是分解那个概念，割断它（按照亚里士多德的理解）联向行动的可靠纽带。受到他自己的潜能-现实之分的启发，亚里士多德区分了两种知识状态——一种是潜在地拥有知识，但不"使用"、"注意"或"激活"之；另一种是实际地据有知识，这时候的知识已经被激发起来并投入运作。根据这个区分，我们可以这样来理解意志软弱现象：这里涉及的那个知识仍然滞留在潜能状态(1146b32—38)。亚里士多德的本意是，通过这样分析知识的概念，割断从知识到行动的"苏格拉底式"纽带。给定上文对苏格拉底的辩论的解读，我们现在会产生这个猜疑：亚里士多德可能从一开始就错误地转述了苏格拉底的知识概念，他实际上夸张地、错误地看待了他自己在意志软弱问题上跟苏格拉底的分歧。但是，我在这里更关心亚里士多德对下面这个日常信念的同情和捍卫："强烈的情感"要对意志软弱的现象负责。亚里士多德的显明论证无疑是失败的，但这个失败将把我的注意力转向其中隐含的另一个论证。就是这个隐含的论证，也许能够更好地传达亚里士多德对日常信念的同情。不过我们也将看到，在根本的意义上，亚里士多德对意志软弱这个问题的理解仍然超越了那些日常信念。

在开始分析亚里士多德对意志软弱现象的解说之前，我们需要提一提另一个区分。这个区分虽然重要，却没有被明说。当亚里士多德一般地谈论"情感"(feelings)时，这个词广泛地包括心灵内部除了"理性"以外的其他所有要素。但是，它的具体内容随着语境的变化而有所不同。为了讨论之便，下文的分析将把这些多样的情形归入两类，一类是"激情"，另一类是"欲望"。

亚里士多德谈论作为激情的情感时,似乎更关心情感对正在进行的实践推理的影响,而不是直接对行动的影响。① 粗略地说,这个影响在两方面发挥作用。一个实践推理的模型是包含大小两个前提的一个三段论——大前提涉及一般(the general),小前提涉及有关的特殊(the particular)。比如,下面这个三段论:(A)没有人被允许打他自己的父亲;(B)这个人是我的父亲;(C)我不被允许打这个人。在这里,A是大前提,B是小前提,C是从A和B推出的结论。一个有效的推理要求兼具关于两个前提的知识。但亚里士多德告诉我们,有时候,一个人也可能仅仅"部分地"具有知识,也就是说,他可能以潜能的状态具有知识但不使用它——没有注意它或者没有激活它(1146b35)。把这个可能性运用于意志软弱现象:意志软弱者在完全的意义上具有关于大前提的知识,但仅仅在潜能的意义上具有关于小前提的知识,所以没能得出本该得出的结论。举例来说:我完全知道没有人被允许打他自己的父亲,但是碰巧有某样东西妨碍了我,以致我没能识别出眼前这个人就是我的父亲(而这是事实),那么很显然,我不会得出结论说,"我不被允许打这个人(因为他是我的父亲)"。若在寻常的情境中,在其他条件同等时,我很容易作出那样的识别,那么,是什么在此时此刻妨碍了我? 某些"强烈的情感"(1147a14),亚里士多德回答说。何种类型的强烈情感? 爱恨之情,性欲,诸如此类(1147a15),亚里士多德列数道——这些情感不仅搅扰我们的肉体,而且妨碍我们的知识,在某些情形中甚至导致"疯狂"(1147a16—17)。也许是为了便于理解,亚里士

---

① 对亚里士多德的显明论述的一个反驳是这样的:如果,只有当一个人具有一个完全且真实的关于行动的判断,而且这个人有能力在行动中践履这个判断,然而他在实际的行动中又背叛了这个判断,这个人才可以被说成是一个意志软弱的人,那么,亚里士多德在辩论中谈论的情形根本就不符合这些条件,因为按照他自己的分析,意志软弱的人对知识的据有实际上是不充分的,不完全的。但是,在我看来,这个批评对亚里士多德不构成挑战。如果可以合法地在亚里士多德身上附会一种从苏格拉底和柏拉图那里沿袭下来的唯理智主义气质,那么我们不妨猜测:不管亚里士多德在辩护关于伦理生活的日常信念时显得多么诚恳,他却仍然信奉理性的最终权威———旦理性已经达到了某些判断,就没有什么东西能够一贯地凌驾那些判断。因此,必定是进行之中的实践推理出了什么差错。那就是为什么,就此而论,亚里士多德对意志软弱现象的显明论述似乎理应说明情感何以妨碍理性有效地作出判断,而不是说明情感何以横刀插入了理性判断和行动之间。

多德作了一些有趣的类比,他把一个在不完全的意义上具有知识的人比作做梦之人、醉酒之人或者疯癫之人(1147a12—14),后来又比作在舞台上背诵台词的演员(1147a19—23);①所有这些人都在一个意义上具有知识,在另一个意义上又不具有知识。

值得注意的是,亚里士多德有意拒绝把潜能-现实之分运用于大前提,只是允许小前提有可能受到情感的不良影响。他对这样的安排自有辩护:在两个前提中,只有小前提代表关于特殊的知识,而由于我们总在感知(perception)中把握特殊,我们的感知觉又特别容易受到强烈情感的影响,所以小前提知识从潜能向现实的转化过程特别容易被打断(1147a25—26);实践推理必须惟独借助小前提来首先引入关于特殊的知识,以便最终指向特殊的行动——由此反推,如果在意志软弱的现象中我们看到实践推理事实上没能抵达特殊的行动,那么我们必定最容易在小前提中追究出原因;假定日常信念对意志软弱的原因的猜测基本上是对的,即行动的失败归根结底在于知识的失败,那么我们可以更加明确地说,知识的这种失败仅仅意味着它没能从它的潜能状态转化成现实状态,这就是说,它仍然停留在不完全的状态;所以,若是我们可以公正地说意志软弱现象根本上是知识的失败,这个失败了的知识就只能是关于小前提的知识(1147a1—3,1147b9—13)。

如果我们从一开始就接受亚里士多德对知识的概念分析,并且始终停留在他所界定的语汇和概念范围内,那么,从逻辑上看,在他对意志软弱现象的这一解说中似乎并没有什么东西不对劲。然而,我们的常识不愿接受他把关于特殊的不完全知识和关于一般的完全知识结合在同一个推理过程

---

① 亚里士多德把这两对类比分别开来是合适的,因为这里提到的那些人显然有一定的区别。但是,就目前的论述而言,演员的类比看起来有点让人疑惑。首先,似乎很难用激情来解释一个演员在背诵台词时并不理解那些台词的真正意义。其次,亚里士多德非常清楚地说过,小前提中的特殊是通过感知觉被把握到的,小前提把这些特殊作为纯粹的事实呈现出来,却不包含任何一般的意义;若此,我们要么知觉到这些特殊,要么根本就没有知觉到。说一个人在一种意义上知觉到了一个特殊,但在另一种意义上,就像演员不具有关于其台词的知识那样,这个人又不具有关于这个知觉的知识,这样说是不可理喻的。

中。假使知识的完全性在于一个事实,即,一个人据有这个知识并且(非常有意识地)注意到这种据有,但是,如果我并未意识到在我面前的这个男人就是我的父亲,我又何以可能注意到"没有人被允许打他自己的父亲",从而何以在亚里士多德所界定的意义上"完全地"据有关于这个命题的知识呢?这个说法似乎更合理:每当涉及实践推理时,一个总是真实的情形是,我们首先识别到某些特殊的情境,然后才会有意识地去选择、运用和激活相关的一般知识。① 因此,如果亚里士多德坚持认为完全的知识必须包含对所知道的东西的注意(在"注意"一词的强的意义上),并且认为意志软弱的现象就是小前提单方面缺乏这种注意,那么,这样的策略似乎就很难有说服力。

这说明,并不是潜能-现实的知识概念的所有逻辑可能性都能被我们的常识所接受。涉及大前提和小前提的知识,一个人要么同时完全拥有二者,要么不完全地拥有二者中的每一个(尽管也不是不可能,一个人完全知道特殊却并不完全知道一般)。把关于一般的完全知识和关于特殊的不完全知识"逻辑地"结合起来,却不符合常识。比如,尽管我总是有一个一般的知识,即没有人被允许打他自己的父亲,这个知识却总需在适当的情境中得到我的注意:如果我没有意识到眼前这个人就是我的父亲,那么在此时,那个一般知识就不会正好作为我不被允许打这个人的理由而被我意识到,更不会在我的实践推理中发挥作用。这样的话,亚里士多德何以能够有意义地说,我虽然不完全知道眼前这个人是我的父亲,同时我却有意识地具有并且注意到——也就是"完全地"据有——"没有人被允许打他自己的父亲"这个

---

① 这一点也许可以帮助我们理解演员的类比。毕竟,意志软弱者有可能在最弱的程度上知觉到他所处的特殊情境,却不理解这个情境的性质,从而也不知道应该运用何种类型的原则。比如,一个人可能知道他在一个家庭中担当父亲的角色,但他对这个角色的声言不过就是口头上说说而已——他并不真正地知道,一个父亲的角色同时还包含了责任和爱,等等。在这样的情形中,这个人关于自己的父亲角色的知识并不保证导向相应的行动,那也就是为什么人们会说这样一个人"根本就不像个父亲"。如果这样的情况确实常见,那么伦理行动就必然不仅要求原则,而且也在同等的重要性程度上要求对特殊情境的理解;而且,这种理解的深浅程度无疑会影响甚至决定对原则的选择和运用。尽管亚里士多德在我们所考察的讨论中并未表达这一点,这却肯定包含在他的"实践智慧"观中。

知识,并把这个知识作为一个前提来推出我不被允许打这个人?

揭示这个结合的失败,有另一层不可忽略的重要意义。一个大前提知识有它自身的真值(truth value),也有它对特殊情境(表现在小前提中)的相关性和可运用性。如果我此时不知道眼前这个人是我的父亲,那么我也就不知道"没有人被允许打他自己的父亲"这个一般知识跟我目前的情境发生了关联。这一点无知并不妨碍我完全知道——即使在亚里士多德的强的意义上来理解知识的"完全性"——那个命题的真值。不管怎样,这样的情况不是不可设想:我虽未意识到眼前这个人是我的父亲,却仍然推论说,我不被允许打这个人;可以从不同的大前提推出这样的结论,例如"没有人被允许打一个无辜的人"。我可能也具有,在某些情况下甚至碰巧还注意到,"没有人被允许打他自己的父亲"。不过,对此时的我来说,这个一般知识不会作为一个大前提来让我推出我不被允许打这个人。因为,这个知识跟我现在所处的特殊情境没有什么被注意到的、对这里所要求的实践推理而言有效的关联。这个观察揭示,在一定程度上,一般知识也许有赖于对特殊情境的感知或理解,才能有效地充当某个实践推理的大前提。甚至可以说,就伦理判断和伦理行动而言,一般知识与特殊情境的相关性比它自身的真值具有更大的重要性,或者起码与后者同等重要。对这个观点,亚里士多德本人在别处显然也是明确支持的。

到此为止,亚里士多德为意志软弱的日常解说所作的显明辩护是不成功的。幸运的是,这些还不是亚里士多德真正要说的东西。当我们进一步试图从这个失败的辩护中挖掘更合理的含义时,我们接近了第二类情感——欲望,发现了它们影响理性的独特方式。

为了演示这种独特的影响方式,不妨考察一下亚里士多德自己提供的吃甜食的案例(1147a29—1147b3)。涉及同一个对象,我们有

S1:如果(a1)我相信甜食总会给我很特别的快感,每当它唾手可得时,我都非常想吃它;而且,

(b1)我现在唾手可得的这个食品是甜的;那么,

(c1) 我非常想吃这个食品。①

S2：如果(a2)有一个一般的信念以充分的理由禁止我吃任何甜食；而且，

(b2) 我现在唾手可得的这个食品是甜的；那么，

(c2) 我不应该吃这个食品。

在此，(a1)看来表达了经常地、稳定地持存在我的欲望结构中的一个欲望。这个欲望有它的渊源，并且(我相信)它总会给我带来"很特别的快感"。对一类事物的某个特性("甜的")的知觉，把这个欲望指向了属于该类事物的"这个食品"。于是，在我真正遭遇这样一个特殊对象时，对它的欲望就会立刻在我的显明意识中"自然地"发生。作为比照，(a2)陈述了一个理性信念，它和上面那个欲望似乎同样经常地、稳定地持存在我这里，②并且同样

---

① 在《尼各马科伦理学》1147a29—31 中，原本在这个地方出现的那个三段论是这样的：如果(a)一切的甜食都应该被尝一尝，且(b)这个特殊的东西是甜的，那么必然地(c)一个人，如果他有能力，如果没有什么东西禁止他，他就应该尝一尝这个东西。在这样一个例子中，(a)看来是跟欲望发生某些正面关系的一个信念——它支持一个人去尝任何甜食。然而，亚里士多德不允许它无条件地发挥效力；相反，他在这里提出了两个"如果"条件句，尤其是第二个条件句。这暗示，尽管我们可能有一些信念来支持特定的欲望，而且这些信念也能用"一切的……都应该……"这样的一般形式来表述，这些信念本身却要受制于其他某些更一般的信念，诸如"如果没有什么东西禁止他"这个条件句所表明的。

出于两个考虑，我对这个原版的三段论做了调整。首先，涉及理性和欲望之间的关系，原版的那个三段论绕了太多的弯路，而我想在理性和欲望能合作于伦理生活之前先把它们从形式上分离开来。其次，这样的调整其更加凸显了亚里士多德在 1147b1—4 中的言下之意，同时也相当符合亚里士多德在 1147a33—34 中提到的另一个三段论的两个前提——一切甜的东西都是令人愉快的，且这个东西是甜的。

② 这里说"经常地、稳定地持存"，对欲望和理性信念而言只有相对的意义。我在这里似乎故意忽略了一些复杂性。其实，"以充分的理由禁止我吃任何甜食"的这个理性信念，它禁止的不仅是而且可能不首先是我吃甜食的行为，而是我吃甜食的欲望。这样的话，这个理性信念的出现本身可能就预设了我已经有一个欲望要去吃甜食，因为否则的话提出禁止就是不必要的。此外也不难想象，如果这个信念总是紧随着我吃甜食的欲望而产生，并且总是成功地妨碍后有效地转化为行动，那么那个欲望自己可能也会逐渐地减弱，甚至于不再出现；不妨想象，由于久已没有实际地经验到甜食一度给我带来的那种特别的快感，我关于那种快乐的记忆已经越来越稀薄，越来越淡漠，直到最后，当甜食出现时，我不再立刻对它曾经能够带来的那种快感产生联想和指望。换句话说，禁止吃甜食的理性信念一方面似乎常常要随着吃甜食的欲望而产生和消长，另一方面也反过来影响那个欲望的命运。但是，本文略去了欲望和理性信念的这种复杂的相互机制。

也因为知觉到一个特殊的对象是"甜的"而跟这个对象联系起来。

正如上文中已经谈到过的,在实践推理中,若是没有首先有意识地知觉到小前提中包含的特殊,那么有关的一般信念也就不可能作为一个大前提来进入有意识的推理过程。这意味着,一般信念被假定应该发挥的功能在某种程度上要受到一个人实际的知觉状态的限制。如果一个人的知觉状态实际上妨碍他充分地意识到某个特定的情境,那么就很难设想,这个人何以在那个一般信念跟这个未被意识到的特殊情境之间注意到任何有意义的关联。但是,事情甚至还要更复杂一些:伴随着我对一个特殊情境的知觉,我的注意力可能不是单纯地指向相应的一般信念。我们在吃甜食的例子中明显地看到,某个欲望也可能要求我去注意,并且在强度上未必弱于那个一般信念的主张。因此,当我知觉到"这个食品是甜的"时,我发现同时有两样东西伴随而来——想吃这个食品的一个欲望,以及指示我不应该吃这个食品的一个一般信念。

很显然,欲望在这里并不像激情那样发挥作用:它并不挫败正在进行的实践推理。这里的欲望是因其"力量"或者"活跃性"(1147a34)而扮演一个角色的;它让 S2 得出的结论在相形之下黯然失色到如此程度,以致最终也许会排挤掉那个结论,让后者无法得到兑现。于是,意志软弱者还是吃了那个食品,而不管他已经意识到他绝不应该吃那样一个食品。尽管如此,在这种情形下,不加分别地谴责欲望却是不公平的。亚里士多德强调,让一个人吃甜食的行为表现出意志软弱的特征的,不是想吃甜食的欲望本身,而是另一个事实,即这个欲望碰巧遭到了正确的理性的反对(1147b2—3)。正是意志软弱者的理性或信念,让他吃甜食的行动显出了意志软弱的特征(1147b1)。我们通常把意志软弱归咎于某些欲望,这有赖于一个假定,即那些欲望怂恿我们背叛了我们的某些一般信念。在上面的案例中,如果一个人根本就没有任何禁止他吃甜食的一般信念,那么,不管是他想吃甜食的欲望,还是他吃甜食的实际行为,都将跟意志软弱没有丝毫瓜葛。

这样,我们在两个层面上梳理了亚里士多德对意志软弱的解说。在他的表面论证中,亚里士多德没有看到这样做有什么困难:把意志软弱者的失败归咎于一个不完全的特殊知识,后者转而又被归咎于"激情"。毕竟,我们可以通过"习惯的养成"这样的计划来驯服激情,让它们重新与理性说和。况且,正如一个人在醉酒状态中的错误行径可以因他在事后回顾时表达的"后悔"而部分地得到补偿,一个人对自己受激情支配的错误行径表达回顾性的后悔,也可能缓解理性受到的威胁,甚至产生一定的积极效果。换句话说,这个人可能从此更好地理解他自己内部的那些激情,并决心为了理性的缘故来驯服它们。然而,我怀疑,甚至亚里士多德本人也不会简单地指望这样一幅光明的图景。

理性面临一个更加困难的挑战。不同于我们从一个多少有些理性主义的角度作出的想象,我们的多数欲望在发挥作用时并不那么武断、任意或者充满偶然性。而是,它们从我们的真实的生活经验中得到了许多支持,它们甚至可能逐渐地积淀下来,作为一些稳定的构成性要素来影响我们对种种情境的反应。也不是不可能,会有某些信念跟这些欲望相互关联而产生出来。然而,另一方面,这些关系到欲望的信念并不无条件地、决定性地发挥作用。因为,一旦涉及人,这些信念总是必须从理性那里请求一个最终的辩护。对神,或者对野兽,意志软弱并不构成一个问题。意志软弱只是人类之人的一个问题,这是因为,被欲望所推动的一个行为本来就已经遭到了理性的反对和禁止。因此,理性面临这个尴尬的问题:一方面,理性无法把这样的欲望简简单单、彻彻底底地放逐出人的生活,因为单单理性绝不足以穷尽对人的处境和人的生活的理解;另一方面,理性如果向欲望作出过大的让步,以致实际上把人交给欲望来指点,它就会失去自己的地盘和基础。

鉴于这样一个困境,有人也许会建议亚里士多德采纳一个新的"观点"来看待目前的问题。这些人也许会跟亚里士多德辩论说,既然你已经承认,单单欲望自身并不造成任何不幸和罪恶,那么为什么不往前再走一步,把怀疑的目标放在禁止一个人按照这些欲望来行动的一般信念上?既然你已经能够接受欲望,那么为什么不进一步抛弃一般信念对欲望的那种终极的优越性,转而批判一般信念——毕竟,这样做也许会帮助我们澄清甚或重构我们的信念框架,使它变得更加适合于引导我们的伦理生活?这个"新的观点"对亚里士多德来说不算新鲜,实际上,他很明白混乱的信念可能使人"受奴役"(1146a13—b5)。然而,亚里士多德反对像苏格拉底那样明确地区分(真正的)信念和知识。因为,至少对某些人来说,在他们的生活中,他们对他们的信念的确信在强烈程度和稳固程度上并不弱于另一些人对他们的知识的确信(1146b25—32)。亚里士多德这样说,不是在混淆信念和知识,而是因为他理解到,对许多人而言,他们的信念就是他们的知识。这样的话,如果我们纠缠于一个意志软弱者在行动中是违背了他的信念还是他的知识,我们就会错过意志软弱现象真正该让我们看到的意义(1146b26—28)。没有一个人的信念体系是完美的。如果苏格拉底知识的重要意义在于充当我们一切理智努力的鹄的,那么,人的信念的这种不完美性恰恰覆盖了信念跟那个知识的远近不同的距离;这些距离取决于我们作为人的存在的必然限度,却不是我们的消极命运,而是为我们的理性提供了发挥积极作用的契机和切入点。

回到意志软弱的案例。通过梳理出亚里士多德对意志软弱的含蓄的解说,我们已经发现了人的条件的两个主要成分——理性和"情感"(尤其是"欲望")。这两个成分结合在一起,可以解释:为什么人需要一种伦理的生活——因为他的理性拒绝让欲望来指使他的生活;为什么人必得通过努力来争取这样一种生活——因为我们的大多数情感实际上经由它们与我们的生活经验的特殊关联而在我们的生活中发挥着作用;此外,人的生活为什么即使到了最高水平也还是一种伦理的生活而不是神圣的生活——因为,尽管理性总是希求、而且努力彻彻底底地超越欲望,理性还是不得不学会直接面对欲望。这些理解基本把握了人的伦理生活的要义,同时也是追求伦理生活的一个恰当的起点。

三

现在,借助两位先哲提供的材料,我们已经把意志软弱粗粗地勾成了一幅立体画。在苏格拉底那里,我们看到人的一种存在状态,人在这种状态中摇摆于现象的世界中，被未经审视的情感、感觉、知觉、意见和信念糊涂了。然而，在这个严厉的、否定性的诊断深处，我们仍然能够感到苏格拉底的一个正面的关切：按照本文的分析，苏格拉底否定和辩驳日常解说，归根结底是要警醒人们注意意志软弱现象所暴露的那种状态，并且最终暗示一条彻底的出路。苏格拉底指出的无疑是一条追求"苏格拉底知识"的道路。不管他的知识概念引起过多大的争议，我们这样解读它仍然是有意义的：至少就它与伦理生活的关联而言，这个知识概念代表并且指引着人战胜现象之武断任意的权威的那些理智努力。

作为对照，亚里士多德相信苏格拉底指出的方向对常人而言是不合适的。作为人与其现象性存在的一个基本关联，"情感"可能跟人的伦理生活发生着相当复杂的关系。有些"情感"几乎可以说是人与生俱来的负担（如果它们终究是负担的话），或者，更准确地说，它们扎根在人性的结构中，并且已然经由人的生活经验而逐渐在人对世界的反应模式中占据了一个比较牢固的地盘。人的理性——亚里士多德说这是人被赋予的唯一一个神圣的要素——执意要反抗"情感"的支配。但是，理性又无法一贯地做到彻底抛弃那些情感而独自升华；相反，理性最好主动地与那些情感达成和谐，提携它们一起"向上"。理性要走的这条与情感一同上升的道路也就是人过伦理生活的道路。

如果我们仅仅注意到，苏格拉底和亚里士多德的论证所共享的那些术语实际上是在非常不同的意义上被使用的，那么我们甚至很难做到让他们真的彼此反对：因为那样的话，他们一直在谈论的事情似乎就互不相干了。但是，如果我们参照他们各自对伦理生活的独特理解来领会他们关于意志软弱的显明论证，那么，他们表面上的针锋相对就容易调和了。在意志软弱现象中，苏格拉底诊断出：伦理生活作为引导人的日常生活的一种方式，如果单纯地依靠普罗塔哥拉式审慎，那么就是脆弱的，无法真正地获得和保持；不过另一方面，不可能一劳永逸地克服伦理生活所面对的现象性局限，也不可能合理地全盘否定人们对审慎的坚持。鉴于对伦理生活的这种理解，苏格拉底必须非常谨慎地界定他的知识概念，如果他终究想让知识有效地引导人的伦理生活的话。结果,最有说服力的做法就是把苏格拉底知识的本质理解成对作为一个整体的伦理生活进行反思的点,而不是对具体行动的直接指针——那是该由判断来做的事情。这样,苏格拉底至少没有必要鄙视伦理生活的现象性的一面。

　　这可以作为苏格拉底对伦理生活的限度和可能性问题的一个回答。显然,不管苏格拉底愿意留出多大的余地来考虑受到现象性约束的人的条件,他的知识概念总是代表一种彻底的解放——彻底地摆脱现象的武断任意的束缚。然而,在亚里士多德看来,这种苏格拉底式的解放很难适用于大多数人。对伦理生活的任何有效的反思都应该从日常生活内部开始——我们应该以日常生活、以我们对这种生活的理解为语境来理解伦理生活。只有采取这样的途径,我们才能真正地理解是什么构成了伦理生活,是什么决定了人要过一种伦理的生活、并且至多只能过那样的生活,又是什么将成全人对伦理生活的这种追求。特别是,意志软弱的情形正好向亚里士多德揭示了:伦理生活是人的生活,而人是同时由情感和理性来界定的;人对一种伦理生活的意向来自他的理性,并且也要理性来成全;因此,一种伦理的生活也就意味着一条道路,理性将沿着这条道路理解情感,并携带情感前行——最后,一切伦理思考,若是不坚持这些基本的要点,就是不恰当的,无所助益的。

　　正是通过这样的定位和分析,我们看到,苏格拉底和亚里士多德关于意志软弱的论证具有真正的深刻性。在讨论意志软弱作为一种现象是否可能并且何以可能时,两位先哲并不肤浅地彼此反对。而是,他们首先都意识到,对理解伦理生活的可能性和必要性而言,现象作为一个整体本身就有不可忽略的重要性。

参 考 书 目

1. Plato, *Protagoras*, tr. S. Lombardo & K. Bell, from *Readings in ancient Greek philosophy: from Thales to Aristotle*, ed. by S. Marc Cohen, Patricia Curd, C. D. C. Reeve, Indianapolis: Hackett Pub. Co.,

1995.
2. Aristotle, *Nicomachean Ethics*, tr. T. Irwin, Indianapolis: Hackett Pub. Co., 1985.
3. Donald Davidson, *Essays on Actions and Events*, Oxford: Clarendon Press, 1980.
4. Justin C. B. Gosling, *Weakness of the Will*, London: Routledge, 1990.
5. Anthony Kenny, *Aristotle's Theory of the Will*, New Haven: Yale University Press, 1979.
6. Gerasimos Santas, "Plato's *Protagoras* and Explanations of Weakness", *The Philosophical Review*, Vol. 75, Issue 1 (Jan. 1966), 3—33.

(作者系北京大学哲学系硕士研究生)

海德格尔的因缘和亚里士多德的"为了善"

● 朱 清 华

海德格尔的此在生存在一个由"为了……"(um-zu)和"为何之故"(Worum-willen)指引关联共同勾连起的世界中。只有在这个因缘整体中,存在者之存在才能显现出来并为人所把握,世界才会对人展开。人对世界的领会以此为根基,人的认识也必以这个因缘整体、这个世界为出发点。海德格尔生存论哲学深深植根于古希腊哲学中,尤其从亚里士多德哲学吸收了许多重要的哲学概念和思想。就本文讨论的范围而言,海德格尔从亚里士多德灵魂揭示真理的诸种方式,尤其是技术(techne)、实践智慧(phronesis)、智慧(sophia)等几个方式中挖掘到了他的存在论根源。从这个角度来说,海德格尔的"为了……"和"为何之故"勾连起来的因缘系统同亚里士多德著名的"幸福论"体系在某种意义上形成对应。海德格尔正是在对亚里士多德这些思想的深刻领会基础上,将它们加以存在论和现象学地阐释后吸收进自己的哲学建构中,成为构造他的生存论哲学的基础。

《存在与时间》中,海德格尔重新解释了世界现象。他认为我们所处的世界并不是多种客观物的聚合,人——"此在"迎面遇上的通常所谓的"物"无一不是用具[①]。不但如此,而且根本不存在单一的用具,用具的一个本质特征是,它们都是出现在无数用具构成的整体中的[②]。只有在用具整体中,用具才是用具。用具在人的实践中

[①] Martin Heidegger, *Being and Time*, trans by John Macquarrie & Edward Robinson (New York: Harper & Row, Publishers, 1962), p. 96. 海德格尔,《存在与时间》,陈嘉映 王庆节译,三联书店 1999 年版,第 79 页。德文见 *Sein und Zeit*,第 7 版,Max Niemeyer, Tubingen 出版社,1953 年(此后按惯例缩写为 *SZ*),SZ68。

[②] 用具指引模式包括用具的效用性和材料的有用性。效用的"何所为"与有用性的"为什么"作为用具的指引变成具体的指引。这些具体化通常被称为用具的特性。〔美〕约瑟夫·科克尔曼斯,《海德格尔的〈存在与时间〉》,陈小文 李超杰等译,北京,商务印书馆,1996 年版,第 143 页。

在使用中成为上手的,用具被消融在使用中,并且往往人对这些用具"日用而不知"。所谓用具,总是一种"um-zu(为了……)",即它们具有指向性或指引性的特征。它指向它的使用目标,同时也指向它的来源——它的材料、材料的来源等等。也可以说,用具是在系统中存在,离开该系统,便找不到它们的任何痕迹,所以实际上用具是生活的因素和环节。海德格尔的存在者构成了一个由"um-zu"勾连起来的因缘整体。因缘整体却不是无限蔓延的,它最终回溯到一个不再"为了"什么而自身却是所有"为了"的目标,这是此在存在的"为何之故 Worum-willen, for the sake of which"。正是这个最后不再有因缘的"为何之故"赋予了前此的 um-zu 因缘关联以意义。它们共同构成了"意蕴"世界①。

"意蕴作为世界就是由生存论上的'为何之故'确定下来的,"②作为共在的此在就生存在一个由"um-zu"和"Worum-willen"共同勾连起来的世界中。只有在这个整体中,存在者之存在才能显现出来并为人所把握,世界才对人展开。人对世界的领会以此为根基,人的认识也必以这个意蕴整体、这个世界为出发点。

海德格尔用 um-zu 为了……和 Worum-willen 因……之故、为何之故勾连起世界并不是空穴来风。他的蓝本就在亚里士多德哲学中。许多中外哲学家已经指出了亚里士多德哲学对海德格尔哲学的巨大影响③。科克尔曼斯指出,"为了……","因……之故"等海德格尔的术语是他在反思亚里士多德的《物理学》和《形而上学》中的 pros, kath'o, to ek tinos, hou heneka

---

① 他人的人生的此在与一般存在者不同:他人的此在(海德格尔称其为 Mit-dasein 共同此在)不是作为用具被遭遇到的,但他们是在工具的使用中、在实践中被遭遇的。因此,此在以及共同此在是以"为何之故(为了自己的存在可能性之故,为了他人之故)"方式一道构成了意蕴,构成了世界。

② Martin Heidegger, *Being and Time*, p.159,海德格尔,《存在与时间》,第 143 页,SZ123。

③ Franco Volpi," Dasein as praxis: the Heideggerian assimilation and radicalization of the practical philosophy of Aristotle," in Christopher Macann, ed. *Critical Heidegger*, Routledge 1996. And in Christopher Macann, ed. *Martin Heidegger, Critical Assessments* Ⅱ, Routledge, 1992.

这些希腊术语"创造性"的翻译的结果①。实际上,不仅如科克尔曼斯指出的,在《物理学》和《形而上学》中可以发现 pros、hou heneka 概念是海德格尔的"um-zu(为了……)"、"为何之故(Worum-willen, for the sake of which,为了自己的存在可能性之故,为了他人之故)"等的概念基础,而且,在亚里士多德的《尼各马科伦理学》中,这种对应性关联尤为明显。这种关联和对应绝不是表面上的近似或巧合,而是海德格尔在对亚里士多德思想的深刻领会基础上,并将它们加以存在论和现象学地阐释后吸收进自己的哲学建构中,成为构造海德格尔存在哲学的基础。甚至亚里士多德著名的"幸福论 eudaemon-ism"②体系在某种意义上也可以在海德格尔的存在论中找到对应,这就是海德格尔的"为了……"和"为何之故"勾连起来的因缘系统。

初看起来海德格尔的 um-zu 和 Worum-willen 的勾连起来的世界与亚里士多德的以最高善为最终目的的"幸福论"系统似乎没有什么内在联系。Um-zu 是工具为了……而使用,它同 Worum-willen 指引关系一起是此在所缘以在世的意蕴。而亚里士多德之"为了……"(pros, hou heneka, etc.)所引出来的是一个目的链条,这个链条的终点是最高的善,即幸福。海德格尔曾多次申明,他的基础存在论不是一种伦理学,他也反对将他的描述理解为任何价值论的(如 sz128)。将他的 um-zu 网络同亚里士多德的幸福论联系在一起,不是恰恰违背了海德格尔的初衷吗?其实并非如此。下面就几个方面来指明,海德格尔正是在吸收亚里士多德"幸福论"基础上提出了自己的因缘世界概念。并且,亚里士多德思想中的"善"的概念非但没有被海德格尔排除;相反亚里士多德的《尼各马科伦理学》中的最高的善和幸福观念都通过海德格尔的解释以某种方式一起被纳入他自己的系统,成就了海德格尔的人生本体论(生存论)。下面通过几个方面来进行分析。

---

① 〔美〕约瑟夫·科克尔曼斯,《海德格尔的〈存在与时间〉》,第 134 页。

② 在国内,过去也同亚里士多德的自然目的论一起,统称"目的论"。

一、技术（techne）活动的指引关系和为了……（um-zu）勾连起的世界

海德格尔重新对世界现象，尤其是世界和此在的关系做出解释的根源在于他对现当代主体—客体二元分立的观念不满。在他看来，近代以来对世界和此在形成的这种观念绝不是本真的认识世界的方式。在这种观念下，世界成了广袤，世界内的存在者就是放在一个容器中的各种各样的物。整个世界就是各种各样物的集合（SZ63）。海德格尔强烈批评了这种观念，"这样一种存在的观念不仅说明了以极端方式规定世内存在者的存在的动机，说明了把世内存在者同一般世界混为一谈的动机，而且这一存在观念同时妨碍了我们从存在论上恰当地把此在的行为收入眼帘。这样一来却又完全错置了视线，从而看不到一切感性觉知与理智上的觉知都另有根基的性质，不能领会此在的各种行为都是在世的可能性。"[①] 以这种方式看待世界实在是误会了世界、存在者和此在，并由此才出现了"我与世界"的二元对立和如何超越这一对立的问题。但在海德格尔看来，并没有这种主体和客体的对立存在，从而也没有必要去寻求一种超越对立的方法。此在在操劳打交道活动中首先碰上的并不是笛卡尔所想象的纯粹的物质实体，而是"用具"。"就用具属于此在的世界而言，此在不可能遇到除用具以外的东西，因为如果不与这种世界的结构交织在一起，上手的东西就是无意义的。因此，环顾寻视着繁忙的此在是在一个用具指引的总体中起作用的。"[②] 用具以 um-zu 为指引勾连起一个因缘整体（SZ68），也就是意蕴世界。世界就是在这个用具整体中作为"操持和参与的事物"[③] 来照面的。Um-zu 指引着形形色色的操劳打交道活动。它所带出来的对世界的领会方式不是此在抽身退

---

① 海德格尔，《存在与时间》，第114—115页。SZ98。

② 〔美〕约瑟夫·科克尔曼斯，《海德格尔的〈存在与时间〉》，第138页。

③ Martin Heidegger, *Ontology The Hermeneutics of Facticity*, Translated by Johm Van Buren(Inceiana University Press, 1988), p. 66.

步的"冷眼直观",而是"寻视 um-sicht",就是在使用工具中按照工具本身的指引关系来领会用具整体。此在之间的打交道也从这一角度得到理解,即是在用具的 um-zu 各环节上遇到的。海德格尔认为对存在者的提问方式不再是"这是什么 what is it?"而是"它是作什么用的? 我们打算拿它怎么办? 它是为谁的? 它应是怎样的? 谁制造了它?"① 存在者的"在此"就是它的"为了……"。② 并且要达到对世界的先行领会就要明白"为了……原始地构造了距我们最近的'此'"③。

海德格尔的工具整体之"为了……"的指引关系的理论根源就在亚里士多德思想中。在《尼各马科伦理学》中,技术(techne)是灵魂揭示真理(aletheuein 解蔽④)的五种方式之一⑤。技术是关于制作和创制的,技术的创制过程就是作品逐渐形成的过程。一切技术都有其目的善,就是产品,"技术思考的是使事物怎样存在(1140a10)",技术就是"为了"这个目的并在达到这个目的的过程中存在的。对亚里士多德的"kai to technazein kai theorein hopos an genetai ti ton endechome-non kai einai kai me einai (1140a11)用技术来思考,就是考察怎样使可以存在也可以不存在的事物产生"这句话海德格尔进行了阐释,指出技术这种思不是为了思而思,而是指向"使事物以怎样的方式产生",就是关于事情怎样被正确地执行,它总是指向一个目标。"技术总是一种预备,"海德格尔解释道,他显然从这儿发现了自己的独特视角:"技术之视/思(theurein)绝不是一种思辨,而是引导着所从事的工作指向一个目标,是'为了 for

---

① "What is it for? What are we supposed to do with it? Who is it for? What is it supposed to be? Who made it?" *Ontology*, p. 72.

② "their being-*there* lies precisely in this 'in order to' and 'for'" *Ontology*, p. 73.

③ *Ontology*, p. 75.

④ 海德格尔在《技术的追问》中明确提出,"技术本身乃是一种设置 einrichtung,用拉丁语讲,是一种工具 instrumentum。"又说,这个词来自希腊语,指 techne 所包含的东西。它的本质在于解蔽。海德格尔还区别了希腊人的 techne 和现代技术的差异。孙周兴,《海德格尔选集》(下),上海三联书店,1996 年版,第 925、931 页。

⑤ 另外四种是 episteme(科学)、phronesis(实践智慧)、sophia(智慧)、nous(理智)。1139b14—15。

which, in order to'"①。他将技术之思的特征作为自己用具勾连起世界的出发点。他又对"estin de techne pasa peri genesin(1140a10) 技术是关于生成的"解释道,"一切技术,作为对事物制作的指引,运动在存在者的环围(circuit)中,这些存在者就是以这种方式处于形成过程中并处在成为自己的存在的路上。"②海德格尔的这一解释使技术活动的指引同他构成世界的因缘指引已经相当接近了。

　　技术不但使存在者走在了存在的路上,而且还勾连起了"始点 arkhe"和作品本身(即制作的终点),这形成了一个由技术的"为了……"指引勾连起来的完整过程。技术的始点(柏拉图称之为型相 eidos)是产品的原型,建筑师建构房屋总要先在心中有了所造房屋的原型,才好用他的技术一步一步构建起真实的房屋。海德格尔说,这个原型或始点并不神秘,这就是对存在者之存在的先行视见(to eidos en te psyche) vergegernwartigt③,它使房屋在将在场但还没有在场时已经预先在场化了。除了对始点和终点的揭示,这种先行视见是一种对"eidos aneu hules 无质料的形式(Met. 1032b12)"揭示,海德格尔认为必须在"存在论意义上"来理解这句话,它是说在构建计划中将原材料(hule)也预先考虑到了,因而它总是已经可以利用的(用海德格尔存在论的术语也可以说是上手的)就是说它也在场了。此外先行视见也预先规划好了为谁之用等等目的环节。原材料——制作——产品——为谁之用……,这样一个关联已经可以算是海德格尔的因缘关联整体了。可见正是在对亚里士多德的技术思想进行存在论阐释的基础上,海德格尔基本上构建起了自己的用具勾连的世界。

　　对这个世界的领会,海德格尔也存在论地改造利用了亚里士多德的技术中的相关思想。亚里士多德说"he oikodomike to eidos tes oikias(Met. 1032b13f)建筑术是房屋的形式。"基于 eidos 词根上"看"的意义,海德格尔将这句话直接翻译为

---

① Martin Heidegger, *Plato's Sophist*, Translated by Richard Rojcewicz and Andre Schuwer (Indiana University Press, 1997), p. 28.
② *Plato's Sophist*, p. 28.
③ *Plato's Sophist*, p. 30.

"建筑术是对房屋的外观(outward look)"。这是一种寻视 circumspection。"技术的寻视最终达到了它由之出发的地方。"技术从形式出发,操作一项一项实施,直到完成产品。寻视也按照这个过程进行,技术如何操作,它的各种"为了"实际如何,对它的领会就如何进行。从始点出发,又回到原点,这样寻视就完成了,对整个因缘勾连也领会到了。"这个寻视没有进行任何理论步骤,而是就在制作活动中,在使之存在的活动中。"① 对世界的认识是在对工具的操作中形成的,世界是在工具整体中被领会的。

通过对亚里士多德技术思想的本体论阐释,海德格尔的 um-zu 因缘勾连的世界基本建立起来了。但此在和世界的关系(他构建了世界并被世界构建)和此在本己的"为何之故"(Worum-willen)还没有着落,接下来的对亚里士多德的 phronesis 实践智慧的分析中我们发现了此在的"为何之故"对世界的构建,并为揭示此在本真的"为何之故"做好了准备。

二、Phronesis(实践智慧)和此在

海德格尔将周围世界的"指引"关系定为"为了……in order to/um-zu",此在靠了这种指引来领会世界。意蕴所蕴含的指引关联与此在的存在联系在一起,不过此在最本己的存在没有这种因缘牵连②。此在就是"为了 for the sake of which"它的存在而存在。此在本己的指引联系就是这个"为了",或说"为何之故"。可以说这是前此一切指引关联的最终目标,无论从前存在论上还是从存在论上都是如此。此在与他人的共在也属于此在的存在,因为人不可能真正地孤身一人,即便是离群索居也是与他人共在,从这个方面说,此在就是"为了他人之故 for the sake of others"。此在与其他存在者和其他此在的打交道、操劳烦神都是为了这个目的,都由这个"为何之故"带出。这一个"为何之故"的指引关系和前

---

① *Plato's Sophist*,p. 32.
② 海德格尔,《存在与时间》,中译本第 143 页。SZ123。

面一个 um-zu 指引关系共同构造了意蕴世界①。海德格尔的这个"为何之故"的来源,也如同因缘牵连的"um-zu 为了……"一样深深扎根于亚里士多德的哲学中。就在对亚里士多德灵魂探索真理的另一种方式"Phronesis"(实践智慧)的存在论的解释中,他找到了自己的"为何之故"指引关联的出发点。

"Phronesis"(实践智慧)所对应的活动是实践(praxis)。亚里士多德的实践概念(praxis)不同于现代使用这个概念所指的广泛意义。在亚里士多德那儿,实践实际上是就人与人之间的交往,在家庭和社会活动中获得善(1142a5—10)。它不是创制活动,和创制也互不包容(1140a1)。在亚里士多德看来,人本质上是政治动物,必然处于家庭和社会之中,实践智慧对人而言也就必不可少。同样在海德格尔这儿与他人的共在属于此在的存在,此在无论是在获取生活必需品的活动中还是在社会政治交往中,都离不开和人打交道。实践智慧体现了此在的"共在"性。作为一种揭示真理的方式,实践智慧是在具体的个别的实践活动中进行,在此在同他人的共在中进行。

在亚里士多德那儿,实践智慧和技术有共同之处:它们的始点和本原(所加以从事的东西)都是可以变化的,都是可以对之加以筹划的;前者的思路是,如果如此如此行为,则会有什么什么结果,后者的推断是,如果怎样怎样的情况出现,则有什么什么事发生②。但实践智慧和技术指导的活动有着本质的差别。techne 对应的活动是创制(poiesis),而 phronesis"对应的活动是实践(praxis)。创制的目的在自己之外——产品,而实践的目的就是良好实践自身(1140b1)。按照海德格尔的解释,技术的创制活动中的指引关联是"为了 in order to",即为了什么之用,创制活动为这一指引关系所引导。而与之相对,实践的目标就是实践本身的善,而不是在

---

① 海德格尔,《存在与时间》:"我们把这些指引关联的关联性质把握为赋予含义。……'为何之故'赋予某种'为了作'以含义;'为了作'赋予某种'所用'以含义;'所用'赋予了却因缘的'何所缘'以含义;而'何所缘'则赋予因缘的'何所因'以含义。……它们作为这种赋予含义恰是如其所是的存在。"中译本第 102 页。SZ87.

② *Sophist*, p. 35.

它自身之外追求其他的善。因此，实践智慧是关于人整个生活之幸福的筹划（1140a25）。也就是说实践和实践智慧的目的是为了人本身，"为了 hou heneka, for the sake of"人本身的整体的善。海德格尔将这一指向人自身的整体的善的指引关系"为了 hou heneka"、"为何之故"作为此在在自身的实现活动中的本质指引关联。

技术的制作和生产活动形成的指引系统，揭示了它所牵连的一切事物的存在。但技术生产的目标是在自身之外，所以它对此在存在的揭示还未形成专题。而实践的目的就是人自身的善，在实践智慧进行筹划时，人就是在思考他自己和自己的行为。它的目的（telos）的展开和保存就是对此在自身的存在的揭示①。实践智慧所思虑的是人的本然存在（the proper Being of man）②，这是一种绝对目标（telos aplous），所有实践活动都是为了（hou heneka, for the sake of）这个目标。这个"为了 for the sake of which"所构成的指引关系不同于技术指引，它不是为了外在的什么目的而作什么这样一种机械的关联。对此在来说，实践智慧这种解蔽方式比技术更为切己根本。人可以不懂技术或不去执行技术，但人必须每时每刻为自己的善筹划，为如何行为做出决断。

因为快乐和痛苦会遮蔽行为的始点和目标（1140b10）。人失去了行为的根据和目标，不知道人自身是怎样的和人为之行为的目的，再好的筹划也于事无补，甚至是南辕北辙。在海德格尔那儿这种情况表现为，此在沉浸在世界之中却常常忘却了自我和存在，成为"常人"。他随波逐流，没有任何个人的判断和选择，欢乐常人的欢乐，痛苦常人的痛苦。欲望是人灵魂主宰行为和真理的三个方面之一（1139a15），所以快乐和痛苦也会常常占据人的灵魂，人就总会有失去始点和目标的危险，总是"处于被遮蔽的危险下"。在这种情况下就总是需要实践智慧（phronesis）来去除遮蔽。Phronesis 总是"牵连进同此在心中的遮蔽倾向作斗争中"③。Phronesis 有一个灵魂的其他理性方式所不具有的

---

① *Sophist*, p. 34.
② *Sophist*, p. 35.
③ *Sophist*, p. 36.

特点,就是它不会被遗忘,而其他可以用理性学习和获得的品性和意见都可以被遗忘(1140b25)。海德格尔对亚里士多德这一点看似平常的论断作了重要的发挥,他认为phronesis实际就是良知。我们已经熟悉了海德格尔《存在与时间》中良知在此在存在论中的重要作用。是良知召唤此在起于沉沦,并向本真的能在作出筹划。海德格尔说phronesis作为不被遗忘的良知,总是唤起自己,使行为不被遮蔽。实践智慧使此在从它自身的遮蔽中敞开。海德格尔认为phronesis所面对的情况每次不同,它需要为之思虑的(hou heneka)也不同,因此它是一种讨论(discussing),作为逻各斯起作用①。在《存在与时间中》逻各斯(logos 话语,言谈)被作为现象学方法,使事物显示自身。

显然,在这儿海德格尔对亚里士多德的phronesis和praxis进行了存在论化,从而使亚里士多德的phronesis和praxis只是灵魂揭示真理的活动之一转换为人的之为人的一种本质活动②,从而又使phronesis和praxis活动的特征作为此在的特征。实践和实践智慧的"为何之故"也就成为此在的指引关联。正由此,海德格尔将实践智慧和实践的目的活动作为他的此在的指引关联 "为何之故 for the sake of which"的理论基础。

实践智慧关注的是人的生存,人最关心的应该莫过于自己的生存状况和生活幸福了。一切的指引关联到此终结,此在的可能性就在实践智慧中显现。那么实践智慧就应该是此在最高的存在可能性最恰如其分的揭示方式了。但是并不完全这样。

三、智慧(Sophia)和最高的善

我们已经在上文中为海德格尔构成世界的两种因缘关联找到了相

---

① *Sophist*, pp.35,36.
② Volpi 认为,深入思考亚里士多德的实践结构和它包含的规定性就会发现,海德格尔从中掇了大量的基本规定性,但他已经不将之作为个别实践的规定性,而是在把实践概念存在论化之后,将这些规定性作为人生的存在论特征。因而在进行生存论分析后就能揭示出在存在论包装下的同亚里士多德的实践概念在概念和术语上的一系列对应。Franco Volpi, "Dasin as Praxis", p.49。

应的亚里士多德思想渊源。此在处在 um-zu 和 Worum-willen 共同构成的意蕴世界中，以这种因缘领会着世界，也以这种因缘领会自身。这个世界就是此在在其中生存的世界。在《存在与时间》中，海德格尔说此在的本质在于它的生存①，又说此在这种存在者与其他存在者不同之处在于，它在自己的存在中为了存在自身而存在②。因此，此在在生存中一方面必须同存在者打交道，另一方面它又是为了存在自身而有所行为。上面找到了此在生存于其中并与之打交道的世界，此在存在的方式。但此在为了存在自身的一个向度中，它最高的存在可能性和揭示这一存在可能性的方式还没有确定，所以这个寻根工作也还没有彻底。

人特有的灵魂活动是 phronesis。它是为了人自身，为了人的整体的善进行的筹划。作为此在的最高的善的那个"为何之故"似乎单独地也能从实践智慧中寻找到。但事实是，phronesis 因自身的局限性不能够像 sophia 那样揭示存在和此在的最高可能性。这是由于实践智慧同实践具有密切关系，实践智慧服务于实践同时又受制于实践，从而使人在许多方面就像奴隶一样（Met. 982b29），是不自由的。在这种情况下，实践智慧就不是自足的。而理论理性是一种纯粹的思辨活动，"实践需要很多条件……一个思辨者对他的思辨则一无所需（1178b5）"，因而理论理性的活动是更为自足的。其中智慧（Sophia）探求关于始点的真理，它的对象和目标是永恒的。亚里士多德称智慧为最荣耀的科学和理智 1141b1，这种活动是最令人快乐的。只有在智慧这种自足的理性活动中，人才能像一个自由人。"完满幸福是一种思辨活动"1178b5，最高的善即最高的幸福就是理论理性的完满活动。它是属神的（1177b30，1178b15）。

而人不是永恒的。作为人的本质灵魂活动的 Phronesis 所筹划的是人在具体的实践中如何如何行为，从而达到怎样怎样的具体的善的目标。这种筹划的始点每次不

---

① 海德格尔，《存在与时间》，中译本第 49 页。英译本 p. 67，SZ42。

② 同上书，中译本第 14 页，英译本 p. 32，SZ12。

同,要达到的目标也不相同,Phronesis每次的决定和选择都是在具体的此时此刻中的。海德格尔的问题是,既然sophia使此在得以自由展开自己的生存可能性,而人又是无往不在枷锁之中的,那么此在有能力达到这样一种生存可能性吗?智慧(Sophia)有可能是此在的品质吗?还有,到底是phronesis,还是sophia可以作为此在自我揭示的最高模式?① 我们发现这也是我们想要回答的问题,即此在的最本己的能在和它的为何之故是怎样的。海德格尔认为这些问题的解决还可以揭示一种伦理学在什么意义上作为科学。

海德格尔将亚里士多德人的幸福,即最高的善的概念进行了分解,认为它有两层含义,其一,它是最高的善,在这个最高的善中人的此在达到完善;其二,它还是人的善,是人的存在的规定性,即不同于其他存在者的此在的规定性。随时可能发生变化的善是第二种,作为此在的可能性,人的善每次也是不同的②。但这并不能说明人的"为何之故"是随意的、随时随刻都在改变的善。人的"为何之故"的善应当是第一种,最高的善③。海德格尔将幸福解释为"构成人的此在之完满存在"。存在即在场,"因为幸福是关于人的完善状态的存在,作为人最高的本体论可能性的完满存在,它必定是人的一种每时每刻恒常如是的存在。"④它是完全自足的。海德格尔把亚里士多德的这一最高的善和幸福拿来,作为此在真正的"为何之故"。此在的存在的真谛就是去揭示其完满的存在,也就是它存在的最大可能性。

phronesis和sophia都能使存在者在其存在的基本模式中被揭示和掌握,因而它们都是存在者自身被展开的最高可能性⑤。phronesis和sophia都是此在的模式,构成了此在存在的模式:sophia是此在朝向世界上所有存在者的向度,而phronesis则是此在朝向此在自身这种存在者的向度。但它们不是平等并列的。亚里士多德说因为只有神能够完全无所欲求地进行思辨,

---

① *Sophist*, p. 89.
② *Sophist*, p. 93.
③ *Sophist*, p. 96.
④ *Sophist*, p. 118.
⑤ *Sophist*, pp. 112—113.

智慧(sophia)是属神的:它为神所有,并且是关于神圣之物的科学(Met. 983a5)。海德格尔认为应该本体论地理解亚里士多德的这个说法,亚里士多德在这儿根本没有神学意味,永恒的神只是指存在者的最高的存在方式。因而这句话的意思是说,智慧(Sophia)研究的对象是那种最无蔽的、最敞亮的存在,它具有最完全的在场;从时间上来说它是永恒的①。智慧是对恒常如一之存在的纯粹思辨,只有智慧活动——理论思辨能够完全自足地对最高的存在进行揭示。Phronesis则不是在思辨中达到它的目标,而是在实践中、在行动中趋向它的目标,它受制于许多其他因素。因而在达到最大幸福和"为何之故"上,智慧比phronesis具有很大的优越性。但是,海德格尔强调,问题不在于哪种灵魂德性更高。必须从本体论层面上来理解亚里士多德提出这个问题的意义,将这些存在模式恰如其分地理解为存在的模式。从这个层面上来讲,就是要决定哪种相应的揭示真理的存在模式更高。

在此在的"为何之故"和存在模式这个意义上,海德格尔也为伦理学指引出了本体论基础。他说希腊人对人的生存的思考完全指向存在的意义自身,也就是指向使人的此在得以永恒的可能性。希腊人从世界的存在中汲取出存在的观念,存在就是绝对在场。他们的伦理学不会有当代伦理学的问题模式,不会去寻求一种结果或意向伦理学(ethics of consequences or ethics of intentions)的代替品②。这实际说明了海德格尔自己的伦理学态度。现代伦理学从问题模式上对人的存在的思考就不是最根本的,海德格尔通过重建存在论,也使伦理学的基本问题模式从根本上得到改变。他通过um-zu和Worum-willen建构起此在存在的世界,并且由此对此在的"为何之故"和此在的存在进行搜求。他说此在在它的存在的可能性中被看作"此"的,无论意向还是实践结果都不能揭示此在的存在。此在生活的幸福就是他最高的生存可能性的把握③。此在

---

① *Sophist*, p. 94.
② *Sophist*, p. 122.
③ 对人而言这个最高的存在可能性是精神(或理智 nous)这种完全在场的活动,人的生命最完满的存在是由精神构成的。

最终的"为何之故"是揭示它最高的存在可能性，对这一可能性的揭示就是此在的最高幸福。这是伦理学由之出发的起点。海德格尔的存在论伦理学给出了伦理学由之产生的存在论基础，伦理学在这个意义上展开成为科学。传统伦理学中的动机和结果的争论，以及规范伦理学——描述伦理学的争论等在此在的对寻求自己本真存在、最大的生存可能性的存在论中没有根基。

虽然有了存在论基础，但海德格尔没有给出具体的实践伦理学，而且在著述中多次强调他的理论和概念都没有伦理学上的评价意义，所以对他的伦理学问题有很多争议，包括他是不是一个道德虚无主义者。Kellner 认为海德格尔从本体论上给出了伦理学的核心概念，所以他不是道德虚无主义者。他指出海德格尔提供了一种建基于描述本体论的新的评价语言，不再将原本就是不可分割的描述和评价分开。他提供的本体论—伦理学模式使传统的描述和评价二元分立的局面不攻自破[①]。他对伦理学的摧毁隐含着建立新的伦理学的可能。

四、"幸福论"体系的对照

在对海德格尔的指引关联体系和他对最高幸福观念的阐释做出说明后，海德格尔存在论同亚里士多德幸福论的对应也渐渐显示了出来。亚里士多德所谓"幸福论"中已经说出了一切技术和研究，一切策划和推断都有目标，它们目标善之间也是以对更高善的追求相连。转换成海德格尔的语言，我们看到，技术上的指引关系"为了……"是此在存在于世界中并同它发生联系的基本方式，而实践智慧的"为何之故"指引关系使此在与他者共在，并最终为了此在的存在，这也是世界的意

---

① Kellner 指出，海德格尔声称自己的存在论分析是纯本体论的，没有伦理学成分。但他的几代读者，包括一些最杰出的哲学家萨特、阿多诺等都证明海德格尔提出了伦理原则。但就他是否取消了传统价值，但不给出或很少给出代替物，因而是一个道德虚无主义者，还是他提供了一个自由的存在法则作为存在主义伦理学的基础的问题上，有着极大的争论。Douglas Kellner, "Authenticity and Heidegger's Challenge to ethical theory", Christopher Macann, ed. *Martin Herdegger-critical assessments*, Volume IV, Routledge, 1992。

蕴构成。这两者勾连成的因缘关联几乎可以囊括此在尤其是它的日常的存在模式。但是此在的"为何之故"被灵魂中另一个向度牵引向更高的善,此在最大的幸福不是获得和体验倏忽来去的人所谓的善和幸福,而是通过智慧的完满实现去把握的永恒的存在。对并不永恒的此在来说,最高的幸福就是自由地去把握人最大的存在可能性。易言之,人追求的最高幸福就是对存在的体认和把握。亚里士多德的《尼各马科伦理学》开篇第一句就提出"每种技术、每种研究,每个活动和每个选择"都有自己的目的。这些目的之间也相互勾连,有的目的还以其他目的为目的(1194a)。但是这个链条不可能是无穷的,总有一个目的是最终的,它以自身为目的,而不以其他任何事物为目的(1194a15—20)。而它是一切其他事物的目的。这就是处于目的链条顶端的最高的善,也就是幸福。亚里士多德这一理论被称为"幸福论"。海德格尔的 um-zu 和 Worum-willen 构成的关联和此在存在方式同亚里士多德的所谓"幸福论"结构的对应是很明显的。他将这个"以自身为目的,而不以其

他任何事物为目的"的最高的善作为人真正的"为何之故"而求索的目标。对存在的体认,对此在最高生存可能性的把握就是链条终端的最高的善。这就是海德格尔的存在论所要揭示的目标。

通过对海德格尔存在论中极其重要的 um-zu 和 Worum-willen 在亚里士多德哲学中对照,可以发现其中的强烈对应。当然这绝不是一种字面上的巧合,也不是对它们的牵强比附,而是在对海德格尔存在论追本溯源中达到的。海德格尔生存论哲学深深植根于古希腊哲学中,并从亚里士多德哲学吸收了许多重要的哲学概念和思想。就本文讨论的范围而言,海德格尔从亚里士多德灵魂揭示真理的诸种方式,尤其是技术、实践智慧、智慧等几个方式中挖掘到了他的存在论根源[①]。当然这种利用不是简单的"拿来",而是建立在海德格尔对亚里士多德思想的存在论改造基础上

---

① 海德格尔对灵魂这种存在者十分青睐,他说,灵魂这种存在者与一切可能的存在者有与生俱来的与众不同,此在对其他存在者的优先地位在这里显露出来。还引述亚里士多德的话说,(人的)灵魂以某种方式是一切存在者。SZ14。

的。他多次强调要对亚里士多德思想进行存在论的理解①,并不反对将一些思想"解释进"亚里士多德思想中,认为这样做只是对亚里士多德真实思想的发生进行理解②。海德格尔对亚里士多德思想的发掘和重新解释也并非偶然,他对存在问题的思考一开始就是受到亚里士多德的存在问题的启发③。他在自己对存在和时间的思考中一再回到亚里士多德,可以说亚里士多德思想对海德格尔的思路历程贯串始终。海德格尔试图通过对亚里士多德思想的现象学的解构、还原和重构④,恢复亚里士多德思想的源始意义,使它从西方的形而上学解释传统中被释放出来。海德格尔认为甚至像耶格尔(Jaeger)这样富有创新的亚里士多德研究家也在某些方面遮蔽了亚里士多德的思想⑤。这种对亚里士多德和希腊哲学的误解和遮蔽在形而上学史上造成了极为不利的影响,并直接导致了现代哲学和认识论的困境。他做的工作就是追本清源,将传统的遮蔽清洗掉,使亚里士多德思想真正的意义显现出来,从而使人类的思想建立在更加坚固的基础上。海德格尔这一工作可以从本文的分析中,在他对亚里士多德思想的借用和重新解释中看出。当然从纯粹的文本考证上看,他对亚里士多德思想的阐发和重新解释是否完全恰当合理,还存在争议。

海德格尔的存在论从亚里士多德思想中汲取了丰富的养料。通过分析认识到他的这一思想源泉,可以更为深刻地理解他的存在论和他思想的发展轨迹。这种创造性的理解方式也真正使亚里士多德思想的丰富矿藏得到充分利用。他为理解亚里士多德的形而上学和伦理学提供了一条新的思路。

(作者系北京大学哲学系
博士研究生)

---

① 如 *sophist*, pp. 94,116 等处。
② *Sophist*, p. 43.
③ 早年他读到弗兰兹·布伦塔诺(Franz Brentano)的博士论文《论存在在亚里士多德那里的多种含义》,受到深刻的启示,开始了对存在问题的思考,这一思考在海德格尔的思想历程中从未中止。
④ 三种方法共称海德格尔的现象学方法。
⑤ Franco Volpi, "Dasein as praxis: the Heideggerian assimilation and radicalization of the practical philosophy of Aristotle," in Christopher Macann, ed. *Martin Heidegger, Critical AssessmentsII* (Routledge, 1992), p. 97.

判定真的标准与塔尔斯基真定义在概念上的区分

● 叶 闯

塔尔斯基真定义,及与其相关的T约定,本身是一种形式的理论。只有在对它进行特定解释时才会具有哲学意义;同时,真定义与判定一个语句、命题是否为真也是两件不同的事情。而当判定本身受一种哲学理论影响时,情况就更是如此。这样一个区分本来在范畴上是清楚的,却在一些哲学文献中经常被忽略或混淆。本文意图在理论上明确这个概念区分,并进而指出,实际上许多哲学争论并非相关于真理定义,或相关于对最基本的真概念之理解,而只相关于判定真理之标准。因此,这种争论并不在塔尔斯基原本意义上属于真定义,或属于相关的元元语言论题。

本文讨论塔尔斯基的真定义[①]与判定真的标准之间的关系,最后的结论是他的真定义与判定真的标准可以相互独立。这里所说的真定义主要用来回答什么叫做真或真理的问题。而真或真理标准指的是如何判定一个陈述,一个命题,或表达它的一个语句是否是真理的方法或准则。根据这样的判准,一个陈述,一个命题,或一个语句被确定为是真的,或是真理。根据上述对真定义与真理标准问题的解说,从概念上和直觉上都能够使人们清楚地意识到,真定义与真理标准确实属于不同

---

 * 本文的初稿曾给北京师范大学哲学系的刘晓力博士和我的同事邢滔滔博士看过,所得到的批评和建议的一部分已体现于现在这个完成的稿子中。关于数学和逻辑的可判定性与真理标准问题方面的结论,其主要的思想得益于与邢滔滔的讨论。在此向二位同仁表示感谢。当然,文中的所有错误属于作者本人。

 ① 在本文中,"真定义"一语经常比形式上那种严格的使用更宽泛一些,它包括塔尔斯基真理论的其他一些内容,特别是他对T语句、T语句模式、T约定等的说明。为什么不干脆用"真理论"?主要是因为我担心读者会联想到流行的一些对塔尔斯基工作的哲学解释,那些解释通常都用"塔尔斯基真理论"这个提法,而那些解释中有许多是我不赞成的。但不管怎么说,为行文的方便,或照顾到语言上的习惯,文中有时也用"真理论"这个表达。

的范畴,确实是两件不同的事情,理解这个区别也不存在什么特殊的困难。在数学或逻辑学中,一般也在经验科学中,说明什么叫做一个东西属于一个类,与判定一个特定的实例是否属于所说的这个类是两件不同的事情,这是普遍可以接受的概念区分,对此人们也应该没有什么理解上的困难。于是,很明显这个区分也对塔尔斯基的真定义与真理标准之间的关系适用,可为什么还要进行专门的讨论呢?

需要专门讨论是由于看到对塔尔斯基工作的许多评论,往往没有特别注意到这个区分,或者干脆混淆了两件不同的事情(这个混淆通常会与其他的混淆交织在一起,比如真定义与对真定义的哲学解释之间的混淆),使得对塔尔斯基真理论常常会得出不准确甚至不正确的结论。塔尔斯基的真理论在哲学讨论中,经常或被指责或被赞扬为真理的符合论,同时又或被指责或被赞扬为真理的冗余论;有时塔尔斯基的结果由于其不能用于一种认识论的判定而被谴责,或被判为无用。塔尔斯基真理论的许多评论者,比如普特南、戴维森,甚至也许还有 H. Field,都没有完全区分清楚这两件事情。缺乏清楚区分既妨碍了对塔尔斯基真理论及其他一些哲学家的真理论的正确解释,也妨碍了对一般真理问题的正确说明。如此,就有必要对真定义与真理标准进行明确的区分,且对其进行充分的理论说明。就像在哲学中,大家也许都知道本体论与认识论是两件事情,但在具体的理论中又常常有人混淆这两件事情,于是乎就有哲学家认真地在理论上区分或澄清这两件事情,我们在此于不同的问题上也在做类似的工作。

再进一步,我们可以这样来说明本文的意图。理解塔尔斯基的工作,起码在两个方面可能产生哲学上重要的意见分歧。第一个可能分歧是:塔尔斯基是真理符合者,真理冗余论者,还是两者都不是,塔尔斯基工作本身不具有直接的形而上学和知识论推论。第二个可能分歧是:塔尔斯基的真定义是否同时必是判定真理的标准。第一个可能分歧其实是一个现实的分歧,因为许多哲学家已经详细地讨论过这个问题。第二个可能分歧是一个需要研究的,由于其所产生的实际上存在的混淆而变得重要的问题,只是它目前还未被充分地讨论。本文将讨论第二个可能分歧,并论证作者对这个问题的看法。①

理解塔尔斯基真定义的诸可能方面

在逻辑上,或至少根据一种可设想的逻辑哲学或语义学观点,我们可以在逻辑中定义任意的真或真概念。比如我们可以作一个任意的定义,把出现在一类特有语境下的语句叫做真的,或把与特有的语句集发生特定关系的语句叫做真的。那么,"任意"是否就是想怎样就怎样,按定义者所希望、所喜爱、所需要的那样去定义,没有任何限制? 应该说,此处的任意是指没有任何逻辑的理由来限制定义的自由,只要定义遵守一切逻辑操作都要遵守的起码逻辑准则,比如遵守无矛盾性的要求。但如果一个逻辑学家或数学家不把给出一个定义作为纯为自娱的符号游戏,他通常不得不考虑知识社会学意义上的限制。比如以往理论中已提出的问题,直觉上的合理性,甚至一般社会学意义上的限制,比如能否有利于申请一项研究基金。在这里,定义者的自由或任意性就受到了限制。

上述的评论应能适用于塔尔斯基的真理论。在形式上,塔尔斯基理论

---

① 本文作者对第一个可能分歧的看法与塔尔斯基曾明确表述的一致。他说:"……我们可以接受真理的语义学概念而并不放弃我们也许有的任何认识论态度;我们仍然可以是素朴实在论者、批判实在论者、唯心论者、经验论者或形而上学家——即可以是我们以前所是的无论什么。语义学概念完全中立于所有这些争论。"在同一篇文章中他又说:"科学史告诉我们,许多概念在其意义得以精确之前,曾被判定为形而上学的……;不管怎么说,一当这些概念接受了严格的形式定义,对它们的不信任就消失了。我们可以提到的典型例子是数学中的负数和虚数概念。我希望类似的命运等待着真概念和其他语义学概念;……若结果是语义学概念失去了哲学兴趣,它们也不过是分享了其他许多科学概念的命运,这并不需要有任何遗憾。"(分别见 Tarski, "The Semantic Conception of Truth and the Foundations of Semantics," *Philosophy and Phenomenological Research*, vol. IV, 1944, p. 362 和 p.364)本文由其主题所限,不准备专门讨论塔尔斯基是否在他的全部著作中都一致地坚持了这一立场,也不准备论证作者本人在相关问题上的主张,而只是简单地给出一个明确看法:语义学问题可以且应该同形而上学及认识论问题分开。

所必须遵从的限制就是逻辑的基本要求,在此要求之下,他有构造他所想要的真定义的自由。① 但在思想史的考虑之下,在知识社会学的考虑之下,他有自己定义的理论目的,有他需要解决的理论问题,而不只是满足对符号游戏的喜爱。实际上,他"在此试图达到古典真概念的一个更准确的解释,它可能代替亚里士多德的构造,并保存它的基本意旨"。② 由此可见,他还是想通过自己的定义来满足一种理论上和知识系统上的需要,他的定义的目标在于,要对满足一定条件的形式系统给出直觉上合理的语义学说明。很明显,他对自己工作的知识社会学的,实践的,思想史上的考虑是有明确自我意识的。他实际上已经谈到这类工作在所述方面的一般考虑:

> 无论什么时候,当一个人要解释(explain)从日常语言中抽取出来的任何词项的意义时,他应该记住,此类解释的目标和逻辑地位在各种情况下是不同的。比如说,此解释也许打算要说明所涉及词项的实际使用,因此就要面对这个说明是否确实是正确的这样的提问。另一些时候,解释也许具有规范的(normative)性质——它是作为词项应以某种确定的方式来使用的建议提出来的,而并未断定此建议符合于该词项实际上被使用的方式;比方说,这样的解释可以从它的有用性的角度来评价,而不从它的正确性的角度。……
>
> 眼下我们想要给出的解释在某种程度上具有混合的性质。在此所提出的应该在原则上被看作以某种确定的方式使用'真'这个词项的建议,但是,此建议的提出伴有这样一个信念,它要与该词项在日常语言中通行的用法相一致。③

---

① 当然,还有一个因素可能会限制他的自由:对某些系统,它们的真概念不能用某些特定的方法定义。比如他用来定义类演算的真概念的方法,就不是在所有系统中适用的。

② Tarski, "Truth and Proof," in Steven R. Givant and Ralph N. McKenzie (ed.), *Collected Papers* (1958—1979), vol. 4, Birkhäuser, 1986, p. 403.

③ Ibid., p. 402.

这段话的意思是如此清楚,以至于根本不需要再进一步地解释了。

至此,似乎对塔尔斯基理论可以引出四个方面的问题。第一个方面,塔尔斯基理论形式上的结果及广义的真定义本身;第二个方面,塔尔斯基对其理论结果的逻辑上的、理论上的、实践上的用途的考虑,以及他对此理论所欲解决的问题的考虑;第三个方面,塔尔斯基理论的哲学解释;第四个方面,塔尔斯基理论作为真理标准。分别讨论这四个方面的问题不是我们在此的任务。我们真正关心的实际上是第四个方面与第一个方面的关系,那是本篇文章的主题。因为这个主要问题的回答要联系到第二、第三个方面同第一个方面的关系,因此,现在讨论的内容就落实到所有其他各方面同第一个方面的关系(当然也涉及其他各项之间的关系)。下面的论证步骤是先从外围开始,即先讨论第二、第三个方面与第一个方面的关系。然后讨论作为本文主题的第一个方面与第四个方面的关系。

第一个方面与第三个方面的关系,即塔尔斯基真定义与真定义的哲学解释的关系。在前面第130页的注①中,我们已经简单地表明了塔尔斯基在此问题上的立场,我认为这是一个正确的立场。只在此补充一点,第一个方面独立于第三个方面这结论有一个间接的支持,即这样一个事实,同一个塔尔斯基的定义,目前至少有两种很流行的解释,一种把塔尔斯基的定义解释成断定了真理符合论,一种从它在形式上具有去引号的功能,把它解释为真理的冗余论。根据刚提到的那个注中说到的理由,在此我们不准备进一步论证第一与第三方面的相互独立性,而把它作为一个直觉上正确的前提接受下来。

对第一个方面与第二个方面的关系,读者从前面的相应引文中应已看到塔尔斯基本人对此问题的部分观点,他谈到在语义的解释和定义中对日常用法,已有的语言习惯如何考虑的问题。这个"考虑"反映出解释者或定义者对日常用法的态度,或者反映出处理日常用法的建议。当然,解释者或定义者还可以考虑哲学上的要求,甚至其他理论或实践的要求。① 比如,塔

---

① 《形式化语言中的真概念》一文中,塔尔斯基在谈到符号的意义和公理的选取等问题时,曾说过:"……就'形式的'这个词的一种特殊的意义来说,我们在此并不对'形式的'语言和科学感兴趣,这样的科学,其符号和表达未被赋予任何实质(material)的意义。对这样的科学来说,此处所讨论的问题完全是不相关的,甚至也不是有意义的。我

尔斯基一直坚持的要考虑亚里士多德式的古典的真概念,使得在定义中体现出亚里士多德真概念的精神。现在还需要进一步考察这个关系的性质。根据前面已有的讨论结果,可以知道,定义本身的强制性要求是逻辑的要求,定义本身的性质是逻辑的或语义学的。这意味着,外在的定义的目的等等考虑,定义要反映什么理论或实践的要素,对定义本身没有逻辑上的强制性。比如对同一个哲学上的考虑,可以有不同的系统来"反映"这个要求。即使对一个比较具体的要求,比如反映数学推理的真理性,在形式系统的构造,初始符号的选择等等方面都有相当的自由。而反过来从逻辑系统或语义系统这方面看,它可以有多种哲学的或其他的解释,作为你想描述的实际的,或提议的某种事物的模型。之所以如此的原因在于,逻辑的结果与产生这个逻辑结果的动机、目的等等属于不同的范畴,是相互独立的。最后,直接处理我们的主题:第一个方面与第四个方面的关系。这个作为本文主题的问题需要详加考察,其顺序是,首先考察对第一个方面本身的理解,然后结合考察第四个方面来讨论两个方面的关系。

对塔尔斯基真定义本身的理解

塔尔斯基是通过满足概念来定义真的。满足的一般情况即开语句为无穷序列所满足。而语句或者说闭语句,可以被理解为自由变元数为零的语句模式,真语句通过满足概念被定义为:

x 是真语句,当且仅当 x 属于 S,并且每一个无穷序列都满足 x。①

们总是赋予出现在我们将要考虑的语言中的符号以很具体的,且对我们来说是可理解的意义。……作为公理出现的那些语句在我们看来应在实质上(materially)是真的,而在选取推导规则的过程中,我们总是遵循这样的原则,当如此规则被使用于真语句的时候,由规则的使用所得到的语句也应该是真的。"("The Concept of Truth in Formalized Languages", *Logic*, *Semantics*, *Metamathematics*, Oxford at the Clarendon Press, 1956, pp. 166—167)

① 这是对塔尔斯基在《形式化语言中的真概念》一文中的定义 23 的修改和扩展,那个定义中,本来塔尔斯基只考虑类演算,其中的"S"指在所考虑范围内全部有意义语句所构成的类。(*Logic*, *Semantics*, *Metamathematics*, p. 195)

虽然真定义本身人们可能给出哲学解释，比如从语言与世界的关系理解"满足"概念等，但在现代分析哲学的讨论中，对塔尔斯基真理论的理解，更多的是关注于对塔尔斯基的所谓"T 句式"，以及该句式的众多实例（比如塔尔斯基自己给出的实例"'雪是白的'是真的，当且仅当雪是白的"）的理解。尽管塔尔斯基由于形式上的困难等考虑不从 T 等值式直接定义真，而只承认 T 等值式的实例为真的"部分定义"（partial definitions），但对塔尔斯基真理论的哲学解释大多是以这种"部分定义"为背景的。除此之外，对塔尔斯基理论作解释的哲学家们，他们参照的塔尔斯基理论的另一个重要内容是他的 T 约定（Convention T）。塔尔斯基用 T 约定来对真定义本身进行约束，就是说，他希望可能的真定义应满足如下条件：一个形式上正确的真定义如果是充分的（adequate），它将有全部 T 语句作为它的逻辑后承，即它将有所有那些类似"'雪是白的'是真的，当且仅当雪是白的"，"'草是绿的'是真的，当且仅当草是绿的"的句子，作为它的逻辑后承。

不考虑哲学的或其他方面的理解，仅就 T 语句，T 句式结构的逻辑意义上看，塔尔斯基的构造是简单明确的，对于"x 是真语句，当且仅当 p"这个语句函项或语句模式，塔尔斯基只规定 x 被给定的对象语言的语句的名字或结构描述代入，而 p 被该语句在元语言中的翻译代入。至于对等值式的实例或 T 语句的理解，举例来说不过是：当语句"雪是白的"为真时雪是白的，而当雪是白的时，语句"雪是白的"为真，即此复合语句的联结词的左右两边等值。这些都足够清楚，几乎不需要更多的解释。只有一点需要特别提请注意，在等值式的右边，除了正在被定义的那个语句或其翻译之外，没有任何别的东西，特别是没有提到任何语言上的概念，比如"语句"，"意义"，也没有谈到超出该语句内容本身的其他方面的内容，比如"符合"，"有确定的证据"。一句话，那里只有所谈到的那个语句，或与它同义的另一个表达式，仅此而已，没有更多的东西。重要的是，就是因为等值式右边的这个特性，为多种解释，也为多种真理标准留出了广阔的空间。

判定真理的标准及其与真定义的关系

　　塔尔斯基的真定义是否同时也就是判定真理的标准？原则上，人们是可以拿真定义作为真理标准。比如，就 T 等值式和 T 语句看，一个人可以坚持说，当 p 发生时，语句 x 是真的；于是乎他也可以坚持说，当张三洗脸时，"张三洗脸"这句话是真的。如此，p 的发生是语句 x 为真的标准；张三洗脸是语句"张三洗脸"为真的标准。直观上看这没有什么问题。仔细分析，事情似乎还不是这么简单。

　　当具体判定一个命题是否为真时，不是给定真的某些条件，甚至也不是给定真的充分必要条件就足够的，因为你要断定一个特定的语句为真，需要知道真值条件被满足，而不仅仅是知道真值条件。换句话说，当你知道一个语句的意义，知道该语句的真值条件（按一种流行的理论这等同于知道意义）时，你不能由此就导出此语句的真，这个语句的真取决于真值条件实际上被满足。而你要有理智地断定此语句的真，以你有根据断定它的真值条件事实上被满足为条件。如何判定真值条件事实上被满足，根据什么来判定这一点，回答这两个问题可以有许多种（如果不是无数种）答案。于是就存在着在同一真定义下，多种真理标准的可能性。比如，如何判定雪事实上是白的，判定的根据是什么。显然，这取决于多种因素，有多种可能的回答。[①] 于是，在不同标准下，即使对同一个命题或其语言学表达，且在证据等有关因素完全一样的情况下，持有不同标准的人，也可以给出真、假、不能判定等不同的结论。甚至在不同标准下，对什么可叫做"证据"等等的看法也会有很大的不同。

　　由此可见，当不同的人有同样的真定义，或有同样的真概念时，他们完全可以有不同的判定真理的标准，也就是说，他们可以在如何才算是真值条

[①] 本文只考虑判定者的信念或理论的系统在判定中所起的作用，也就是说考虑这种比较确定的因素，而不考虑判定的具体场合等时间敏感因素对判定者的理论、信念，以及由此而来的对标准和判定的影响。

件实际上被满足,什么是这件事情的标准等等问题上有不同的甚至彼此冲突的意见。但上述说法绝不蕴涵如下断定:真定义是无关紧要的,塔尔斯基的真定义是许多同样不重要的真定义中的一种,而重要的只是判定真理的标准。如果这样,T 约定将被平凡化。真定义,特别是 T 约定的平凡化,受到塔尔斯基明确反对。因 T 约定之所以成为一个约定或限制条件,关键的考虑在于使真理论反映某种古典的真理观或常识观点,而其他真理概念有可能蕴涵与 T 约定不一致的结果(至少在塔尔斯基看来是如此),故 T 约定有所需要的过滤功能。所以塔尔斯基写道:

> ……我将试图获得有关这种真概念的信息,……它不包含最素朴的实在论中的逻辑。我推测这种概念必定和语义学概念不相容。如此一来,就必定存在着一些语句,它们在一个概念下为真而在另一个概念下不为真。①

塔尔斯基举了我们最熟知的那个例子,即按他本人的真理论有:
> 语句"雪是白的"是真的,当且仅当雪是白的。

而按某些其他的真理论可能有:
> 语句"雪是白的"是真的,当且仅当雪不是白的。

于是塔尔斯基再一次肯定了 T 约定的实质性的意义:

> 无论如何,意识到与语义学概念不相容的每一个真概念都会引出此类结果,在我看来是很重要的。②

T 约定将排除不相容于古典真概念的真的定义。在 T 约定限制下一个重要的结果是:……定义的实质充分性条件唯一地决定了"真的"这个词项的

---

① Tarski, "The Semantic Conception of Truth and the Foundations of Semantics," *Philosophy and Phenomenological Research*, vol. IV, p. 362.
② Ibid., p. 362.

外延。因此,每一个实质上充分的真定义都必然等价于实际所构造的那个定义。如此说来,真的语义学概念并未给出在这个概念的各种各样的不等价定义之间进行选择的可能性。①

在保卫 T 约定的重要性这个问题上,我们与塔尔斯基站在一起。我们甚至认为,如果按塔尔斯基真定义的戴维森式的理解,塔尔斯基真概念是我们一般人对于真的正确的直觉看法,是我们判定任何问题的真时先已假定的观念,而不是随便一个真概念。因此,在这种理解下,我们认为 T 约定是非常重要的一个元语义学的规定。故此,T 约定的重要性,不仅在于它有一些性质为某些哲学家看重,而且它确实是人的直觉真概念的某种表达,它可能反映的是一个人类学事实。因此,戴维森说这种真概念是原初的(primitive)。在他看来,这其实是一切所谓"客观性的"的思想的基础,也就是信念的基础。在这个意义上,它是最基本的,先在的。"'雪是白的'是真的,当且仅当雪是白的","'草是绿的'是真的,当且仅当草是绿的",正常情况下,这就是人们对真先有的基本理解,几乎没有人会认真地反对它。我们不能用其他的什么来解释它,而是有了它,我们才有解释、理解或判定等等其他的"思想"。也许正是由于塔尔斯基真定义在直观上显明的合理性,可能让人们觉得做这样的定义或断定根本没有什么真正的内容。

以上讨论如果是足够清楚的,就能使人们明白,我们在这里断定的只是:即使我们都有共同的真概念,即塔尔斯基真定义的特定解释下的真概念,且我们可能都接受 T 约定,我们也可以有判定一个命题、句子,或陈述是否为真的不同的标准,我们也可以根据不同的准则或作为其背景的一个信念集,来判定在所考虑的情况下真值条件是否被满足。即使塔尔斯基考虑了日常用法,但他的真定义(狭义的)毕竟是一个形式的构造,T 语句和 T 约定也只是语句,命题函项,或者是对形式的真定义的限制条件。由前面对塔尔斯基真定义性质和特征的分析,可知塔尔斯基的 T 语句等等由其内容决定了,它为多种解释和多种运用留下了宽广的空间。那里还只是提到 T

---

① Ibid., pp. 353—354.

句式右边在内容上的特性,而我们从刚刚进行的分析中应该又看到,塔尔斯基的真定义"反映出"一种很少会有疑义的真的最小化说明。"最小化"当然只是个形象的说法,它意思是说,在我们通常的关于真的观念中,最最起码的东西,那是任何真概念几乎都要认可的起码要素。

使用标准所进行的判定:几个案例

使用标准所进行的判定,其情形之差异取决于所判定的对象(命题、语句、陈述等)和判定所使用的标准。在数学中,有时可以找到比较简单的实例,其判定真理的标准与真的定义有较大的一致性。[①] 比如"4 是方程'$x+2=6$'的解"是个数学命题。按塔尔斯基有:语句"4 是方程'$x+2=6$'的解"是真的,当且仅当 4 是方程"$x+2=6$"的解。那么如何判定此真值条件是否被满足,通常要做的只是把 4 代入,看结果是否能使方程两边相等。这个判定的标准在内容上或意义上与真定义是一致的。因为,所谓"x"是一个方程的解,即意味着把 x 代入这个方程,能使得该方程两边相等。此点表明判定真理的标准在这种情形下至少是暗含于 T 语句之中,也似乎表明了,在这里判定真理的标准可以从真定义本身的语义内容中直接导出。[②] 数学中也有一些较复杂的例子,判定真理的标准与真定义之间的关系也许比上例更复杂。比如对费马大定理,按塔尔斯基有:语句"n 大于 2 时,$x^n + y^n = z^n$ 没有整数解"是真的,当且仅当 n 大于 2 时,$x^n + y^n = z^n$ 没有整数解。判定这个语句的真,至少可以想到有两个证明的办法,它们可能被用来作为判定真的标准。第一个是直接证明,对于任意给的非零整数 x, y, z,都有 $x^n + y^n \neq z^n$;第二个是反证法,假设在 n 大于 2 时,此方程有解,将导致

[①] 自然这里只是举一个例子,不想且我认为也不能就此得出关于数学命题判定方面的一般结论。

[②] 但即便如此,真与判断真的标准也属于不同的范畴,虽然在事实上,我们可以在这里把定义真的程序用于判定真。一般对于一个递归的定义,我们可以使用定义中的程序给出一个事物是否满足该定义的能行的判定。但也同样,设此点成立,递归定义与判定本身仍是两件不同的事情。

矛盾或与已证的数学定理冲突。这是两种不同的真理标准，背后也许对应着不同的数学观念。后一种真理标准，数学的直觉主义者就不赞成。不管怎么说，对于上述的数学例子，要定义或判定其真的语句在语义上是确定的，对其容易形成一致的理解，也就是对 T 语句的右边能够形成一致的理解。比较起后面我们要讨论的经验科学的、伦理的、文化的、历史的其他具有更丰富题材的语句，数学中判定真理的标准也许是更受限制的。

在社会生活和实践中，在比逻辑和数学更丰富的理论中，判定真理的标准具有更大的复杂性。在有关真理的问题上，经验科学虽然比较起数学和逻辑要复杂一些，但比较起社会文化方面的陈述语句来，还是要容易把握一些。因为至少自然科学的语句在语义上是比较明确的，没有多少含混性，判定真理的标准虽然各时代或不同科学共同体之间有着差别，比如对同一类实验的可靠性方面，对判决性实验性质的看法上面都可能存在争议，但在整个科学共同体中，大体上对判定真理问题还是有着较高的一致性。

可是，一进入社会人文诸领域，事情就远远要复杂得多。那里有双重的复杂，即复杂性不但表现在判定真理的标准方面，而且表现在对所考虑的语句的语义理解上面。在社会人文领域，也在日常经验的领域，表达信念的语句的语义经常是含糊的，或者是非常宽泛的，可以有多种解释和理解，这是个众所周知的事实，不需要多说。至于在真理标准方面，所说的这些领域中不可能有统一的说明，标准往往与判定者所拥有的理论或文化习俗有密切的联系。即使在日常判定中，陈述同一个经验事实的语句的真值判定也受判定者已有知识背景和习惯影响。比如，当一个人 A 看到他的一个同事 B 一上午都面带笑容，工作效率很高，于是 A 对他的另一个同事 C 说："B 今天上午很高兴。"（称其为语句"Ab"）A 相信他所说的这句话是真的，且他的这个信念是被判为合理的（justified），因为他了解 B，知道 B 在高兴的时候通常都这样。他判定"B 今天上午很高兴"这类语句为真的标准是：他清楚地看到某类事件发生时通常所具有的特征。而 C 可能是个多疑且细心的人，即使对"B 今天上午很高兴"这样的日常语句的日常用法，他也用更复杂的标准来判定其真假。除对 A 来说是必要的那个标准或条件外，他还需要进一步的证据或条件,比如与 B 本人进行有关问题的语言交流,且交流的内容支持所涉及的断定,又比如他了解最近几天可能影响 B 的情绪的有关事件,如此等等。对 C 来说,满足条件 a(假定 a 就是看到某类事件发生时所通常具有的特征)只是判定 Ab 为真的条件之一,而要最终断定其真,条件应是 a 与 b(假定 b 就是与 B 本人进行有关问题的语言交流,且交流的内容支持所涉及的断定),与 c(假定 c 就是他了解最近几天可能影响 B 的情绪的有关事件),甚至更多其他条件的合取。

在对日常的判定的日常理解下,尚可能有如此丰富的判断真的标准,那么在对日常判定进行非正常的理解时,判断真的标准肯定就更加丰富。比如对语句 Ab 之真的条件做哲学的考察,或者把这句话作为哲学认识论讨论的一个实例时,则此类情况下真的标准将取决于真之判定者所坚持的哲学立场。唯我论者,行为主义者和经验论者都可能会有不同的标准。更进一步的复杂情况也许出现在科学中,对同一个语句在不同的科学理论背景下可能有不同的语义解释。与日常断定相似,有时,在语义解释相同时,判断真理的标准也可能会有很大的不同。比如对量子力学中的许多命题,或表达命题的语句,爱因斯坦要求更具有决定论特征的条件来断定其真或假,而这个断定真的标准与量子力学的波尔解释,或者哥本哈根解释所要求的标准并不一致。

在哲学中,不用说情况要更加复杂一些。即使在赞成塔尔斯基真定义的前提下,也会有不同的真理标准,特别是对真理问题喜欢作认识论理解的哲学家,更是对真理的判定问题给出了五花八门的标准。值得注意的是,戴维森对塔尔斯基真定义的理解,以及在此基础上他对真理标准问题的理解。在哲学家中,对塔尔斯基的真理论给予最实质性的应用的当数戴维森。他对塔尔斯基理论的运用,其特色不仅在于他把真定义运用于自然语言语义学和语言的解释问题,而更突出地表现为,他对塔尔斯基真定义作了独特的理解。塔尔斯基式的真定义不只是一个可用于表达语句的意义的形式模式,而且,他认为在这个定义(广义的,包括 T 约定等等)中包含了人对真的最原初的理解,是一切信念,或有信念的条件。不但如此,他还认为,塔尔斯基理论有一个塔尔斯式本人并未引入,而由他加以扩展的应用,就是让真定义之模式,特别是 T 语句形式,在判定一个真理论是否是适用于一个语言的真理论(即它的意义理论)上起作用。① 于是,在戴维森的理论中,塔尔斯基的真定义与真理的判定问题有了一个直接的结合。尽管按我们的分析,真定义仍独立于真理判定问题,但真定义的模式确实在后者那里得到某种直接的运用。不过,那也不是原封不动地搬过去,而是根据他所设想的 radical interpretation 的思想实验作了必要的变换。在假定善意原则(principle of charity)正确的前提下,最简单的观察语句的真理判定标准可由如下实例(为清楚和便于理解,已作了必要的简化)来显示:

"现在这里正在下雪"这句话可合理地被解释者判定为真,当且仅当(1)说话者说出并认为这句话成立;(2)当说话者说出这句话时,他所在的地方正在下雪;(3)解释者认知地把握(1)和(2)。

不管怎么说,尽管戴维森在判定语言表达的真假时,实质性地运用了塔尔斯基的真定义,但这绝不意味着真定义与判定真具有范畴上的或概念上的同一性,或者弱一点,从真定义到真理标准具有可推导性。在这里,范畴上或概念上的区分是很明显的,一方面,是作为语义学定义的真概念,此外还有引申出来的作为人的基本思想模式的真模式(对 T 语句的直观理解等等);另一方面,是判定真定义中所蕴涵、所要求之条件或要素是否被满足的标准。当此标准运用于实际的语言理解中或其他实践中时,即可判定具体的语句或语句集的真值。此时问题就转变成语言理解或实践判定中的经验问题。

似乎在直观上,实用主义真理论可被认为是把真的定义与判定真的标

---

① 戴维森多次谈到这个看法,比较典型的可见他在 "Radical Interpretation"(*Inquiries into Truth and Interpretation*, Oxford: Clarendon Press, 1984, pp. 125—139)和 "The Structure and Content of Truth"(*The Journal of Philosophy*, vol. 87, 1990, pp. 279—328)两篇文章中的讨论。

准相统一(如果不是同一)的典型。真即是能产生所需的效用,这既是定义,又是判别的标准。但从概念上来分析,真定义与判别真理标准的范畴区别,对实用主义真理论与对其他真理论都是同样适用的,并无本质上的不同。即使实用主义者自己也并非不明白这个概念上的区分,詹姆士就明确说过:

> 像任何一本字典都会告诉你们的那样,真理是我们某些观念的一种性质。那意味着观念与"实在""一致"(agreement),而对于错误,则意味着它们与实在不一致。实用主义者和理智主义者(intellectualists)双方都把这个定义作为理所当然的事情接受下来。只是在问到"一致"这个词意味什么时,以及当实在被看作我们的观念与其相一致的某种东西,而问到"实在"这个词意味什么时,争论才会开始。①

像塔尔斯基那种类型的真定义,其内容之单纯,以及由单纯和"正确"(至少在戴维森等人看来)所具有的基本性,确实可以使争论的双方都接受它。接受它(自然是指接受与塔尔斯基的真定义一致的某种观念,而不是在历史的意义上实际接受塔尔斯基的理论)并容纳实用主义的真理判定标准,这正是在詹姆士的理论构造中所发生的事实。"一致"(或用更通常的叫法作"符合")的话,就一定有 T 语句成立,实用主义真定义并不与塔尔斯基真定义必然冲突。实用主义者若想判定是否 p,可以用他的实用主义标准,比如效用,判定 p 是否正在被证实。证实可以不像许多哲学家所理解的那样是一次完成的,而是一个过程,可能会一直进行下去,永无止息(这正是实用主义在真理问题上的一个有特色的思想)。但这个判定过程,与塔尔斯基真定义一点也不冲突,甚至是"按照它来进行的"。所谓"符合",不就相当于"我们说是的,它就是","我们说不是的,它就不是",不就是这个意思吗?这

---

① William James, *Pragmatism and Four Essays From THE MEANING OF TRUTH*, New American Library, 1974, p.132.

是詹姆士和他的对手共同接受的,关键是看什么是"符合"的进一步的含义。那被证实的,那有效用的,就是"符合"的意思,在这里就提出了真理标准。①

当詹姆士说真"意味"着在实践中形成的一种过程本身的性质时,虽然这里用到"意味"这个说法,似乎是指语义的,或通常都认为它就是定义的另一种说法,但在此处它确实是指:就此我们可判定具有这一性质者为真,就是说,它指的是如何判定一个"观念"(詹姆士用语)的真值的办法或标准。因为标准也在某种角度下,比如詹姆士的角度下,可能是"意味着"什么。也就是这个"意味"具有的迷惑作用,使人们通常没看清,这个说法的真实性质。此处的"意味"与定义中用的"意味"是不同的。

其实,实用主义者完全可以不坚持对真的一种塔尔斯基式的定义,而坚持或创造某种其他的定义,但这时他也许至少不属于我们大家所熟悉的那类实用主义者了(如果他还能叫做"实用主义者"的话)。"我们大家所熟悉的"那类实用主义者坚持塔尔斯基式的真定义(或其中反映出的对真的某种直观的理解),同时坚持一种实用主义的判定真理的标准,这一点从前面所引的詹姆士的那段话中可以看得清楚。② 不管怎么说,我们最关心的倒不是詹姆士所采用的真定义到底是什么,而是以某些具体的哲学理论或语义学理论为例来谈一个一般性的概念问题。如此,我们可以试着设想詹姆士把"效用"加入到他的真定义中。即便如此,他仍然像现在的处境一样,需要考察在实践的真值判定中,什么是"效用"的标准,也即什么是判定真的标准。当然,加上"效用"成分的扩充的真定义是否还满足本文的全部结论,本文的论证还不能回答这个问题,因为本文的论证只限于塔尔斯基真定义这

---

① 自然,我们不否认实用主义与理智主义的冲突除了在真理标准问题上,非常重要的还在对真的纯哲学的解释上,甚至理智主义者也许认为只有后一个方面才是他们的根本分歧。但这个事实对我们在此想用詹姆士案例说明的东西没有实质的影响。

② 恐怕有人会说,塔尔斯基并不支持我在这里提出的对实用主义的解释。在《真的语义学观念和语义学的基础》一文的第 14 节,特别是其中的倒数第二个自然段,塔尔斯基实际上认为实用主义观念与古典真理观念是不同的。(*Philosophy and Phenomenological Research*, vol. IV, pp. 355—356)但根据本文第一节关于塔尔斯基理论的解释的四个方面的分类,应能导出对这个问题的适当的说明。

个有限的目标。但有一点是可以肯定的,从这个扩充中,还没发现有否定真定义与真理标准在概念和范畴上区分之重要性和必要性的实质证据。

全文意旨述要

我们在真理问题上作真定义和真理标准之间的区分,原本的目的就是要说明哲学上的争论和问题,特别是这些争论和问题的性质。整个论文考虑做如下几件事情:

(1)对理解塔尔斯基的真理论提供一点一般性的概念上的建议。在第一节中提到的对塔尔斯基理论的理解所涉及的四个方面,是对塔尔斯基理论理解上的一种概念的区分。此文中,我论证了,真理标准之独立于塔尔斯基真定义的范畴上的正确性。不但如此,真理标准在原则上也可以独立于对真定义的哲学说明,尽管在事实上,对大多数哲学家来说,真定义的哲学解释经常实质性地影响到真理标准。

(2)全文或直接或迂回地都意在说明,即便在最实质性地使用了塔尔斯基真理论的戴维森的哲学中,也没有直接把塔尔斯基的真定义作为真理标准。至于无数其他的有关真理的理论,更是有诸多不同的标准,但使用和支持这些不同真理标准的人,却可能且经常(我在此文中并未论证其必然,尽管我相信对塔尔斯基定义的最简单的那种直接的理解,是内在于人一般在作断定时所用的框架的)共同认可塔尔斯基真定义中那个原本的,未加进一步解释的内容。显然,我的目的不是要说明塔尔斯基真定义本身作为思想模式的意义(虽然那是也极有意义的另一个重要问题),而是说明就在定义所把握的范围内,完全给独立的真理标准在概念的可能性上留出了足够的空间。

(3)提请真理问题的讨论者注意到以下事实,许多所谓真理问题的争论,看起来好像是关于真的定义的,其实是关于真的标准的。因此,反对塔尔斯基的真理论的某些批评,在逻辑的意义上就完全可能无关于塔尔斯基理论本身,而是一些塔尔斯基本人也许根本不需要反对的真理标准方面的结论。因此,这个分析不但对于弄清塔尔斯基所做的,而且对于弄清反对他的人所做的(不是他们认为他们所做的),都有促使概念明晰方面的好处。

(作者系北京大学哲学系副教授)

论意图的聚合原则*

● 朱　菁

意图的聚合原则由迈克尔·布拉特曼（Michael Bratman）最先提出，被称为是"一种对意图的天然约束"。根据这一原则，一位理性能动者的意图应该具有聚合性。本文首先对意图的聚合原则作出进一步的阐释和辨析，这一阐述不仅与布拉特曼所主张的意图的规划理论以及植根于该理论的关于意图的一致性原则是合拍的，而且还揭示出关于实践理性的一些深刻的基本原理。本文还将讨论针对意图的聚合原则的一些主要反例和异议，并为该原则提供辩护，以论证这一原则在经过本文提出的适当修正和完善之后，能够经受严格的概念分析和心理学考量。

一、引言

迈克尔·布拉特曼（Michael Bratman）提出了关于意图的聚合原则（the Principle of Intention Agglomeration，以下简称 PIA），并称之为"一种对意图的天然约束"。[①]这一原则要求一位理性的能动者（rational agent）的意图应该具有聚合性。更确切地说，PIA 要求：

如果在某一个时刻一位能动者同时分别合理地拥有意图 A 和意图 B，那么对这位能动者而言，拥有

---

* 作者感谢 Andrei Buckareff 对本文的初稿提出了许多建设性的评论和建议。本文大部分内容曾于 2003 年 12 月 28 日在美国哲学学会东部年会的分组讨论会上宣读，评论人 Edward Hinchman 以及在场的许多同行提出了宝贵的批评和建议，在此一并致谢。此项研究得到了 2003 年度中国科学院研究生院院长基金的支持。

① Michael Bratman, 'Davidson's Theory of Intention', in B. Vermazen and M. Hintikka (eds.), *Essays on Davidson: Actions and Events*, (Oxford: Clarendon Press, 1985), pp. 13—26, esp. 22. Reprinted in his *Faces of Intention: Selected Essays on Intention and Agency* (Cambridge: Cambridge University Press, 1999), pp. 209—224.

一个聚合的意图 A 且 B,也应当是合理的。

鉴于意图在人们的实践推理中所占据的重要角色,布拉特曼指出:"对一位能动者而言,有一种理性的压力要求他将他的各种意图聚合而成一个较大的意图。"[①]

但是布拉特曼未能对 PIA 作出明确的阐释和辩护,许多与该原则有关的关键问题未能得到解决:意图聚合的"理性压力"的来源是什么?当两个意图进行聚合时需满足哪些约束条件?PIA 到底是要求聚合后的复合意图取代参与聚合的子意图,还是在原有意图的基础上增加一个复合意图?由于这些问题未能得到适当的处理,致使 PIA 面临着许多致命的反例和异议。[②]

本文将首先对 PIA 作出进一步的阐释和辨析,这一阐述不仅与布拉特曼所主张的意图的规划理论(the planning theory of intention)以及植根于该理论的关于意图的一致性原则是合拍的,而且还揭示出关于实践理性的一些深刻的基本原理。本文还将讨论针对意图的聚合原则的一些主要反例和异议,并为该原则提供辩护,以论证这一原则在经过本文提出的适当修正和完善后,能够经受严格的概念分析和心理学考量。

二、对 PIA 的进一步阐述

在过去的 20 余年间,在关于行动(action)的哲学理论中最重要的进展恐怕要算对意图的深入研究。一系列的研究成果有力地阐明了意图作为一种独特的、不可还原的心理状态在人们的自愿行为中所发挥的不可或缺的作用。[③]意图在人

---

① Michael Bratman, *Intention, Plans, and Practical Reason* (Cambridge, MA: Harvard University Press, 1987), p. 134.

② Hugh McCann, 'Rationality and the Range of Intentions', in P. French, T. Uehling, and H. Wettstein (eds.), *Midwest Studies of Philosophy X* (Minneapolis: University of Minnesota Press, 1986), pp. 191—211; Steven Sverdlik, 'Consistency among Intentions and the "Simple View"', *Canadian Journal of Philosophy* 26 (1996), pp. 515—522.

③ M. Brand, *Intending and Acting: Toward a Naturalized Action Theory* (Cambridge, MA: MIT Press, 1984); M. Bratman, *Intention, Plans, and Practical Reason* (Cambridge, MA: Harvard University Press, 1987); *Faces*

们的实践推理和行动中扮演着关键性的角色，在概念上无法将其还原为其他类型的心理状态，如信念（beliefs）、愿望（desires）或希望（wishes）等。① 我们常常会形成指向未来的意图（future-directed intentions），这往往是我们的行动计划的有机组成部分。这样的意图对于我们进行实践思考以及筹划合理的社会行为都是至关重要的，因为它既能促进人际间的协调与合作，也便于我们合理地安排自己的个人生活，并使得我们当前的思维与决策能够有效地影响到我们未来的行为。② 正如布拉特曼所言："意图是构成计划的砖瓦，而计划则是扩大化的意图。"③ 近前的（proximal）或指向当前的意图（present-directed intentions）涉及人们当下就要做的或者正在做的事情，它们在有意行为（intentional behavior）的发生、控制和完成的过程中具有关键性的作用，使得一位能动者能够有效地实现先前确定的意图和计划，并在执行过程中指导和监控其行为的发生。④

意图所具有的一些特性能够将其与其他类型的心理状态区别开来。首先，正如许多哲学家已经注

---

of Intention: Selected Essays on Intention and Agency (Cambridge: Cambridge University Press, 1999); G. Harman, 'Practical reasoning,' *Review of Metaphysics* 79 (1976), pp. 431—463; 'Willing and intending,' in R. E. Grandy and R. Warner (eds.), *Philosophical Grounds of Rationality: Intentions, Categories, Ends* (Oxford: Clarendon Press, 1986), pp. 363—382; *Change in View* (Cambridge, MA: MIT Press, 1986), chs. 8&9; A. Mele, *Springs of Action: Understanding Intentional Behavior* (New York: Oxford University Press, 1992); J. Searle, *Intentionality* (Cambridge: Cambridge University Press, 1983), ch. 3.

① 有关意图可以还原为其他类型的心理状态的哲学讨论，参见 Robert Audi, 'Intending', *Journal of Philosophy* 70 (1973), pp. 387—403, reprinted in his *Action, Intention, and Reason* (Ithaca, NY: Cornell University Press, 1993), pp. 36—73; Audi, 'Intending and Its Place in the Theory of Action', in G. Holmeström-Hintikka and R. Tuomela (eds.), *Contemporary Action Theory*, Volume 1: Individual Action (Dordrecht: Kluwer Academic Publishers, 1997) 177—196; Wayne Davis, 'A Causal Theory of Intending', *American Philosophical Quarterly* 21 (1984), pp. 43—54, reprinted in A. R. Mele ed., *The Philosophy of Action* (Oxford: Oxford University Press, 1997), pp. 131—148.

② 见 Bratman, *Intention, Plans, and Practical Reason*, chs. 2&3.

③ 同上，p. 8.

④ 见 Mele, *Springs of Action*, ch. 10.

意到的,意图意味着一种心理学上的或者实践意义上的承诺:当一个能动者拥有某个意图的时候,他就已经决定了或承诺了要介入到该意图所指向的蓄意行为中去,无论该行为是发生在当前还是属于未来,尽管这样的承诺并非不可更改或者被撤销。① 其次,意图常常拒斥对自身的反思和修正。一旦某个意图已经形成,环境或条件的轻微变化往往不足以促使该意图的持有者重新考虑该意图的适当性,然后重新展开思量与决策。这也就是说,意图在人们的实践推理中"具有一种特有的稳定性或惯性"。② 意图的这两个特性,即意图的设定性(settledness)和惯性,有助于我们理解意图在人们的实践推理和社会交往中所扮演的特殊角色,因为对他人行为的理性预期往往需要建立在对其意图的恰当理解和判断的基础上,这对于人际间的协调与合作无疑是必要的;而当我们对自己未来的行动进行筹划时,也需要认真对待我们先前已确立的意图。

按照布拉特曼提出的关于意图的规划理论,对一位理性的能动者的意图和计划,存在着一些约束条件。③ 首先,意图受制于一致性约束(consistency constraints)。处于同一个计划中的不同意图,在其他条件均等的情况下,应该满足内部的一致性。假如一位能动者在蓄意做 A 的同时又蓄意不做 A,那么在通常情况下,他就犯了一种应该受到批评的缺乏一致性的错误。此外,在其他条件均等的情况下,一位能动者的意图应当与他所持有的信念保持一致,如果他的信念之间本身是满足一致性的。比方说,如果我相信我不可能在同一天既参加一个会议又去观看一场足球比赛,那么我就不应当故意在当天做这两件事情。第二,一位理性能动者的意图和计划应当满足目标-手段的和谐性(means-end coherence)。我们的意图和计划通常是按照分层结构组织的:涉及目标的总计划往往包含着涉及手段的子计划,而一般性的意图往往包含着特殊性的意

---

① 见 Bratman, *Intention, Plans, and Practical Reason*, pp. 15—18; Mele, *Springs of Action*, ch. 9.

② Bratman, *Intention, Plans, and Practical Reason*, p. 16.

③ 同上, pp. 30—32。

图。① 满足目标-手段的和谐就要求每一位理性的能动者能够合理地安排他的计划和意图,以便有效地加以实施。

如果在一个时刻一位理性的能动者同时拥有两个不同的意图,那么这两个意图通常应该满足上面提到的两个重要的约束条件:它们应该在内部是一致的,而且应该与该能动者的信念保持一致;同时,它们还应该满足目标—手段的和谐性。然而,有必要在这两个意图上再施加一个额外的约束,即意图的聚合原则 PIA 吗?对这样一位能动者来说,将两个意图合并为一个较大的意图的"理性压力"的来源究竟是什么?

正如一些 PIA 的批评者已指出的,不加限制、无所不包的 PIA 明显是不合理的。② 例如,李红拥有的一个意图是在四年以后她大学毕业时报考医学院的研究生,她还有一个意图是当天晚上回家吃饭。好像不存在任何"理性压力"要求李红形成这样一个复合意图,其内容是"既在四年之后报考医学院的研究生又在当晚回家吃饭"。斯蒂文·斯维德里克指出:

确实,如果对 PIA 不加任何限制,即一位理性的能动者总是将她所拥有的意图聚合起来,那么每一位理性的能动者就会拥有一个巨大无比的复合意图来指导其行为。而这样一个过大的意图更有可能是妨碍,而不是方便人们去满足自己的愿望。③

那么,两个意图的聚合应该满足怎样的约束或限制?当一位理性的能动者将两个不同的意图合并成为一个较大的意图时,这两个意图最起码应该是相关的。如果两个意图彼此互不搭界,就像上面李红的例子所表明的,令意图进行聚合的"理性压力"似乎无从谈起。

一位理性能动者的不同的意图彼此有关系的方式可以有很多种,

---

① Bratman, *Intention*, *Plans*, *and Practical Reason*, p. 16.
② McCann, 'Rationality and the Range of Intentions', p. 198; Sverdlik, 'Consistency among Intentions and the "Simple View"', p. 517.
③ Sverdlik, 'Consistency among Intentions and the "Simple View"', p. 517.

但并非所有的相关性都会导致意图的聚合。李红有意在大学毕业后报考医学院的研究生，为此她要学好医学方面的专业基础课。她学好各种专业基础课的意图与她报考研究生的意图显然是相关的：前者是实现后者的手段。但在这里似乎并没有什么特别的理由让李红将这两个意图聚合起来，因为前者已经包含在后者里面了。基于同样的目的，李红决定还要学好一些研究生入学考试中的规定课程，如政治、英语等。这一意图与她学好专业基础课的意图也是相关的：二者是实现同一个目标的手段。但好像仍然不存在什么特殊的理由要求将这两个意图合二为一。

本文认为，当一位能动者同时拥有多个在执行时相互竞争的意图时，有一种"理性的压力"要求将这些意图整合成为一个单独的、较大的意图。两个意图在执行上的竞争性可以定义如下：

如果对其中一个意图的执行会显著地减少执行另一个意图所必须的资源（物理的、心理的，或二者皆有），那么这两个意图在执行时就是相互竞争的。

在这里，有必要对这个定义做一些说明。首先，任何有意行为的执行都会消耗一定量的资源，对这一点应该是没有太大疑义的。这些资源可以是物理性的，如时间、精力、可以支配的身体器官，等等；也可以是心理性的，如注意、记忆、信息加工的容量、进入意识的通道，等等。对有些意图的执行，比如回忆起一位朋友的电话号码，所要求的资源可能是微不足道的，而有些意图，比如撰写一部著作，可能会要求使用相当多的资源。在理论上，不存在在执行过程中完全不需要资源的意图。其次，两个意图在执行时可能发生资源竞争的方式至少有两种：共时性竞争和历时性竞争。在白天参加了一次高强度的考试之后，李红可能会觉得很累，在晚上就没有精力再进行有质量的学习了。在这个例子中，对参加考试这个意图的执行与随后对进行有质量的学习这个意图的执行，就发生了历时性竞争。与此成对照的是，如果一位能动者同时执行多个意图，那么对每一个意图的执行通常就与对其他意图的执行是共时性竞争的。第三，两个意图还可以发生在其他意义上的竞争。例如，李红想通过体育锻炼而保持体型的意图与她想多吃一些卡路里含量过高的食品的意图，可能在效果上是相互竞争的。不过，意图在这个意义上的竞争性不在本文讨论的范围之内。

在我们的日常生活中，我们需要经常应付在执行时相互竞争的意图。像大多数学生一样，李红每个学期都要选修多门课程。尽管可能有很多的课程是她想学的，她必须慎重地从中做出她的选择。首先，她不应当选择在时间上相互冲突的课程，因为她不可能在同一时间出现在不同的教室里。其次，她需要避免所选择的课程密度过大或负担过重，以至于她无法应付。比如，在同一天上四门课，对她来说可能就负担太重了。毕竟，我们所拥有的资源是有限的。① 我们不可能在同一时间做无穷多的事情；在周期性地施展了我们的能动性（agency）之后，我们也会感到疲劳、辛苦、乏味甚至筋疲力尽。所以当我们在规划那些在执行时可能发生竞争的活动时，我们必须严肃地考虑到我们资源的极限。不仅如此，资源的极限还有可能制约我们怎样去实现那些相互竞争的意图。对李红来说，如果她在某一门课上花费了过多的时间和精力，她可能就面临学不好其他课程的危险。因此，如何合理地分配她的资源，以求在她选修的所有课程上获得满意的成绩，对她来说就是一件非常重要的事情。

于是，我们可以理解为什么一位能动者会处在"理性的压力"之下将其所有的在执行时相互竞争的意图合并为一个较大的意图。首先，正如布拉特曼已经有力地加以论证了的，早先的意图和计划为后续的实践思索和规划提供了一个背景框架，这一背景框架为确定进一步的行动方案设立了相关性和可接受性的标准，将思考权衡的范围缩小到一个有限的备选集，并划定了实现其意图的可行性手段。② 如果一位能动者已经具有了多个在执行时相

----

① 参见 Bratman, *Intention, Plans, and Practical Reason*, pp. 10—11, 28—30, 关于我们心理活动所需资源的有限性对于我们的实践思考和筹划活动所产生的影响。

② Bratman, *Intention, Plans, and Practical Reason*, pp. 32—35.

互竞争的意图,当她在盘算和规划后面的行动时,她的实践推理必须在由已有的竞争性意图所设定的统一的背景框架内进行。比如,在学期的中段,李红有一个机会参与一个非常有意思的研究课题,她需要考虑参与这个课题是否会与她所选修的所有课程发生冲突,因为课题的工作会消耗掉她本来可以投入到她的课程学习当中去的时间和精力。一个将所有的竞争性意图包容在内的复合意图因而可以为建立统一的背景框架所需的心理表征提供基础。其次,意图在指导、监测和协调人们执行有意行为的过程中扮演着极为重要的角色。当一位能动者具有多个执行时相互竞争的意图时,由一个复合型的意图来指导、监测及协调对这些竞争性的有意行为的执行,就显得十分自然了。李红可能会发现她对她正在选修的某一门课程特别感兴趣,并愿意通过那门课学到更多的东西,而有一个复合意图会提醒她、指导她将她的资源合理地分配到所有她正在选修的课程上去。

那么,意图的聚合原则是意谓着由复合意图取代原先的子意图,抑或是在原有意图的基础上添加一个复合意图呢?如果是从心理学空间的经济性上考虑,我们似乎应该倾向于接受前者。① 然而,单独拥有一个较大的复合意图并不意谓着在未来的规划和执行活动中会来得更经济些。当李红坐在某一门课的课堂上时,她并不需要时时反思她的整个学习计划。她现在所需要做的,是集中精力完成对当前的特定意图的执行。她不需要为如何安排她的其他课程而担心,因为那些问题早已通过她先前的深思熟虑解决了,并体现在她所拥有的整合性的意图之中。正如布拉特曼所揭示的,意图和计划往往具有分层结构:特殊意图通常是被包含在一般性的意图当中的。所以,在不同的意图被整合进一个较大的意图之后,这一复合意图就作为一个一般性的、整体性的意图负责指导、监测和协调竞争性意图的执行,而将具体实现的细节留给了包含在复合意图之内的较特殊的子意图。

意图的聚合原则的另一个值得

---

① 见 Sverdlik, 'Consistency among Intentions and the "Simple View"', p.516.

注意的特点是,当人们执行多个相互竞争的意图时,通常执行其中某些意图时的性能会相应地打折扣。① 假如李红是一门一门地完成她所选修的五门课程,她或许可以在每一门课上都拿到"优秀"的成绩。但如果她必须在一个学期内完成这五门课,对她来说每门课都获得"优秀"就是一件极为困难的事情。意图之间的竞争可能还会导致对其中某些意图的心理承诺的削减。比如,李红可以在学期开始的时候预选了六门课,如果她发现课程负担过重,或者有些不如她想象的那么有意思,她就会放弃其中的部分课程。

根据意图在人们实践推理和行动中的独特作用,本节对意图的聚合原则作出了详细的阐释和辨析。我们是资源有限的理性能动者,而且我们需要合理地处理那些在执行时相互竞争的意图。当一位能动者同时具有多个竞争性的意图时,存在着一种理性的压力要求将这些意图整合到一个较大的意图当中。这样一个复合意图为进一步的实践思考和规划提供了一个统一的背景框架,并且指导、监测和协调着那些相互竞争的意图的执行。

三、为 PIA 辩护

本文的余下部分将讨论针对意图的聚合原则 PIA 的一些主要的反例和异议,并为 PIA 辩护。

(甲)一些怀疑者发现 PIA 刻画了"是一种很古怪的心理态度,因为大多数的心理状态并不具有聚合性"。② 例如,聚合原则并不适用于愿望(desires)。③ 一个人可以同时分别拥有去听音乐会的愿望和上图书馆的愿望,但不一定有同时做这两件事情的愿望。所以,PIA 似乎显得有些不同寻常。这种责难是毫无根据的。与愿望不同,意图意谓着实践意义上的承诺,因而受制于

---

① 这一点也许会有例外。比如,在开车的同时与人交谈,可以使司机免于疲劳和乏味。不过,在这个例子中,驾驶与交谈对这位司机却很难被看作是两个具有竞争性的行为。

② McCann, 'Rationality and the Range of Intentions', p. 198.

③ Bratman, *Intention*, *Plans*, *and Practical Reason*, pp. 137—138; Alfred Mele, 'Motivation, Self-Control, and the Agglomeration of Desires', *Facta Philosophica* 1 (1999), pp. 77—86.

较强的实践理性的约束,比如前面提到的一致性约束以及目标—手段和谐性的约束。在上文中已经阐明,当一位能动者具有在执行时相互竞争的意图时,这些意图会在理性的压力下聚合在一起,这并没有什么可奇怪的。在这一点上,愿望不具有聚合性也很容易得到理解。

休·麦坎(Hugh McCann)提出,对于信念(beliefs)来说,这一要求也不存在:

> 在我看来,在一次有一千个人参加的抽奖活动中,让我相信当中的某一位购买了彩票的个人不会获奖,这是完全合理的。然而,如果让我把这一千个关于个别人的信念聚合起来,我还相信没有人会获奖,这就不合理了。可是,如果把一千个"此人不会获奖"的信念聚拢起来,我所得到的复合信念就是那样的。所以,信念的聚合原则是不合理的。①

但这样的分析是有问题的。② 事实上,每一位彩券的持有者至少有千分之一的概率获奖,而这一点应该反映在关于此人获奖的理性信念中。所以,如果麦坎将他的这些信念聚合起来,他就应该相信彩券购买者当中有一人,而不是无一人,会获奖。与麦坎不同,另一些哲学家认为一个人的信念是受制于整合性或者聚合性原则的:我们应当保持我们信念的融贯性和一致性,并将它们放入到一个较大的、全局性的总信念中。③

---

① McCann, 'Rationality and the Range of Intentions', p. 198.

② 上面的例子来源于有名的"抽彩悖论",是由亨利·凯伯格最先提出来的(Henry Kyburg, *Probability and the Logic of Rational Belief* (Middletown: Wesleyan University Press, 1961))。"抽彩悖论"涉及确定性与知识之间的关系,关于这个问题的近期的讨论,参见 Igor Douven, 'A new solution to the paradoxes of rational acceptability', *The British Journal for the Philosophy of Science* 53 (2002), pp. 391—410; Ruth Weintraub, 'The lottery: A paradox regained and resolved', *Synthese* 129 (2001), pp. 439—449; Dana Nelkin, 'The lottery paradox, knowledge, and rationality', *Philosophical Review* 109 (2000), pp. 373—409.

③ Bratman, 'Practical Reasoning and Acceptance in a Context', *Mind* 101 (1992), pp. 1—14, reprinted in his *Faces of Intention*, pp. 15—34. Pascal Engel, 'Believing, Holding True, and Accepting', *Philosophical Explorations* 1 (1998), pp. 140—151. Raimo Tuomela, 'Belief versus Acceptance', *Philosophical Explorations* 3 (2000), pp. 122—137.

(乙)针对 PIA 的另一种反对意见认为:如果意图需要满足一致性约束和目标—手段和谐性,那么 PIA 就是多余的。如果一位能动者既有做事情 A 的意图,又有做事情 B 的意图,那么不管这两个意图是处于分立的状态还是处于合取的状态,它们都必须相互一致并且与信念保持一致。"分立但不相容的意图,一旦被我识别,将随后掣肘我的规划活动的每一步,这与将它们聚合起来没有实质上的区别。把它们整合为一个单独的意图,较之未合并之前,既不会增加我的规划活动的复杂性,也不会带来什么新的问题。"①

假设我已经有了两个在执行时相互竞争的意图 A 和 B,它们为我进一步的实践推理和行动提供了背景框架和指南。现在我要考虑一个新的活动 C,它与 A 和 B 具有潜在的竞争性。在我的思考中,我不仅要考虑 C 是否会与我所有的信念以及我先前确定的意图 A 和 B 分别发生冲突,对我来说很重要的一点是,我还需要弄清楚 C 的执行是否会与对 A 和 B 的执行同时发生冲突。我能够同时进行三个动作当中的任何两个,并不意味着我就能够同时完成这三个动作。但如果 C 与 A 和 B 在同时执行时是兼容的,则蕴涵了 C 与 A 和 B 分别是兼容的。如果在其后的实践推理中,在考虑新的意图时,我总是需要在对先前的意图进行合取,以便能够检验意图之间的一致性,或者合理地在相互竞争的意图之间分配资源,为什么我不应当把先前已确定的意图整合为一个较大的复合型意图,使我能够免于遗忘、忽略、费时费工的记忆搜索以及重复性的计算?所以,对一位能动者而言,将执行时相互竞争的意图聚合成为一个较大的意图以方便未来的实践推理,完全是合理的。

(丙)如果我们能够设计一个例子,在这样的例子中一位能动者同时合理地拥有多个意图,而在此之上再拥有一个聚合性的意图对他来说却是不合理的,那么 PIA 就是错的。

下面讨论麦坎给出的一个针对

---

① McCann, 'Rationality and the Range of Intentions', p. 198.

PIA 的反例。① 一位警官正在追捕两名正朝着两个方向迅速逃跑的罪犯。这位警官是一名神枪手,用两只手同时开枪都能做到百发百中。他身上恰好带了两支枪,但其中只有一支装了子弹。这位警官是知道这一点的,但他忘了到底是哪支枪里有子弹。在经过简略的计算之后,他决定同时拔出两支枪来,分别瞄准一名逃犯,然后同时扣动扳机。这样做可以使得他击中其中一名逃犯的几率得以最大化,尽管另一名罪犯会逃脱掉。他由此采取了相应的行动,而且获得了成功。

毫无疑问,这名警官用双手分别扣动两支枪扳机的行为是有意的。按照对有意行为的"简单观点"(Simply View,以下简称 SV)的理解(这是麦坎所接受的),每当一位能动者有意做一件事 A,他必须在做这件事的时候拥有做 A 的意图。因而这名警官必须拥有两个分立的意图操作双枪向两名逃犯分别射击。然而根据 PIA,这名警官还会同时拥有一个复合意图向他们同时射击。但这样一个聚合性的意图直接同这名警官的知识发生矛盾,因为他清楚地知道只有其中的一支枪里有子弹,所以他不可能击倒两名逃犯。如果我们认为警官的行为是理性的,而且他所有的意图与他的信念是一致的,那么,麦坎认为,PIA 就一定是错误的。

布拉特曼则认为我们应该保留 PIA 而放弃 SV。② 按照布拉特曼的看法,一名能动者的有意行为 A 并不必然地蕴涵着一个做 A 的意图。所以尽管该警官用双枪射击两名逃犯的行为是有意的,这并不意谓着他就拥有分别向他们射击的两个意图。因此,这个案例并不能构成对 PIA 的任何威胁。

本文认为,SV 是对的。③ 但我

---

① McCann, 'Rationality and the Range of Intentions', p. 199. 这个例子以布拉特曼用过的另一个例子为模本,参见 Bratman, *Intention, Plans, and Practical Reason*, pp. 113—118。

② Bratman, 'Two Faces of Intention', *Philosophical Review* 93 (1984), pp. 375—405; *Intention, Plans, and Practical Reason*, chs. 8 & 9.

③ 对"简单观点"的阐释和辩护,参见 McCann, 'Rationality and the Range of Intentions'; 'Settled Objectives and Rational Constraints', *American Philosophical Quarterly* 28 (1991), pp. 25—36, reprinted in A. R. Mele ed., *The Philosophy of Action* (Oxford: Oxford University Press, 1997), pp. 204—222; Frederick Adams, 'Intention and Intentional Action: The

们仍然有可能在对上述案例所给出一个更为合理的理解的基础之上保留PIA。在规划的开始阶段,警官并不是先拥有两个分立的意图,其内容是分别向两名逃犯开枪,而是先形成了一个更具有全局性的意图,这个意图的内容是举双枪射击但只击倒其中一名逃犯,因为警官知道他的两支枪当中只有一支是装有子弹的。他用双手同时操作两支枪并扣动扳机的行为,可以看成是在这样一个全局性意图的指导和协调下所进行的复杂行为。随后,警官才具有了从先前的全局性意图所导出的两个更为特殊的意图,分别用于指导他的每只手的动作。但是,对这两个导出的意图并不具有百分之百的自信度。对其中每一个意图来说,这名警官只有50%的自信度击倒逃犯。① 毕竟,他知道其中只有一支枪是装了子弹的,而且并未指望他能够将两名逃犯都击倒,这一点肯定与他在知道两支枪都有子弹的情况下所可能形成的意图是不一样的。这样,在对案例给出一个更合理的分析的基础上,我们可以同时保留SV和PIA。

(丁)斯维德里克注意到在某些情况下一位能动者可以合理地拥有多个相互不兼容的意图,并认为这样一种心理现象对PIA构成了威胁:

> ……例如,在预测到部分旅客有可能临时取消旅行计划的情况下,航空公司可以合理地对某些航班超额预订出一些座位。同样,在某些时候个人也可以合理地采用这种策略,即作出一些预先知道将来不会履行的承诺。比方说,根据顾客活动的规律,一名出租车司机在下午四点钟的时候会同意搭载六名乘客,虽然她知道她基本上不可能完成这么多的任务,但是在她下班之前,她极有可能载运到五名乘客,从而获得最大的利润。(作出一个认真的承诺通常可以看作是形成

Simple View', *Mind and Language* 1 (1986), pp. 281—301; David Chan, 'A Not-So-Simple View of Intentional Action', *Pacific Philosophical Quarterly* 80 (1999), pp. 1—16.

① 关于意图的自信度的概念,见David Chan, 'A Not-So-Simple View of Intentional Action'.

一个打算执行的意图。）……一名能动者可以合理地有意做A，合理地有意做B，……而且合理地有意做G，而不必合理地有意做A且B……且G。①

正如一家精明的航空公司根据其掌握的在某些确定时段的客流量的统计知识，可以采用"超额预售策略"以求获取利润的最大化，

一位理性的能动者在类似的情况下，也可以运用类似的策略，合理地形成一些她明确知道不会最终实现的意图，以求最大可能地满足她自己的愿望。在这种条件下，她这么做是合理的，因为拥有这些意图可能是实现她的目标的最佳策略。……在这样的情况下，一位理性能动者没有必要将她的意图加以聚合，因为这样做会与一致性要求直接发生冲突。②

正如斯维德里克自己已经意识到，"超额预售策略"可以合理地运用的情形，不仅仅只对PIA是一个挑战，对于意图的种种一致性约束，也构成了威胁。③ 即便聚合性意图缺失，那位出租车司机对六位乘客作出的承诺，也与她所拥有的不可能搭载六名乘客的信念是不一致的。为什么这是合理的？下文将阐明PIA实际上能够为在"超额预售策略"可以合理地使用的场合中保留意图的一致性约束提供帮助。

意图通常意谓着在实践上的承诺，但并非所有的意图都会得到执行，并非所有的意图都蕴涵着同等程度的承诺。对于某些意图，比如履践某个极为重要的商业会谈，我们会竭尽全力来实现其承诺。但某些意图会最终流产，因为条件有了变化，或者人们改变了想法。当一位能动者具有多个在执行时相互竞争的意图时，通常他是希望将他有限的资源合理地运用到极至。但事物是在不断发生变化的，环境因素也难以预测，所以一位理性的能动者应当随时准备在必要的时候放弃或悬置对部分意图的执行，以便能够实现更重要的意图或者满足更具

---

① Sverdlik, 'Consistency among Intentions and the "Simple View"', p. 517.
② 同上。
③ 同上，p. 518。

有优先性的目标。

当某家航空公司对某次航班超额预售了一些座位,比如说,一架100个座位的航班预售了105张机票,这家公司对其(部分)乘客的承诺就相应地削减了:在超额预售前,每一位订了票的乘客都能保证有座位;在超额预售之后,航空公司就不能再声称它能保证每一位订购了机票的乘客都能登机,因为在理论上,如果所有预订了机票的乘客都按照计划旅行,他们的要求是不可能得到满足的;如果这种情况发生,一些乘客将不得不改变行程。上文提到的出租车司机并不相信她能搭载六名乘客,但基于她的统计知识,她认为对这六名乘客分别作出承诺可能是能够使得最终有五名乘客前来乘车的最佳策略。很明显,这增加的第六个意图使得她所拥有的六个意图相互竞争她有限的资源,这就显著地削减了她对先前的五个意图的承诺。在此之前,她可以明确地承诺她会执行所有五个意图,但现在她知道其中一个很可能无法兑现了。因而对她来说,很有必要将这六个意图合并为一个较大的意图,这样一个复合意图可用于指导她随后的活动,以决定其中的哪一个意图将被放弃,这样她能够最终搭乘到五名乘客。这种情况很像是一名学生在刚开学时预选了六门课程,他知道他并没有能力选修所有这些课程,但却合理地采用了超额预订的策略,先对这六门课进行试听,然后再逐步弄清楚其中的哪五门课是他能够胜任并且最想选修的,并最终放弃掉另一门。如果不借助于一个包容了每个个别意图的复合意图,这样一种复杂的思维活动是很难得到清楚的说明的。

(作者系中国科学院研究生院人文学院副教授)

不是"世界的图画"而是"语言游戏"
——从《哲学研究》看维特根斯坦Ⅱ的语言观

● 孟令朋

《哲学研究》采用的是苏格拉底式的论辩方式,维特根斯坦演的是双簧戏(Spiel)。他所持的观点是语言游戏说(Sprachspiel),攻击的靶子是语言图画论,反驳"私人语言"的论证也是贯穿这条主线,他的主要根据是对日常语言的分析。从语言游戏说中,我们可以窥见他的意义理论,也可以重新给诗定位。

维特根斯坦说"哲学家诊治一个问题;就像诊治一种疾病。"(PI. 255)[①]在《哲学研究》中,维特根斯坦诊治的其中一种"病"就是:语言图画论。语言是世界的图画,语言像镜子一样反映出世界,把语言仅仅当成一种工具,这就是语言图画论的观点。

一、语言不是世界的图画而是"游戏"

前期维特根斯坦认为,我们生活于其中的现实世界及其可能世界是由事实或事态组成的,是事实、事态的总汇。而且,他认为这样构成的世界有一个本质

---

① 维特根斯坦:《哲学研究》(PI),陈嘉映译,上海人民出版社,2001年版(下同)。

结构。世界的本质是由可以为命题所描述的事实或事态组成的封闭的、完成了的整体。①

思想被一个光轮环绕。——思想的本质,即逻辑,表现着一种秩序,世界的先验秩序;即世界和思想必定共同具有的种种可能性的秩序。但这种秩序似乎必定是最简单的。它先于一切经验,必定贯穿一切经验;它自己却不可沾染任何经验的浑浊或不确——它倒必定是最纯粹的晶体。这种晶体却又不是作为抽象出现的,而是作为某种具体的东西,简直是最具体的,就像是世界上最坚实的东西。(《逻辑哲学论》第 5.5563)及(PI.97)

思想、语言似乎是世界的独特对应物,世界的图画。句子、语言、思想、世界,这些概念前后排成一列,每一个都和另一个相等。(PI.96)

实际的语言中并没有这样一个"水晶"般纯粹的逻辑结构,语言也不是世界的图画。语言图画论的基本假定是用"名称—对象"来说明语言与世界的关系。

指物定义就是典型的"名称—对象"模式。维特根斯坦在《哲学研究》的一开头就批评了以指物定义来理解语言的方式。

奥古斯丁,《忏悔录》卷一第八节:当成年人称谓某个对象,同时转向这个对象的时候,我会对此有所觉察,并明了当他们要指向这个对象的时候,他们就发出声音,通过这声音来指称它。……。

在我看来,我们在上面这段话里得到的是人类语言本质的一幅特定的图画,即:语言中的语词是对象的名称——句子是这样一些名称的联系。——在语言的这幅图画里,我们发现了以下观念的根源:每个词都有一个含义;含义与语词一一对应;含义即语词所代表的对象。(PI. 1)

---

① 韩林合:《维特根斯坦哲学之路》,昆明:云南大学出版社,1996 年版,第 143 页。

接下来维特根斯坦就对这种理解方式作了批评:

> 现在来想一下语言的这种用法:我派某人去买东西,给他一张纸条,上面写着"五个红苹果"。他拿着这张纸条到了水果店,店主打开标着有"苹果"字样的贮藏柜,然后在一张表格里找出"红"这个词,在其相应的位置上找到一个色样,嘴里数着一串基数词——假定他能熟记这些数字——一直数到"五",每数一个数字就从柜子里拿出一个色样和颜色相同的苹果。——人们以这种方式或类似的方式和词语打交道。——"但他怎么知道应该在什么地方用什么办法查找'红'这个词呢?他怎么知道他该拿'五'这个词干什么呢?"……——刚才根本不是在谈什么含义;谈的只是"五"这个词是怎样使用的。(PI. 1)

"名称—对象"模式解释不了"红"、"五"这两个词是怎样使用的。维特根斯坦又进一步对这个模式作了说明:

> 让我们设想一种符合于奥古斯丁所作的那类描述的语言:建筑师傅 A 和他的助手 B 用这种语言进行交流。A 在用各种石料盖房子,这些石料是:方石、柱石、板石和条石。B 必须依照 A 需要石料的顺序把这些石料递给他。为了这个目的,他们使用一种由"方石"、"柱石"、"板石"和"条石"这几个词组成的语言。A 喊出这些词,B 就把石料递过来。(PI. 2)

在这个场景里仿佛说的是"方石"、"柱石"、"板石"和"条石"与外在的对象一一对应。但这并不是一个完整的交流系统。维特根斯坦说"板石"是一个"蜕化句",或者说是"省略"句,是"拿给我一块板石"这个句子的一种缩略形式。"拿给我一块板石"才表明这个交流系统是如何运作的。

语言中的每一个词都标示着某种东西，这时候还什么都没有说出来。(PI. 13)

人们以为学习语言就在于叫出事物的名称。即叫出人、形状、色彩、疼痛、情绪、数字等等的名称。我们已经说过——命名就像给一件东西贴上标签。可以说这是使用语词前的一种准备工作。但这种准备为的是做什么呢？(PI. 26)

是用来做"语言游戏"。我们使用语言，就是在做各样语言游戏。描述、报道、推测、编故事、演戏、唱歌、请求、感谢、谩骂、问候、祈祷等等，这些无一不是在做语言游戏。奥古斯丁描述的那个交流系统，只是语言游戏的一种。

离开了象棋游戏，问"棋子是什么"是没有意义的。同样，离开了语言游戏(语言的具体运用)，没法说清楚"词是什么"。我们有一个错觉：可以单独举出一个"词"，问它是什么意思。之所以能这么做，是因为我们已经熟悉了它的具体用法，如果面对一个生僻的词，你就茫然了，你能说出"厽"的意思是什么吗？索绪尔也持相同看法，他是这样说的，"比方一枚卒子，本身是不是下棋的要素呢？当然不是。因为只凭它的纯物质性，离开了它在棋盘上的位置和其他下棋的条件，它对下棋的人来说是毫无意义的。只有当它披上自己的价值，并与这价值结为一体，才成为现实的和具体的要素。假如在下棋的时候，这个棋子弄坏了或丢失了，我们可不可以用另外一个等价的来代替它呢？当然可以。不但可以换上另外一枚卒子，甚至可以换上一个外形上完全不同的棋子。只要我们授以相同的价值，照样可以宣布它是同一个东西。"[1]

命名和描述并不在同一个平面上：命名是描述的准备。命名还根本不是语言游戏的一步——就像在棋盘上把棋子摆好并非走了一步棋。可以说：为一事物命名，还什么都没有完成。除了在语言游戏里，

---

[1] 索绪尔：《普通语言学教程》，北京：商务印书馆，1996年版，第193页。

事物甚至没有名称。(PI.49)

　　指着象棋里的王对一个人说:"这是王",这并没有对他解释这个棋子的用法。向某人解释象棋,一开始就指着一个棋子说:"这是王,它可以这样走,等等。"——在这种情况下,我们要说:只有当学习者"已经知道棋子在游戏中是什么东西","这是王"(或"这叫'王'")这样的话才是对语词的解释。即只有当他做过这种游戏或者看过别人做这种游戏而且"看懂了",——以及诸如此类的情况。也只有在这些情况下他才能够在学习这种游戏之际切实地询问:"这个叫什么?"——即这个棋子叫什么。可以说:只有已经知道名称是干什么的人,才能有意义地问到一个名称。(PI.31)

一个棋子只有在象棋游戏中才有意义,才能谈到它的用法,同样,

　　一个词怎样起作用,猜是猜不出来的。必须审视它的用法,从中学习。(PI.340)

　　"一个词到底是什么?"这个问题类似于"棋子是什么?"(PI.108)

一个词的用法比一枚卒子的走法更灵活。"把那个绿瓶子给我","花红了,柳绿了",而"春风又绿江南岸"则另有一番气象,一个"绿"字把春天的气息、春天的形势带出来了。我们只有从"春风又绿江南岸"这个用法中才能理解"绿"字的这个含义。

二、认为有"私人语言"存在,这完全是语言图画论在作怪

　　是否可以设想这样一种语言:

　　这种语言的语词指涉只有讲话人能够知道的东西;指涉他的直接

的、私有的感觉。因此另一个人无法理解这种语言。(PI. 243)

我们来想象下面的情况。我将为某种反复出现的特定感觉做一份日记。为此,我把它同符号 E 联系起来,凡是有这种感觉的日子我都在一本日历上写下这个符号。——我首先要注明,这个符号的定义是说不出来的。——但我总可以用指物定义的方式为自己给出个定义来啊!——怎么个给法?我能指向感觉吗?在通常意思上这不可能。(PI. 258)

这里要问的是:每个人怎么给自己的"私人感觉"命名?每个人是如何判定两种感觉是"相同"的?

认为有"私人语言"存在,实际上是受语言图画论的影响。按照"对象和名称"的模型来构造感觉表达式,把"疼痛"与某种私人经验对象对应起来,仿佛我们是通过"疼痛"的感觉来定义"疼痛"这个词的,这是经不起推敲的。他用甲虫的例子作出说明。

假设每个人都有一个盒子,盒子里装着我们称之为"甲虫"的东西。谁都不能看别人的盒子,所以每个人都说,他只是通过看自己的盒子里的东西才知道什么是甲虫的。——在这种情况下,很可能每个人的盒子里装着不一样的东西。甚至可以设想这样一个东西在不断变化。盒子里的东西根本不是语言游戏的一部分;因为盒子里的东西也可能是空的。我们可以用盒子里的这个东西去"约简";不管它是什么东西,它都会被消掉。

这就是说:如果我们根据"对象和名称"的模型来构造感觉表达式语法,那么对象就因为不相干而不在考虑之列。(PI. 293)

如果我们是从每个人的内在经验来定义"疼痛"这个词,那么内在经验在语言游戏之中,就可以像"甲虫"一样消掉,成了可有可无的东西。我们是从"疼痛"的用法中学会使用"疼痛"的,不是由一个内在经验来指示定义"疼痛"。

因此，这样的私人语言是不存在的：一个人可以用其他人无法理解的语言写下或说出他的内心经验，他的直接的、私有的感觉。唯一讲起来有意义的是主体间的公共语言。表示感觉的词也属于这一公共语言，并且从一开始就这样；这些词并非原来是用以表示在个人意识世界中发生的事件而后来才成为语言的一部分的："你是在学会语言的同时，学会'疼痛'这个概念的"（PI. 384）。① "疼痛"与其他词一样，都是在使用中学会的。我们在说"疼痛"的时候，"疼痛"一词的意思是大家都清楚的。

> 我可以展示疼痛，其方式一如我展示红色，展示直和曲，展示树和石头。——我们恰恰把这称为"展示"。（PI. 313）

没有私人语言，可是常识告诉我们，我们有"内在的私人经验"。比如，莫名的愁、兴奋、畏、烦，说不上来的不自在、尴尬、腻歪、害羞。我们可以这样说，我们并不缺乏私人经验，而是不会如何表达，没有表达的技术。表达的困难在哪里呢？我们面临的不是一个"对象"化的东西，它们很难捉摸，稍纵即逝。如果我们套用"名称—对象"的模式，就无从下手的。而诗人就可以表达出来"莫名"的愁，"白云飘飘，舍我高翔；青云徘徊，为我愁肠。""茕茕子立，形影相吊。""月落乌啼霜满天，江枫渔火对愁眠。""和衣拥被不成眠，一枕万回千转。"也可以表达"莫名的"高兴，"春风得意马蹄疾，一日看尽长安花。""两岸猿声啼不住，轻舟已过万重山。""日出江花红胜火，春来江水绿如兰。"也可以表达害羞，"洞房昨夜停红烛，待晓堂前拜舅姑。妆罢低声问夫婿，画眉深浅入时无。""见有人来，袜铲金钗溜。和羞走，倚门回首，却把青梅嗅。"

---

① 施太格缪勒：《当代哲学主流》，王炳文等译，北京：商务印书馆，2000年版，第637页。

三、语言与意象

1. 有一种用法,就有一种含义;有一个语言游戏,就有一种意象。

我们说一个词的一种用法表达出来的是含义,一个命题显示出的是意义,一篇论文表达的是思想,一首诗展示的是意象。它们各不相同,但我们不妨把它们归为一类,把语言游戏所展示出来的,统称为意象。那什么是意象?

> 必须问的不是:什么是意象,或具有意象的时候发生的是什么;而是"意象"一词是怎样用的。……。追问意象本质的问题谈论的也是"意象"这个词。而我说的是,这个问题不是可以通过指向什么东西得到解释的——无论对于具有意象的那个人还是对于别人都是这样;这也不是可以通过对任何过程的描述得到解释的。(PI. 370)

"桃花潭水深千尺,不及汪伦送我情","人间二月芳菲尽,山寺桃花始盛开","去年今日此门中,人面桃花相映红。"每首诗展示出来的意象都不同,我们也不能说这几个"桃花"是一个含义。虽都是"桃花",它们的用法各不相同,含义也不一样。

> 在使用"含义"一词的一大类情况下——尽管不是在所有情况下——可以这么解释"含义":一个词的含义是它在语言中的用法。(PI.43)

维特根斯坦说一个词的含义在于它的用法,其实就是说一个词在不同用法中表现出来的含义是各不相同的,有一种用法就有一种含义。我们做各种语言游戏,而每种游戏表现出来的意象绝不相同,而且是独一无二的。

在诗里,语言与意象水乳交融,浑然一体,意象就是诗本身。我们阅读中国古人留下的诗篇时,就像仰望满天繁星。这些优美的诗篇像一颗颗星,有的亮一些,大一些,那是李杜的诗,有的就小一些,不那么耀眼。它们虽然有相似之处,但绝不相同。它们只是"家族相似"。

我们有一个错觉,仿佛"含义"是一个词的"影子",是固定的,这个词用到什么地方,"含义"就如影随形般地跟着它,意义好像"捆绑"在这个词上。字典也可以采用这样的编法,只给出每个语词的"定义",那么,字典就像是中药店,柜子的每个抽屉上面标着各种药名,里面放着相应的药材。只知道定义,我们还是无法应用某个语词,如果盲目使用,往往要出笑话。我们还应该注意到字典里语词的"定义"已经是一种用法或者是简化的语言游戏。

2."红"的意象

可有谁曾向我展示过蓝色的意象并告诉我它就是蓝色的意象?"这个意象"这话的含义是什么?怎么指向一个意象?怎样两次指向一样的意象?(PI. 382)

两个意象一样,标准是什么?——一个意象是"红"的,标准是什么?对我来说,要是别人有这个意象,标准就是:他的所说所为;要是我有这个意象,标准就是:根本没有。(PI. 377)

我们只有从"红"的具体使用中,看出"红"是什么。一个红盘子、一块红布、一朵红花,"红"的意象不能离开语言游戏而存在,"红"总是某种红的东西。这也是"一个词的意义在于它的用法"所要说的意思。

思想和现实一致、和谐,这在于:当我错误地说某种东西是红的,那东西不管怎么说,它就不是红的。而当我要对某个人解释"那不是红的"这句话里的"红"字,我这时指的是某种红的东西。(PI. 429)

试着描述咖啡的香气!——为什么不行?我们没有语词?我们没有干什么的语词?——但认为一定能够作出这样一种描述的想法从何而来?你可曾缺少过这样一种描述?你可曾尝试描述这香气却做不

到?

>我会说"这些音符述说着某种壮丽的东西,但我不知道是些什么"。这些音符是一种强烈的姿态,但我无法把任何东西放在它们旁边来解释它们。(PI. 610)

看过《老残游记》里的"明湖湖边美人绝调"(明湖居听书)就能"想象"出来王小玉唱的曲调吗?离开了具体的载体,我们就不能经验到咖啡的香气,乐调。同样的道理,我们只有在具体的语言游戏中,才能说意象是什么。

3. 意象不是图画

>"意象一定比任何图画都更像它的对象。因为无论我把图画作得多像它所表现的东西,它总还可以是其他的什么东西的图画。但意象的本性就在于它是这一个的意象而不是其他任何东西的意象。"于是竟可以进一步把意象视作一种超级图像了。(PI. 389)

有个人说:"我疼痛。"然后我们看到他面部扭曲的表情。在这种情况下,人们往往想到这样一幅图画:"锅里的水在沸腾,蒸汽就从锅里冒出来;蒸汽的图画也是从锅子的图画里冒出来的。"(PI. 297)但是,一个"沸腾的锅"的意象绝不是一个关于这个"沸腾的锅"的图画,但这个图画可与它对应。扭曲的表情的图画也可以对应"疼痛",但它绝不是"疼痛"的意象。

>说"疼痛的图画随着'疼痛'这话进入了语言游戏"是一种误解。疼痛的意象不是一幅图画,在语言游戏里,这个意象也不能由我们称之为图画的那类东西取代——疼痛的意象在某种意义上是进入了语言游戏;只不过不是作为图画。(PI. 300)

常识告诉我们:想象一幅图画是可能的。

例如，对我说"立方体"这个词，我知道它的含义是什么。但我这样理解它的时候，这个词的全部使用能够在我们心里浮现出来吗？
......
好吧，假定你听见"立方体"一词的时候，心里的确浮现出一幅图画。例如一幅立方体的草图。......
立方体当然提示了一种特定的用法，但我还是能够以不同的方式使用它。(PI. 139)

并不是"立方体"每一种用法所表现的意象都可以相应地想象一幅图画，而且这个图画对于理解语言并不必要：

听到一句话后是不是根据它勾画一幅图画，这对理解这一句话无关紧要；听到一句话是不是设想什么东西也并不更重要。(PI. 396)
教师用手指着对象，把孩子的注意力引向这些对象，同时说出一个词；例如指着板石形状说出"板石"一词。(维特根斯坦把它称作"指物识字法"不是称为"指物定义"。)......。可以说指物识字法是要在词与物之间建立一种联想式的联系。但"联想式的联系"说的是什么？说的可以是各式各样的东西。但人们首先想到的大概是：孩子听到词语，事物的图像就在他心里浮现出来。就算这样的时候——但这就是词语的目的吗？——它的确可以是目的。......。但是在第2节的语言里，语词的目的不是要唤起意象。(PI. 6)

一个孤立的语词是不能有意象的，也不会有关于它的图画。我们听到"桃花"，仿佛一个图画就浮现出来。其实，我们也是把"桃花"这个词放到一个具体的语言游戏中，这个图画才能浮现出来，因为我们本来就是在具体的用法中才理解这个语词的。这幅图画也并不是"捆绑"在这个词上的，对于这个词的另外一种用法，就不会有这个图画。浮现这幅图画并不妨碍有其他的用法："桃花潭"、"人面桃花"、"山寺桃花"等等。

经验一个含义和经验一幅意象图画。人们要说,"在两种情况下都在经验,只是所经验的东西不同。向意识呈现出了不同的内容——摆在意识前的是不同的内容。"——什么是意象经验的内容?答案是一幅画或一个描述。什么是含义经验的内容?我不知道该怎么回答。——如果那个说法有任何意义,这意义就是:意象经验和含义经验这两个概念就像"红"和"蓝"这两个概念一样相互类似;而这是错误的。(PI. 第二部分 5)

我们能像保持一幅意象图画那样保持对含义的理解吗?也就是说,如果我突然明白了某个词的一种含义,——这也能持留在我心里吗?(PI. 第二部分 6)

某个词的一种含义浮现出来而你没有再忘掉它,你就能够以这种方式使用这个词。含义对你浮现,你就知道含义,这个浮现就是知道的开始。那么这个浮现怎么和某种意象经验相似呢?(PI. 第二部分 9)

我们经验一个含义(意象)和经验一幅图画并不一样。我们不需要一个"图画"或一个其他的什么"中介"来理解一个语言游戏。如果在我们的理解与语言游戏之间加上"图画"这个中介,或把意象当成图画,那我们岂不是把原来一体的语言与意象分开了吗?

4. 思想与语言也是不能分开的

当我们边想边说或边想边写——我的意思是像我们平常做的那样——我们一般不会说我们想得比说得快,在这里,思想似乎不和表述分离。但另一方面,我们也谈论思想的迅速:思想闪电般掠过脑海;问题一下子变得清楚了,等等。(PI. 318)

当我用语言思想、语词表达式之外,并不再有"含义"向我浮现;而语言本身就是思想的载体。(PI. 329)

我们努力寻找——例如在写信的时候——正确地表达我们思想

的语词之际,发生的是什么?这种说法把上述过程同翻译和描述的过程等量齐观:思想就在那里(可说先在那里),我们只是在寻找思想的表达式。……。若有人也问:"你在有表达式之前有没有思想?"——我们须回答什么?又该怎么回答这个问题:"在表达式之前就已存在的思想是由什么组成的"?(PI. 335)

思想并不是什么无形的过程,给予言谈以生命和意义,而我们可以把它从言谈上剥下来,就像魔鬼把笨人的影子从地上捡走。(PI. 339)

海德格尔说,切近与道说(die Naehe und Sage)作为语言的本质现身是同一的东西。切近之本质在空间和时间之外,是无赖于空间和时间的,切近是相互面对(das Gegen-einander-ueber)。① 语言与意象是如此"切近",所以语言不能从思想上"剥下来"。

索绪尔作过这样的比喻,"语言还可以比作一张纸:思想是正面,声音是反面,我们不能切开正面不切开反面,同样在语言里,我们不能使声音离开思想,也不能使思想离开声音。"② 如果把文字也包括进来,那么声音(或文字)与意象就像纸的两面。当然这是抽象分析出来的,事实上它们是一体的。我们其实应该做一个强调:你见过只有一面的纸吗?

但在句子一开始我的意图不就在于句子的整体形式等等吗?所以没说出句子之前它就已经在我心里了!——既然在心里了,它一般就不会有另一种词序。但我们在这里再次构造了一幅引起误解的"意图"图画——这个词的用法的图画。意图镶嵌在处境、人类习俗和建制之中。若没有象棋技术,我就不可能有下棋的意图。(PI. 337)

只有学会了说(sprench)才能有所说(sagen)。因此,愿有所说,就

---

① 海德格尔:"语言的本质",见《海德格尔选集》(下),孙周兴编,上海三联书店,1996年版,第1114、1118页。

② 索绪尔:《普通语言学教程》,北京:商务印书馆,1996年版,第158页。

必须掌握一种语言;但显然,可以愿说却不说。就像一个人也可以愿跳舞却不跳。(PI. 338)

当我们在默默地思考时。

四、语言游戏与"世界"的关系

维特根斯坦一直谈的是语言问题,那"世界"与语言的关系是什么?

"语言游戏"这个用语在这里是要强调,用语言来说话是某种行为举止的一部分,或某种生活形式的一部分。(PI. 23)

我还将把语言和活动——那些和语言编织成一片的活动——所组成的整体称作"语言游戏"。

除了在语言游戏里,事物甚至没有名称。(PI. 49)

并非:"没有语言我们就不能交流"——而是:没有语言我们就不能以如此这般的方式影响别人;不能建造街衢和机器,等等。而且:不使用话语和文字,人就不能交流。

可见,"世界"不是一个"对象"(Gegenstand)摆在我们面前,我们用语言来描述它。"世界"是被编织在我们的语言游戏之中的。我们不能把语言—世界用二元对立的方法分开,我们和世界的关系从根本上说,并不是认识与被认识的关系,认识是从属于语言游戏的。

语言游戏对于我们来说,就是整个世界。

按照一个对象的外观来描述它,或按照它的量度来描述它——
根据描述(绘图)构造一个对象——
报道一个事件——
对这个事件的经过作出推测——
提出及检验的一种假设——

用图表表示一个实验的结果——
编故事；读故事——
演戏——
唱歌——
猜谜——
编笑话；讲故事——
解一道应用算术题——
把一种语言翻译成另一种语言——
请求、感谢、谩骂、问候、祈祷。(PI. 23)

我们总认为，按照一个对象的外观来描述它，或按照它的量度来描述它，根据描述（绘图）构造一个对象，这才是语言基本功能，这是语言图画论的观点。在 PI. 2 游戏中，"方石"、"柱石"、"板石"和"条石"这些语词指称外在一个对象。相类似地，我们看一个电器的说明书时，首先要把每个名称与这个名称所指的电器上的某个部分一一对应起来，然后进行操作。在这两种游戏中，语言造就的意象"空间"完全被挤压掉了，名称所指的那个事物仿佛就是这个名称的意义了。而按照语言游戏的观点，这些名称之所以有意义，是因为处在一个语言游戏之中，游戏赋予它们以意义，它们的意义并不在那些外在的"对象"上。

如果我们并不是用语言去对描述、构造"现实对象"，那么，语言的意象就"盘旋起来"。"空山新雨后，天气晚来秋。明月松间照，清泉石上流。竹喧归浣女，莲动下渔舟。随意春芳歇，王孙自可留。"（王维的《山居秋暝》）在这首诗里，它"一下子"把形势、势态、气氛表现出来了。

诗不是对现实的诉说吗？它不过是以另一种方式诉说罢了，在"名称—对象"模式起不了作用的地方，诗就可以大显身手。"大江东去，浪淘尽千古风流人物。""寻寻觅觅，冷冷清清，凄凄惨惨戚戚。乍暖还寒时候，最难将息。""千古江山，英雄无觅，孙仲谋处。舞榭歌台，风流总被雨打风吹去。"描述的何尝不是这个世界。

我们的思维模式受到语言图画论的影响太深了。拿战争来说,它被当成是由一些事实或事态组成的,军事教科书的内容是描述这些事实或事态的命题,它也是一个操作手册。"电子模拟战"、"电子信息战"成了主角,高级指挥官完全可以在屏幕面前指挥战争了。战争完全是在计算性的思维审视之下了,武器、技术发挥着越来越大的作用,你制造飞毛腿,我就用爱国者来对抗;你用F16,我就购买苏27。战争越来越依赖技术了。

我们翻翻历史书,就会看到那长长的战争画卷(这又是一种语言图画论的观点)。历史没有重演过,战争也一样。我们在其中找"规律",然后用来指导下一次战争?有人说《孙子兵法》是一部理论高度概括的兵书,揭示了战争的一些重要规律,如"知彼知己,百战不殆"等,用它来指导实践,以不变应万变,这岂不是说孙武找到的战争的"逻辑结构"。战争有"逻辑结构"吗?以语言图画论的模式来刻画世界,难免圆凿方枘。

孙武的曾祖父、祖父都是齐国名将,在对内对外战争中立过赫赫战功,他也是身经百战,出生入死,不像赵括,只会"纸上谈兵"。《孙子兵法》是孙武的诗作,是一组"诗"。不过,这些"诗"可不是为了抒发离愁别恨,慨叹世事无常,白云苍狗,战争可是关乎生死存亡的大事。他用诗的方式来显示出波谲云诡的战争:"兵者,国之大事,死生之地,存亡之道,不可不察也。""兵者,诡道也。""用兵之法,全国为上。""不战而屈人之兵,善之善者也。""知己知彼,百战不殆。""决积水于千仞之溪。""转圆石于千仞之山"。"激水之疾。""鸷鸟之疾。""凡战者,以正合,以奇胜。故善出奇者,无穷如天地,不竭如江海。""故善战者,其势险,其节短。势如彍弩,节如发机。""夫兵形象水,水之行避高而趋下,兵之形避实而击虚。""非圣贤不能用间,非仁义不能使间,非微妙不能得间之实。""投之亡地然后存,陷之死地然后生。"这些是对战争"整体"的把握,是全景式的展示,里面并没有一个个孤立的对象。"问君能有几多愁,恰似一江春水向东流。"我们能领会"愁",也就能领会"战争"。

五、语言游戏是"绵延之流"（Das Sprachspiel spielt）

理解一个句子就是说：理解一种语言。理解一种语言就是说：掌握一种技术。(PI. 199)

在语言游戏中，诗歌是很难掌握的技术。《红楼梦》中林黛玉教香菱学作诗：你真要学诗，首先读一百首王维的五言律，再读一二百首杜甫的七言律，一二百首李白的七言绝句。肚子里先有了这三个人作底子，然后再把陶渊明、应玚、谢灵运、阮籍、庾信、鲍照等人的诗看一看，不用一年工夫，不愁不是诗翁了（大意）。要掌握现代的科学技术知识，也是不容易的。从小学、中学、大学要看多少本教材，才能掌握一门技术。

语言游戏具有多样性、无限可能性，它没有本质，语言游戏本身使意义生发出来。我们可以说，游戏规则本身就是游戏，两者是一回事。诗歌的游戏规则是什么？中国的近体诗（律诗和绝句）对平仄、押韵要求非常严格，这就是它的"游戏规则"。由于平仄、用韵的要求，以至于"五四"以来，有人说近体诗不能表达现代人的感情，认为"带着镣铐不能跳舞"。这就如同说，围棋规则太复杂，我把它简化一下，甚至于把规则取消了，那下出来的，还是围棋吗？规则都不存在了，游戏本身还存在吗？

平仄、押韵是对我们诗性思维的限制吗？恰恰相反，我们之所以能写诗，完全是依赖的平仄和韵脚。把它们一脚踢开，我们就完全找不着北了，不知从何处开启诗的运思。我们说，我们的运思选择平仄、韵脚，也可以说，诗借助平仄、韵脚展示它本身。我们琢磨平仄、韵脚，我们就是在开启着诗的运思，我们就是在做语言游戏。

在德文里，游戏一词 Spiel 还有"戏剧"、"演出"的意思，游戏就是戏剧，游戏就是在显示什么。而且舞台上的戏剧，也就是语言游戏的一种。语言游戏是永不谢幕的演出。它变换着花样，不断涌动出来，展现出来，我们可以说"Das Sprachspiel spielt"。一个游戏包含着多个游戏,游戏之间也不是泾渭分明,它们互相融贯,前后交叉,形成一个绵延之流。在诗的海洋里,我们更能体会到这股"绵延之流"。从这种意义来说,语言游戏就是我们的世界,动物是没有世界的。

(作者系北京大学哲学系博士研究生)

Philosophical Investigations §§ 1—693: An Elementary Exposition[*]

David Stern

One of the recurrent themes of *Philosophical Investigations* is that we cannot give a word a meaning merely by giving it a one-off attachment to a thing. What is needed is a sustained contribution from us as we continue to use the word, an established practice of applying it in a way that we all take to be the same… [T]he indefinitely prolonged sequence of correct applications of a word cannot be fixed unequivocally by any example or set of examples. It will always be possible to continue the sequence in more than one way. Nor can we eliminate this latitude by falling back on something in our minds, like a picture or a rule or a mental act. For a picture too can always be applied in more than one way, and the same is true of any words that may be used in the formulation of a rule, and a mental act may have more than one sequel. The correct continuation of a series can be determined only by what we, who continue it, find it natural to do. So if our contribution is ignored, it will not be possible to pick out the right continuation from the others. Anything will pass as correct, and the distinction between obeying the rule and disobeying it will collapse. This distinction must be based on our practice, which cannot be completely anticipated by any self-contained thing. We do not, and cannot, rely on any instant talisman. ①

---

* This paper is based on chapter 1 of Stern 2003. References in footnotes to "chapter m" or section "m. n" are to subsequent parts of that book.

① Pears 1988, 208—209.

1.1 The "method of §2"

In the *Philosophical Investigations*, topics are repeatedly introduced in the following way.

Stage 1. A brief statement of a philosophical position that Wittgenstein opposes, which usually emerges out of an exchange with another voice. Thus, in §1, we are presented with a conception of meaning that arises out of Wittgenstein's reading of a passage from Augustine's *Confessions*:

> Every word has a meaning. The meaning is correlated with the word. It is the object for which the word stands. (§1) ①

Stage 2. The description of a quite specific set of circumstances in which that position is appropriate:

> That philosophical conception of meaning has its place in a primitive idea of the way language functions. But one can also say that it is the idea of a language more primitive than ours.
>   Let us imagine a language for which the description given by Augustine is right… (§2)

In §2 of the *Philosophical Investigations*, the passage just quoted leads in to the famous story of "Wittgenstein's builders," a tribe who only have

---

① For references to the *Philosophical Investigations*, I provide section numbers, or page numbers, in parentheses. All translations from that book are my own. References to Wittgenstein's other works in the text and footnotes are by name; for other writers, I use the name and date of publication; for full information, see the Bibliography at the end of the f.

four words, each of which is used by a builder to instruct his assistant to bring one of four kinds of building blocks.

Stage 3. The deflationary observation that the circumstances in question are quite limited, and that once we move beyond them, the position becomes inappropriate:

> Augustine, we might say, does describe a system of communication; only not everything that we call language is this system. And one has to say this in many cases where the question arises "Is this an appropriate description or not?" The answer is: "Yes, it is appropriate, but only for this narrowly circumscribed region, not for the whole of what you were claiming to describe." (§3)

To drive the point home, Wittgenstein later adds other uses of signs that don't fit Aufgustine's description: §8 describes an expansion of the language in §2 to include numerals, demonstratives and colour samples, and §15 adds names for particular objects. ①

This three-stage argument scheme suggests a more general recipe for unsettling philosophical preconceptions. First, describe a case the preconception fits as well as possible, "a language-game for which this account is really valid" (§48), then change just enough about the case in question, either by adding or removing some aspect, or by changing the context or our point of view, so that we run up against the limitations of the preconception. This "method of §2," as Wittgenstein calls it in §48, is used repeatedly in the remarks that follow.

It is also characteristic of Wittgenstein's use of this argument-scheme

---

① For further discussion of §1, see 4.1.

that all three stages follow each other so quickly. In §§ 1—3 and §§ 46—48, each stage of the argument is presented quite explicitly; in many other cases the argument is only sketched, and Stage 3 may be left as an exercise for the reader. Because he aims, not to solve philosophical problems, but to undo, or "dissolve" them, Wittgenstein frequently presents the materials for a Stage 3 reply immediately before setting out Stage 2. The aim of the reply in Stage 3 is not to articulate a philosophical answer to the protophilosophical question with which we began, but to get us to give up the question. The story of the grocer and his different ways of using words in § 1d plays this role in the argument of §§ 1—3. Similarly, § 47's multiplication of examples of alternative conceptions of complexity comes between Socrates's Stage 1 discussion of simples, the 'primary 'elements' out of which the world is made in § 46, and the use of the "method of § 2" in § 48 to attack the very idea of a 'primary element.'①

One might reply, in defence of the first moves towards philosophical

---

① Wittgenstein frequently uses a complementary method: attend more closely to the "best cases" we come up with in Stage 2, to get us to see that they themselves unravel when one pushes them a little; that ultimately we cannot even make sense of what at first sight seem like the most straightforward applications of a given account. In the three-stage argument above, we are expected to take it as a matter of course that words stand for objects, or that the story of the builders in § 2b, like the grocer in § 1d, makes perfect sense. The complementary strategy is to approach these matters of course in a way that defamiliarizes them, and so makes us see how much we took for granted when we took them at face value. This is already anticipated in the final words of § 2, separated from the story of the builders by a double dash, usually an indication of a change of voice: "——Conceive this as a complete primitive language." For despite the repeated insistence that we "could imagine that the language of § 2 was the *whole* language of A and B; even the whole language of a tribe" (§ 6), it is far from clear that we can. Of course, we can speak the words, and imagine many ways of performing or filming the scenario Wittgenstein describes. But can we fill out such a story: can we make sense of a tribe whose linguistic abilities were exhausted by the routines described in § 2?

theorizing Wittgenstein is criticizing, and the theories they give rise to, that the approach to philosophy he opposes aims at a "view from nowhere," a position that is correct for all possible circumstances and contexts, not just a position that fits a few carefully selected cases. In defence of Wittgenstein's "method of § 2," one can say that if we grant, for the sake of argument, that such philosophical accounts do work at all, they must be applicable to specific cases, and ultimately these must include not only the "best cases", but the problem cases, too. Furthermore, Wittgenstein will suggest, the "view from nowhere" is a distinctively philosophical fiction, a fiction that always starts out from a quite specific somewhere, and begins its theorizing with particular examples of familiar objects and activities. The philosophy Wittgenstein takes as his target begins, in other words, with our taking familiar matters out of context, and taking them as the model for a universal account, true everywhere and at any time, of how things must be.

The relationship between everyday life, science, and philosophy, is a central concern throughout the course of Wittgenstein's writing. He regarded philosophy, properly conducted, as an autonomous activity, a matter of clarifying our understanding of language. Wittgenstein thought philosophy should state the obvious as a way of disabusing us of the desire to formulate philosophical theories of meaning, knowledge, language, or science, and was deeply opposed to the naturalist view that philosophy is a form of science.

Confronted with § 2-type examples, the Socratic philosopher dismisses the concrete cases as irrelevant, insisting that what matters is to get clear about the rules that determine which cases the term really applies to, and what they have in common. In 1944, when Wittgenstein was putting the first part of the *Philosophical Investigations* into its final form, he told a friend that he was reading Plato's *Theaetetus*, and that "'Plato in this dialogue is occupied with the same problems that I am writing about.'"① Wittgenstein owned a five volume German translation of Plato by Preisendanz, and refers to passages in Plato quite frequently in his writings. The philosophical discussion in the *Theaetetus* begins with Socrates's asking Theaetetus "what is knowledge?" His first answer is as follows:

> Th. I think the things Theodorus teaches are knowledge—I mean geometry and the subjects you enumerated just now. Then again there are the crafts such as cobbling, whether you take them together or separately. They must be knowledge, surely.
>
> Soc.: That is certainly a frank and indeed a generous answer, my dear lad. I ask you for one thing and you have given me many; I wanted something simple, and I have got a variety. ··· You were not asked to say what one may have knowledge of, or how many branches of knowledge there are. It was not with any idea of counting these up that the question was asked; we wanted to know what knowledge itself is. — Or am I talking nonsense?②

We can see much of Wittgenstein's later philosophy as an extended defence of Theaetetus's initial answer—the best we can do in answering questions about the essence of a word such as "knowledge" is to give examples, with the aim of showing that Socrates *is* talking nonsense, and so "bring words back from their metaphysical to their everyday use"

---

① Drury 1984, 149.
② Plato 1997, 162—163; *Theaeletus* 146c—e.

(§116). ① In the *Blue Book*, Wittgenstein explicitly opposes his approach to Socrates's:

> When Socrates asks the question, "what is knowledge?" he does not even regard it as a *preliminary* answer to enumerate cases of knowledge… . the discussion begins with the pupil giving an example of an exact definition, and then analogous to this a definition of the word "knowledge" is asked for. ② As the problem is put, it seems that there is something wrong with the ordinary use of the word "knowledge." It appears we don't know what it means, and that therefore, perhaps, we have no right to use it. We should reply: "There is no one exact usage of the word 'knowledge'; but we can make up several such usages, which will more or less agree with the ways the word is actually used" (*Blue Book*, 20, 27).

On the other hand, there are also deep affinities between Wittgenstein's and Plato's dialogues: each of the definitions of knowledge Socrates proposes in the *Theaetetus* proves unsuccessful.

In the early 1930s, Wittgenstein emphatically rejected systematic approaches to understanding language and knowledge. His answer to the Socratic question about the nature of knowledge is that it has no nature, no essence, and so it is a mistake to think one can give a single systematic answer:

> If I was asked what knowledge is, I would list items of knowledge and add "and suchlike." There is no common element to be found in all

---

① For further discussion of §116, see 2.3.
② See *Theaeletus* 146 ff.

of them, because there isn't one.①

In the *Philosophical Investigations*, one of the principal reasons for Wittgenstein's opposition to systematic philosophical theorizing is that our use of language, our grasp of its meaning, depends on a background of common behaviour and shared practices—not on agreement in opinions but in "form of life" (§242).②

1.2 The central arguments of the *Philosophical Investigations*

There is a sense in which the argument of §2 is over almost before it has begun, for the limitations of the language proposed in §2 are anticipated in §1d and set out quite explicitly in §3 and the sections immediately following. On the other hand, the further discussion of the language game of §2 connects many of the remaining sections of Part I in a number of far-reaching ways.

There are a large number of explicit cross-references between sections in the first 186 sections of Part I, and almost all of these links ultimately lead back to the language game of §2③. This cat's-cradle of cross-refer-

---

① Wittgenstein, MS 302, "Diktat für Schlick" 1931—1933. For further discussion of the *Theaetetus*, see 4.4. See also Stern 1991, or 1995, 6.1 on Wittgenstein's use of Heraclitus's and Plato's river imagery.

② See 5.2 for further discussion of §242.

③ Thus there are explicit references to §2 in §§6—8, §§18—19, §27, §37, §48 and §86, and one can find language-games that extend or draw on the example of §2 throughout the book. However, §8, §15, §48 and §86 play a particularly prominent role, for each of these three variations on §2 generates its own sequence of subsequent cross-references. §8, §15, and §86 each introduce language-games by making additions to the game described in §2: numerals, colours, "this" and "there" in §8, names in §15, and a table of instructions in §86. There are references to §8 in §13, §§16—18, §27, §38 and §41; references to §15 in §41 and §60; and a reference to §86 in §163. The language-game described in §48 is not an extension of §2, but it is said to "apply the method of §2"; there are references to §48 in §§50—51, §53 and §64.

ences, which ultimately extend as far as § 185, not only give this part of the book a strongly interlinked and hypertextual character; they also draw our attention to many of the crucial turning points in the overall argument of the first 242 sections of the book. ①

While there are no chapter or section headings, and no table of contents, the text of the *Philosophical Investigations* does contain many passages that clearly and explicitly indicate the topics under discussion, some of the principal links between them, and where they begin and end. Thus, just as § 1b identifies one of the principal topics of §§ 1—38, § 39 identifies the point of departure for §§ 39—64: "a name ought really to signify a simple." The language-games of § 2 and § 8, repeatedly cited and discussed throughout much of §§ 1—38, provide a point of reference that connects the various threads of this discussion. The language-game of § 48, itself modeled on the "method of § 2", plays a very similar role in §§ 48—64. A further trail of explicit cross-references leads from § 2, via § 86, to § 143, § 151, §§ 162—164, § 179, § 183 and § 185.

The argument of Part I of the book can be divided into four main chapters, of which the first two focus on language, and the last two on the philosophy of mind. The central theme of the first chapter, §§ 1—64, is a critique of the idea that our words get their meaning by standing for something independent of language. The second chapter concerns what

---

① The first 188 remarks were the first part of the book to be written. The "early" pre-war version, which for the most part closely corresponds to § 1— § 188, was written out in a manuscript dating from November and December 1936, and typed up in 1937. In 1939 Wittgenstein considered publishing this version; Rush Rhees drafted a translation of the first 100 or so remarks, and Wittgenstein made extensive corrections to Rhees' translation. The next draft, the "intermediate" version, dates from around 1943, and is numbered up to § 300; the new material consists of approximately half of the remarks we now know as § 189— § 421. The typescript of late draft, the basis for the published text of Part I, was probably produced in 1945.

might seem like the natural alternative to the view that words get their meaning by standing for something independent of language, that we must look within language for a theory of meaning. Thus, Chapter 2, §§ 65—242, is a critique of the idea that linguistic or logical rules are the basis of the meaning of words and sentences. Chapter 3, §§ 243—427, begins with a critique of the idea of a private language, "a language which describes my experiences and which only I myself can understand," (§ 256) and the related notion that our psychological concepts get their meaning by standing for objects in the mind. The principal concepts under discussion in § 243— § 315 are those of sensation and visual experience; the main topics of the remainder of this chapter are thought (§ 316— § 362), imagination (§ 363— § 397) and the self and consciousness (§ 398— § 427). Chapter 4, §§ 428—693, is less focused and concerns a wide range of inter-related topics, but intentionality is the principal topic of the opening part (§ 428— § 465) and a theme that runs through the rest of Part I. Other topics include negation (§ 446— § 448, § 547— § 557), meaning (§ 449— § 468, § 503— § 524, § 558— § 570, § 661— § 693) understanding (§ 525— § 546) intending (§ 629— § 660), and willing (§ 611— § 628).

The three-stage argument of §§ 1—3 marks the beginning of an extended critique of the notion, prominent in § 1, that every word has a meaning, the object for which it stands. This critique, which occupies much of §§ 1—64, can be divided into two distinct units. The first unit, §§ 1—38, is an attack on the idea that the meaning of a word consists in its standing for a familiar object of one kind or another. One of the principal approaches under discussion in §§ 1—38 is the view that ostensive definition—explaining a word's meaning by pointing at an object—is the basis of meaning. The second unit, §§ 39—64, looks at an approach that promises to avoid some of the difficulties that have arisen in §§ 1—38, the view that words stand for simple objects. §§ 39—45 consider the possibility that familiar things could be simples; §§ 47—64 examine the notion that ultimately words get their meaning by standing for "simple objects," objects that we reach by analyzing familiar objects, which are complex, into their ultimate, primitive components, or "ur-elements," on an overly literal translation.

A three-stage argument starts from questions about something apparently unphilosophical—language learning, or giving a name to a thing; but this draws the narrator's alter ego into Stage 1, a preliminary formulation of a philosophical thesis. Stages 2 and 3 bring us back to earth, by first proposing as prosaic and simple an example as possible, and then pointing out its limitations. However, the method of three-stage argument can only get us so far; replying to Socrates with a list of different kinds of knowledge, or the denotationalist with a list of different uses of words, may perhaps make us suspicious of the idea that we must be able to give a unitary specification of knowledge, naming, or the use of words, but it runs the danger of giving the impression that the only thing that is wrong with such theories is that they need refining. For this reason, Wittgenstein's narrator replies to many different Socratic lines of thought in §§ 1—38 and §§ 65—88. However, the problems and paradoxes Wittgenstein's narrator produces provoke his alter ego to dig deeper, and look for something hidden, a structure that supposedly underlies, or a hidden process that somehow animates, our everyday lives and language. Wittgenstein speaks of this movement, from the Socratic questions that typically initiate philosophical inquiry, to the counter-examples and paradoxes that such questions inevitably produce, and from there to the Platonic vision of a reality behind the phenomena as a "tendency to sublime the logic of our language" (§ 39, cf. § 89). [1] For this reason, the Socratic questions about naming and reference in

---

[1] For further discussion of Wittgenstein's conception of "subliming", see 4.3—4.4 and 5.2.

the opening sections of the *Philosophical Investigations* lead up to the formulation of a paradox about ostensive definition: "an ostensive definition can be variously interpreted in *every* case" (§§ 26—31; see 4.3). This results in a discussion of "sublime names": names that must stand for their objects, and so cannot be variously interpreted (§§ 39—64; see 4.4). This larger argumentative cycle, beginning with initial puzzlement, leading to the formulation of a paradox, to the further reaches of the sublime, and then back to the everyday, provides an overarching plot for the main "units" that comprise Part I: § 1— § 64 (chapter 4), § 65— § 133 (chapter 5 and 2.3), § 134— § 242 (chapter 6), § 243— § 427 (chapter 7), and § 428— § 693 (chapter 4.4 and 5.2).

Within chapter 2, we can identify two principal units. The first turns on the idea that understanding a word or a sentence involves commitment to definite rules for its use (§ 65— § 88; see 5.1). ① Wittgenstein's response to Socratic demands for an analysis of what words mean in terms of

---

① Like the remarks that open the two principal parts of chapter 1 (§ 1: Augustine; and § 46: Plato's Socrates), each of the three parts of chapter 2 begins with a clear invocation of the words of another philosopher and a particular philosophical picture. In § 65 and § 134 it is the "author of the *Tractatus Logico-Philosophicus*" (§ 23) and the notion of a "general form of the proposition": a logical form that every meaningful proposition must share (*Tractatus* 5.47ff). § 65 addresses Wittgenstein's rejection of the Tractarian view that every proposition shares the same general form, and § 134 returns to this topic, quoting, without giving a citation, the words the *Tractatus* tells us state the general form of the proposition: "This is how things are" (*Tractatus* 4.5). § 89 returns to Augustine's *Confessions*, quoting a passage in which he tries to answer the question "What, then, is time?" Another aspect of the intricate argumentative structure of this portion of the book is that in both the first and the third units of chapter 2, passages linked to § 2 are key points in the argumentative structure of each unit. §§ 65 —88 begins by making what appears to be a sharp break with the discussion of simples and § 48. It responds to the *Tractatus's* quite general idea about the shared nature of all language by offering a close examination of the variety of ways we use a single word, the word "game", but it culminates in a paradox that is set out using a language-game based on the one in § 2, a paradox that reappears in a slightly different form as the leitmotif of §§ 134—242.

rules for their use culminates in the formulation of a paradox about explanation: any explanation hangs in the air unless supported by another one (§ 87). This, in turn, leads up to a discussion of "sublime logic", rules that supposedly state the essence of language (§§ 89—133; see 5. 2). Here Wittgenstein attends to the idea that the rules on which our use of language depends are the rules of logic. The second part of Chapter 2, §§ 134—242 concerns the "paradox of rule-following": the problem that any rule can be interpreted in a number of mutually incompatible ways. Consequently, it can seem as if any interpretation—any statement of what a word or rule means—hangs in the air unless supported by another. Famously, Wittgenstein summarizes this predicament in § 201: "This was our paradox: no course of action could be determined by a rule, because every course of action can be made out to accord with the rule." While it generally recognized that this is a recapitulation of a previous train of argument, the full implications of the fact that it is a continuation of an argument that begins in the opening sections of the book are rarely acknowledged.[1]

A key paradox that occurs over and over again, in one form or another, throughout the first two hundred sections of the *Philosophical Investigations* is that nothing is intrinsically meaningful, for all determination of meaning, by such means as definitions, rules, thoughts or images, is dependent on interpretation. Given any candidate meaning-determiner, it is always, in principle, open to a further, deviant, interpretation. No act of defining or intending, grasping a rule or deciding to go on in a certain way, can give the supposed meaning-determiner the power to determine our future actions, because there is always the question of how it is to be

---

[1] See Kripke 1982, Stroud 2000.

interpreted. Only if we ignore the context can we think that some isolated act or event can have a determinate meaning regardless of its context. A change in the context of application can yield a change in meaning, and therefore meaning cannot be identified with anything independent of context. Leading examples include the wayward child who learns to add small numbers correctly but systematically miscalculates, all the while insisting that he is going on the same way (§143, §185) the drawing of an old man walking up a steep path, resting on a stick, that a Martian might describe as a man sliding downhill (p. 54), and deviant ways following arrows or signposts (§§85—86), or interpreting a drawing of a cube (§§139—141.)

The resolution of these paradoxes, like the resolution of a three-stage argument, turns on considering the wider context in which our words are used. In response to a proto-philosophical theory, a three-stage argument draws our attention to the circumstances it fits, and those it does not fit. Similarly, in replying to a philosophical paradox, Wittgenstein's narrator points out that the paradox does not arise in our everyday lives, and draws our attention to the way in which it turns on a failure to pay attention to the circumstances in which those words are ordinarily used. Ordinarily, the paradox does not arise, because it is already clear how the words or actions in question are to be understood. Thus Wittgenstein's reply to the paradox of ostension turns on the point that "ostensive definition explains the use — the meaning — of the word if it is already clear what kind of role the word is to play in language" (§30). A parallel paradox about explanation—that any explanation of the meaning of a word hangs in the air unless supported by another one—receives a similar response: "*One* explanation may rest on another explanation which has been given, but no explanation needs another — unless *we* need it to avoid a misunderstanding"

(§ 87). Analogous paradoxes about understanding, interpreting, and following a rule are the principal concern of § § 134—242; by the time Wittgenstein sums up the paradox of rule-following and provides his response in § 201, he expects the paradox to be so familiar that his treatment takes the form of a summary that begins by referring back to the previous discussion.

1.3 Seeing the *Philosophical Investigations* as a dialogue

The previous paragraph attributes a clear-cut set of answers to the paradoxes of ostension, explanation and rule-following to Wittgenstein. There can be no denying that these answers are present in the text; they can be compared to a prominent and repeated pattern in the weave of the *Philosophical Investigations's* argumentative fabric. Most interpreters attribute this argumentative strand to Wittgenstein without any pause. But the connection between this train of thought and the author's intentions is far from clear and so I will usually qualify this by attributing them to "Wittgenstein's narrator."

If we take Wittgenstein's narrator to be a behaviourist, or an ordinary language philosopher who maintains that the rules of our language guarantee that we are mostly right, then the sceptical paradoxes—namely, that ostension, explanation and rule-following can always be undermined by sceptical possibilities—receive what Kripke calls a 'straight' solution: we really can provide a positive answer to the paradoxes, because the expressions in question can be defined in terms of public behaviour, or the rules of grammar that govern our use of language. If, on the other hand, we follow Kripke in taking Wittgenstein to be a sceptic who endorses the paradoxes he has formulated, then the appeal to what the community ordinarily does in its use of these terms is only a negative answer to the sceptical problem (Kripke calls this a "sceptical" solution): recognizing that we cannot solve the problem, we instead appeal to what we ordinarily do as a way of indicating the best reply available, albeit one that does not really solve the paradoxes. ①

Rather than seeing these arguments as exchanges between "Wittgenstein" and "his interlocutor", I propose that we approach them as an exchange between a number of different voices, none of which can be unproblematically identified with the author's. For these reasons, in discussing passages of dialogue in the *Philosophical Investigations*, I prefer to speak of dialogues between "Wittgenstein's narrator" and "an interlocutory voice," rather than "Wittgenstein" and "the interlocutor." In some places, and particularly in those parts of the text that are most critical of the *Tractatus*—principally §§ 39—142—the narratorial voice sets out the case against philosophical positions set out in Wittgenstein's first book, in opposition to voices that express Tractarian convictions. In §§ 140—693, the narratorial voice is frequently used to set out behaviourist, verificationist and anti-essentialist objections to traditional philosophical views, in opposition to an anti-behaviourist voice that expresses mentalist, verification-transcendent and essentialist intuitions and convictions.

In addition to these opposing voices, voices that play different parts at different points in the text, we also meet with a third voice. This third voice, which is not always clearly distinct from the narratorial voice, provides an ironic commentary on their exchanges, a commentary consisting partly of objections to assumptions the debaters take for granted, and partly of platitudes about language and everyday life they have both over-

---

① For further discussion of Kripke and rule-following, see chapter 6.

looked.① Most readers treat both of these voices as expressions of "Wittgenstein's" views, with the result that they are unable to reconcile the trenchant and provocative theses advocated by the narrator and the commentator's rejection of all philosophical theses.

Despite my emphasis on the variety, diversity and ambiguity of the voices in the *Philosophical Investigations*, I do not aim to replace those black and white readings on which the *Philosophical Investigations* is an attack on a single "Augustinian picture," or a continuous dialogue between "Wittgenstein" and "his interlocutor," by endless shades of gray or a kaleidoscopic hall of mirrors. On the contrary, I have outlined the argumentative strategies that structure the *Philosophical Investigations*, both at the micro-level of individual remarks or groups of remarks, and the macro-level of the themes and concerns that link these smaller units. On the reading advocated here, the "straight" and the "sceptical" solutions

---

① The commentator's role is comparable to that of the leading character in Nestroy's plays; see the discussion of Nestroy in 3.2. The voices of the narrator, interlocutor and commentator play roles quite similar to Demea, Cleanthes and Philo in Hume's *Dialogues Concerning Natural Religion*, another posthumously published work whose conclusions have been much debated. Cleanthes, a rather naive deist, believes in God much as the interlocutor believes in the mind and its powers. An advocate of the argument from design for God's existence, Cleanthes sees evidence of God's handiwork everywhere he looks and cannot comprehend how anyone could deny the plain fact of a Designer's existence. Demea, a dogmatic rationalist, thinks the existence of God is established by a priori proof, not by an appeal to evidence for Design. Just as Demea finds Philo's conception of God as an unseen cause of the world insupportable, the narrator treats the interlocutor's view of the mind as a mythological misunderstanding. Demea thinks God's existence can be proved by rational argument; the narrator maintains that statements about the mind are logically linked—by means of "criteria"—to public behaviour. Philo, often identified as the mouthpiece for Hume's own view by his readers, plays a role similar to the commentator's: he rises above the standard arguments offered by the others. Philo provides a minimalist standpoint that offers so little support to traditional approaches to proofs of God's existence, that despite his professions of deism, many have taken Hume to be using Philo to provide the coup de grace to deism.

are equally misguided, for they both misunderstand the character and methods of the *Philosophical Investigations*. They mistakenly identify the viewpoint defended in a particular strand of argument—in one case, the reasons Wittgenstein's narrator gives us for thinking that the problem of rule-following can be solved, in the other, a sceptical problem that the narrator claims the interlocutor faces—as equivalent to the views that are advocated by the author, or the book as a whole. Wittgenstein, I contend, provided neither a straight solution nor a sceptical solution to the philosophical problems discussed in the *Philosophical Investigations*; rather, he aimed to dissolve those problems, by means of a dialogue between opposing voices, a dialogue in which the commentator comes closer to expressing the author's viewpoint than either of his leading protagonists do.

The following passage provides a convenient summary of the commentator's approach, not only to disputes over realism and idealism, but also to the exchanges between narrator and interlocutor, the voice of correctness and the voice of temptation:

> For *this* is what disputes between idealists, solipsists, and realists look like. One side attacks the normal form of expression as if they were attacking a statement; the others defend it, as if they were stating facts recognized by every reasonable human being. (§ 402b)

Most of the *Philosophical Investigations* does consist of a debate for and against "the normal form of expression." The narrator is usually taken to be arguing for Wittgenstein's own philosophical position, "ordinary language philosophy," while the interlocutor attacks our ordinary way of speaking, arguing that it does not do justice to his intuitions and his arguments. While the *Philosophical Investigations* is, for the most part, made up of conversation, questions, jokes, and diagnoses, it is not straightforwardly identifiable as a dialogue, a confession, therapy, or philosophy of language, though it certainly contains elements of all these. The book plays upon, and offends against, multiple styles and genres, while resisting identification with any one of them. What kind of a book is the *Philosophical Investigations*, then? On the one hand, it is in large part made up of Socratic dialogues in which a hero aims to find the truth through rational argument with others. It certainly makes liberal use of both of the basic devices of Socratic dialogue: syncrisis—a debate between opposed viewpoints on a given topic—and anacrisis—forcing an interlocutor to express his opinion thoroughly and subjecting it to critical appraisal. Thus there certainly is good reason to read the book as belonging to the familiar philosophical genre of the dialogue.

On the other hand, unlike traditional philosophical dialogues, the *Philosophical Investigations* contains no named characters to whom parts are assigned. Jane Heal observes that while there is no uniform syntactic device that signals the beginning and end of parts in the dialogue, such as dashes or quotation marks, what does make the use of the term "dialogue"

> seem entirely apt is the strong impression that, from time to time, a voice other than Wittgenstein's speaks, i. e. that some thought other than one endorsed by Wittgenstein himself is being expressed.[1]

This is, I think, the right way to read the dialogue in the *Blue Book* and the *Brown Book*, which clearly do set out views endorsed by their author,

---

[1] Heal 1995,68.

interspersed with occasional objections, but not the *Philosophical Investigations*, where matters are not always so simple. Most interpreters share Heal's assumption that the dialogue is between two clearly identifiable voices, and the leading voice expresses the author's considered convictions. But this prevents us from seeing how Wittgenstein's second masterpiece is not simply the result of simply putting together what he had already achieved, even though most of the words of Part I of the *Philosophical Investigations* had been drafted by the time Wittgenstein finished dictating the *Brown Book*.① While it is certainly possible to construe large swatches of that book as exchanges between "Wittgenstein" and "his interlocutor," or a doctrinaire behaviourist and a querulous anti-behaviourist, we should not identify the outlook of the author with every passage that we attribute to his leading narrator. The closest the author of the *Philosophical Investigations* comes to expressing his own views is not in the person of his narrator, the aggressively anti-Socratic protagonist we meet in the book's three-step arguments, but rather in the moments when he steps back from this serio-comedy and offers us a striking simile, or draws our attention to platitudes that philosophers don't take seriously. ②

For this reason, all this talk of Wittgenstein's argument, and of the positions he opposes, while unavoidable, is potentially deeply misleading. For it implies that he thinks of the views he is opposing as intelligible, albeit mistaken. It also makes it tempting to suppose that Wittgenstein's distinctive contribution to philosophy turns on a clear distinction between unproblematic, "everyday" uses of language, and their mirror image, the

---

① At this point, most of the remarks in Part I had been written, but nothing resembling the *Philosophical Investigations* more closely than the *Brown Book* had been assembled; nearly all of §§ 1—188 was put in its present order around the end of 1936.

② This claim is discussed and defended at greater length in chapters 2—3.

"metaphysical" uses of language that are characteristic of traditional philosophy. ① However, if Wittgenstein is correct, the accounts offered by all the participants in his dialogues are nonsense, and so cannot, in the end, be true or false. Ultimately, Wittgenstein's view is that the proto-philosophical accounts of meaning and mind that his interlocutor proposes, and his narrator opposes, cannot be understood, and that neither the descriptions of simple situations his narrator offers in Stage 2, nor the sublime truths about the essence of the world and language his interlocutor aims for, will do justice to those ideas and intuitions with which philosophical discussion begins. On this reading, Wittgenstein is neither saying that a solution to the sceptical paradoxes, or a "private language" is possible, nor proving that such things are impossible. Rather, Wittgenstein holds that such words do no useful work at all:

> What we 'are tempted to say' in such a case is, of course, not philosophy; but it is its raw material. Thus, for example, what a mathematician is inclined to say about the objectivity and reality of mathematical facts, is not a philosophy of mathematics, but something for philosophical *treatment*.
>
> 255. The philosopher treats a question; like an illness. (§§ 254—255)

If we follow the author's advice, rather than those of the protagonists in his dialogues, we will give up both behaviourism and anti-behaviourism. The result of his discussion of philosophical problems is not sup-

---

① For further discussion of § 116 on metaphysical and everyday language, see 2.3.

posed to be an endorsement of one of the views he discusses; rather, "a combination of words is being excluded from the language, withdrawn from circulation" (§500).

Nevertheless, in order to "turn something that isn't obviously nonsense"— such as the initial expression of a philosophical account of meaning we find in §1—"into obvious nonsense," (§464; cf. §524c) we must first try to make sense of it, and in so doing, come to see that we cannot. There are few better ways of beginning to do this than to try to think of cases the proposed account does fit as well as possible, and then seeing how it fails to fit when the context or circumstances change. Wittgenstein sums up this predicament and his response to it in the following words:

> 374. The great difficulty here is not to represent the matter as if there were something one *couldn't* do… ——And the best that I can propose is that we should yield to the temptation to use this picture, but then investigate how the *application* of the picture goes (§374).

However, in our investigation of what Wittgenstein has to say about yielding to philosophical temptation, I am proposing that we should not simply assume that everything that is said in opposition to these temptations must be taken as a straightforward statement of its author's philosophical convictions.

In my own earlier work on Wittgenstein, I approached his post-*Tractatus* writing as a dialogue with various different stages of his own earlier work, stressing the extent to which the views that receive close critical attention in the *Philosophical Investigations* are not only the logical atomism of the *Tractatus*, but also ones that he himself had set out in writings from 1929 and the early 1930s.① In particular, I emphasized both the continuities and the contrasts between Tractarian logical atomism, the "logical holism" of the 1929—1934 period with the "practical holism" of the later 1930s. The principal continuity is that, in each of these phases, Wittgenstein emphasizes the primacy of context, but his conception of that context changes decisively in the course of his working out the implications of the language-game comparison. Tractarian logical atomism takes it for granted that every context is always governed by formal logic, and that logic, properly expressed, is self-explanatory: "Logic must take care of itself."② In the "logical holist" work from the early 1930s, Wittgenstein frequently compares particular parts of our language with a calculus, a formal system governed by clearly defined rules, and the context in question is usually a matter of publicly verifiable behaviour. Language takes the place of logic: "Language has to speak for itself."③ In the later "practical holist" work, Wittgenstein stresses the open-ended and interconnected character of language, and the context in question is much broader, including the whole range of human life and the various settings in which it takes place. Even formal rules depend on a practical background for their sense: "rules leave loop-holes open, and the practice has to speak for itself."④

The principal discontinuities separating the *Tractatus* and the subsequent phases of Wittgenstein's work have to do with his changing conception of the mind and meaning. The *Tractatus* has very little to say about

---

① See 6.1 and Stern 1995, 4.4.
② *Notebooks* 1914—1916, p. 2; *Tractatus*, 5.473.
③ *Philosophical Grammar*, § 2 and § 27.
④ *On Certainty*, § 139. For further discussion of theoretical and practical holism, see chapter 6.

the philosophy of mind, but in 1929, a dualism of a "primary" mental world and a "secondary" physical world took on a leading role in the further development of the main ideas he took from his previous work. If we look at the first post-*Tractatus* manuscripts, begun almost immediately after his return to Cambridge in January 1929, we find him developing a whole metaphysics of experience, barely hinted at in the *Tractatus*. It was based on a fundamental distinction between two realms, the "primary" and the "secondary." The primary is the world of my present experience; the secondary is everything else: not only the "external world," but also other minds, and most of my mental life. He repeatedly made use of a cinematic analogy, comparing the primary, "inner" world to the picture one sees in the cinema, the secondary, "outer" world to the pictures on the film passing through the projector. But by October of that year, he decisively rejected this whole approach. He came to see that the primary and secondary were not two different worlds, but rather two different ways of talking, and he thought of philosophy as a matter of clarifying those uses of language.

The anti-behaviourist views that are voiced by the interlocutory voice in the *Philosophical Investigations*, and especially the view that there must be intrinsically meaningful mental processes that give life to our use of language, have a great deal in common with the views voiced in Wittgenstein's writings from 1929. The behaviourist responses voiced by the narrator of the *Philosophical Investigations*, and especially the idea that mental processes only have the meaning that they do within a particular context, are first drafted in writings from the first half of the 1930s, writings that are often a direct response to his the anti-behaviourist views one finds in Wittgenstein's 1929 manuscripts.

Wittgenstein aimed to end philosophy, yet in doing so, he was continually struggling with philosophical problems. In order to understand the *Investigations*, we have to see that the tension between philosophy as therapy and philosophy as constructive argument operates there in a number of different ways. First, as is well known, many passages take the form of a debate between different voices. Often, one proposes a certain philosophical argument or theory—Wittgenstein's interlocutor, or the "voice of temptation,"—and the other argues against it—the "voice of the everyday."[①] Second, the voice that argues against philosophical theorizing and attempts to return us to everyday life can also be read as articulating positive philosophical views. These passages have usually been the basis for the theories that commentators have attributed to the author of the *Investigations*. However, interpreting them as the key to the systematic philosophical views that supposedly lie behind the text of the *Investigations* immediately raises the problem faced by any irresolute reading: how can we do justice to Wittgenstein's scepticism about traditional philosophy and attribute a traditional philosophical theory to him? Indeed, many of Wittgenstein's harshest critics take these passages to show that he was inconsistent, and had a philosophical theory that he pretended was composed of platitudes about ordinary language. Instead, I propose that we approach them as further sketches of the landscape, examples of how "ending philosophy" and "doing philosophy" are interwoven in the *Investigations*.

If we give up our reliance on simple stories about how to do philosophy, or how to bring philosophy to an end, we are still left with all the hard questions. To paraphrase Wittgenstein, someone might object against me "You take the easy way out! You talk about all sorts of lan-

---

[①] These expressions are taken from Cavell 1979 and 1996.

guage-games, but have nowhere said what makes them Wittgenstein's philosophy. So you let yourself off the very part of the investigation that once gave you yourself most headache, the part about the *general form of Wittgenstein's philosophy.*" In reply, I would quote Wittgenstein's own answer to a similar question:

"Don't say: There *must* be something common…" but *look and see* whether there is anything common to all. —For if you look at them you will not see something that is common to *all*, but similarities, relationship, and a whole series of them at that. To repeat: don't think, but look! … And the result of this examination is: we see a complicated network of similarities overlapping and criss-crossing: sometimes overall similarities, sometimes similarities of detail. (§66)

Most readers have taken the *Philosophical Investigations* and the *Tractatus* to offer opposed views about the nature of mind, world and language; a small minority have argued that they are in basic agreement. But nearly all of them take Wittgenstein to be primarily interested in advocating some quite specific view about what there is and what philosophy should be. I have been proposing that we approach both books in a less dogmatic spirit, as two very different approaches to the question about the nature of philosophy.

One measure of the power of the *Investigations* is that it has inspired such a wide spectrum of readings. However, these readings can cast a long shadow on the text, and can make it seem much more forbidding and difficult than it really is. Rather than trying to adjudicate between those readings, this book aims to help the reader approach the text of the *Investigations* for himself or herself. While we will inevitably do so by discussing the views we find there, the *Investigations* is primarily about how philosophical theorizing gets started, not the polished theories professional philosophers usually produce. For this reason, it is best read by discussing the questions it raises, rather than beginning by trying to formulate a consistent theory about what its author must have meant. This is not to deny that it is possible to do so. However, "the author" and "what he must have meant" are themselves just the sort of problematic philosophical concepts that the *Philosophical Investigations* places in question.

Bibliography

Cavell, Stanley: 1979 *The Claim of Reason*. Oxford, Oxford University Press.

Cavell, Stanley: 1996 "Notes and Afterthoughts on the Opening of Wittgenstein's *Investigations*" in Sluga and Stern 1996, 261—295.

Drury, M. O'C.: 1984 "Recollections of Wittgenstein" in Rhees (1984).

Kripke, Saul: 1982 *Wittgenstein on Rules and Private Language*, Harvard University Press, Cambridge, MA.

Pears, David: 1988 *The False Prison* Vol. II. Oxford, Clarendon Press.

Plato: 1997 *Complete Works*, ed. John Cooper. Indianapolis, IN, Hackett. The translation of the *Theaetetus* is by M. J. Levett, revised by Myles F. Burnyeat.

Stern, David G.: 1991 "Heraclitus' and Wittgenstein's river images: stepping twice into the same river." *The Monist* 74, 579—604.

Stern, David G.: 1995 *Wittgenstein on mind and language*. Oxford University Press, Oxford.

Stern, David G.: 2003 *Wittgenstein's Philosophical Investigations: An Introduction*. Cambridge University Press, Cambridge.

Stroud, Barry: 2000 *Meaning, Understanding, and Practice*. Oxford University Press, Oxford.

Wittgenstein, Ludwig: 1922 *Tractatus Logico-Philosophicus*, translation on facing pages by C. K. Ogden. Routledge and Kegan Paul, London. Second edition, 1933.

Wittgenstein, Ludwig: 1953 *Philosophical Investigations*, edited by G. E. M. Anscombe and R. Rhees, translation on facing pages by G. E. M. Anscombe. Blackwell, Oxford. Second edition, 1958. Revised edition, 2001.

Wittgenstein, Ludwig: 1958 *The Blue and Brown Books. Preliminary studies for the "Philosophical investigations"*. References are to the *Blue Book* or *Brown Book*. Second edition, 1969. Blackwell, Oxford.

Wittgenstein, Ludwig: 1961 *Notebooks, 1914—1916*, edited by G. H. von Wright and G. E. M. Anscombe, translation on facing pages by G. E. M. Anscombe. Second edition, 1979.

Wittgenstein, Ludwig: 1969, *Philosophical Grammar*, first published as Philosophische Grammatik, German text only, edited by R. Rhees, Oxford: Blackwell. English translation by A. Kenny, 1974, Blackwell, Oxford.

Wittgenstein, Ludwig: 1969a *On Certainty*, edited by G. E. M. Anscombe and G. H. von Wright, translated by G. E. M. Anscombe and D. Paul, Blackwell, Oxford.

Wittgenstein, Ludwig: 2000 *Wittgenstein's Nachlass: The Bergen Electronic Edition*. Oxford University Press, Oxford.

Wittgenstein, Ludwig: 2001 *Philosophische Untersuchungen. Kritisch-genetische Edition* [Philosophical Investigations. Critical-genetic edition] ed. Joachim Schulte. Suhrkamp, Frankfurt am Main.

（作者系美国爱荷华大学哲学系教授）

Kripke's Paradox, Humean Solution and the Nature of Normativity

徐 向 东

This paper is an attempt to understand and rethink the paradox Saul Kripke poses about the following of rule from a *genuinely* Humean point of view.[1] I made the emphasis because Kripke himself had actually treated the paradox as essentially skeptical and attempted to dissolve it by analogizing it with Hume's classical skepticism. I shall rethink the paradox from a Humean point of view because I find out that the skeptical solution Kripke offers is not Humean enough. Indeed, there are many similarities between Kripke and Hume with regard to an account of the nature of rules and rule-following as well as between Wittgenstein and Hume.[2] Yet when

---

[1] Saul Kripke (1982), *Wittgenstein on Rules and Private Language* (Cambridge: Harvard University Press). Page numbers appearing in the text will be referred to this book.

[2] Even though it had been reported that Wittgenstein found out that it was "a torture" to read Hume probably because Wittgenstein did not share Hume's ideas on the nature of mental states and especially his theory of the derivation of ideas from impressions, some similarities between Wittgenstein and Hume are substantively apparent in that both of them share a naturalistic notion of human knowledge. Kripke's solution to the skeptical paradox is itself based on the analogy to Hume's skeptical solution to causal skepticism. Yet, as I shall show, Wittgenstein did not have to fear Hume because the reading of Hume as an empiricist is seriously flawed. And when the naturalistic spectrum in Hume's philosophy is recognized and emphasized, the similarity between Wittgenstein and Hume will overshadow the apparent difference.

The essential similarity between Wittgenstein and Hume has been observed by some writers. Anscombe had early drawn attention to the similarity between Wittgenstein's

Kripke has not proceeded to explicate the nature and origin of rules, Hume does go on to do this job. This is important because, as I shall show, it is the aspect in which Kripke's solution to the paradox is most likely to be challenged. In fact, the analogy Kripke makes between Hume's classical skepticism and his new style of skepticism is not complete. We can in fact draw on Hume to supplement and enrich the Kripkean solution because the solution has some very important implications for philosophy of mind and philosophy of mathematics as well. Most importantly, the community view, which is central to Kripke's solution, in my view, exemplifies a right approach to normativity. This is why it is worthy of being defended against some possible objections and criticisms.

Kripke has initially warned that his "formulations and recastings" of Wittgenstein's argument against private language "are done in a way Wittgenstein would not himself approve". His expositions of the argument are "neither Wittgenstein's nor Kripke's; rather Wittgenstein's argument as it struck Kripke, as it presented a problem for him" (WRPL, p. 5). Like Kripke, I will not be particularly concerned whether Kripke's reconstruction of Wittgenstein's argument has done justice to Wittgenstein. I will then not discuss the kind of critique of Kripke that says that Kripke's exegesis of Wittgenstein is simply wrong,① even though I still

---

account of rules and Hume's approach to morality. See G. E. M. Anscombe (1969), "On Promising and Its Justice, and Whether it need be respected in foro interno" and (1978), "Rules, Rights and Promises", both reprinted in Anscombe (1981), *Ethics, Politics and Religion: The Collected Papers*, Vol. Ⅲ (Oxford: Blackwell). For some further account of the similarity especially with regard to their respective commitment to naturalism, see David Pears (1988), *False Prison* (Oxford: Clarendon Press), Vol. II, especially pp. 507ff, and Peter Strawson (1985), *Naturalism and Scepticism* (New York: Columbia University Press), pp. 14ff.

① McDowell has questioned the soundness of attributing the "skeptical paradox" need to say something about what Wittgenstein had actually said in the regard. This means that I shall mainly focus on the issues Kripke poses about the normativity of meaning and the nature of rule-following, and say little about what may be a right interpretation of Wittgenstein.

Then, in the first section, I briefly outline the skeptical paradox as Kripke sees it and the solution Kripke provides. In doing this, I have supposed that the reader has some knowledge of Wittgenstein's argument against private language and Kripke's interpretation of it. In the second section, I discuss some main challenges to the Kripkean solution and give some responses I think to be plausible. The discussions to be undertaken in the section then also express my own understanding of the paradox. In the third section, which is also the main body of the paper, I show in some detail how Hume deals with the problem of normativity and expound how the Humean account can significantly supplement and reinforce the line of thought along which Kripke works out the skeptical solution. Here, my reading of Hume is significantly different from Kripke's appeal

---

to Wittgenstein as Kripke really does on the ground that Wittgenstein himself does not endorse the reasoning Kripke makes in constructing the argument (McDowell, (1984), "Wittgenstein on Following a Rule", reprinted in McDowell (1998), *Mind, World, and Value*, Cambridge: Harvard University Press, pp. 221—262). Furthermore, it has been argued, among others, by Philip Pettit, that a solution to the "skeptical"challenge need not be skeptical in the Humean sense. Pettit's answer to the challenge is based on the idea, which seems to me not to be ultimately different from Kripke's"skeptical"solution, that a finite set of examples can *exemplify* a determinate rule for an agent and that a suitable connection between the rule and the agent's inclination can be *a posteriori* established probably by some repeated pattern of response to the rule by the agent under favorable conditions. See Pettit (1990), "The Reality of Rule-Following", *Mind* 99 (393): 1—20.

to Hume in constructing the skeptical solution. Hume, like Kripke, may actually hold that we cannot decide whether one follows rules rightly or not apart from a community. But Hume does go on to say something more about how rules (or, in Hume's words, conventions) emerge and how they constitute a community. Hume's understanding of normativity, in my view, is then more naturalistic than Kripke has allowed—in fact, it is much closer to Wittgenstein's essential spirit. In the final section, I give a brief account of why—and in what sense—the Kripkean paradox is still a skeptical one. Taken as whole, the paper then defends the community interpretation of rule-following against some leading criticisms and objections, and moderately develops it from a Humean perspective.

1. The Skeptical Paradox and Kripke's Solution

Despite Wittgenstein's style of thinking about and composing philosophy, it is not improper to hold that the central purpose of *Philosophical Investigation* is to attack and refute an Augustinian conception of language, especially an Augustinian understanding of the relations between language and mind.[①] As a result, Wittgenstein attempts to establish the idea of language as a form of life, which is to set over against the idea of language as an abstract system of symbols. When Wittgenstein claims that "to imagine a language means to imagine a form of life" (PI §19), he means that language and language communication are embedded in the significantly structured lives of groups of activity human agents. Against his critique of Augustine, Wittgenstein can be thought, through the PI, to establish three negative theses and a positive thesis, as follows:[②]

[①] L. Wittgenstein, *Philosophical Investigation* (trans. G. E. M. Anscombe, New York: Macmillan, 1968). Sections 1—38 of the PI are concentrated on such a critique.
[②] Cf. Colin McGinn(1984), *Wittgenstein on Meaning* (Oxford: Basil Blackwell), p. 3.

(1) To mean something by a sign is not to be the subject of inner state or process.
(2) To understand a sign is not to interpret it in a particular way.
(3) Using a sign in accordance with a rule is not founded upon reasons.
(4) To understand a sign is to have mastery of a technique or custom of using it.

These points can be briefly explicated by focusing on Wittgenstein's attack on the classical view to the effect that 'understanding' and its allied concepts ('grasping a rule', 'following a rule', and the like) is a mental state or process.

Against the claim Wittgenstein wants to advocate, namely, that "the meaning is the *use* we make of the word", the classical view says that "we *understand* the meaning of a word when we hear or say it; we grasp it in a flash, and what we grasp in this way is surely something different from the 'use' which is extended in time!" (PI § 138). On this view, in understanding the meaning of a word, we are seeking something that (1) can come before the mind and be grasped "in a flash", in other words, something isolable, but (2) can serve as a guide for certain future actions, and also (3) can set a standard for the correctness of those actions. This view thus takes a rule to serve both as a guide to the individual with regard to her determination as to what she will do or say, and as a basis for justifying or assessing what she does or says. If this is correct, we are naturally led to the idea of the epistemic primacy of the rule as a standard for assessing the correctness of the applications of it. The fact that our applications of a rule can be evaluated at all seems to imply that the standard of correctness is independent of the applications. ①

However, the idea that there must be something that can perform the assigned roles and that is different from the use, Wittgenstein argues, is an illusion. For nothing could meet (1) and yet perform the task set out in (2). Wittgenstein attempts to illuminate this point by calling our attention to the difference between a picture of a cube, which might be thought to be the meaning of the word 'cube, and the method of projection for using this picture. When I have a picture of a cube in my mind, I can always conceive different methods of projecting it, and thus give more than one interpretation to it. This means that "the same thing can come before our minds when we hear the word and the application still be different" (PI § 140). A picture I take to give the meaning of a word can then have different or multiple applications. It may be suggested that I could always understand every application of it by giving an interpretation of the application. But interpreting something is nothing more than translating one sign into another sign. An interpretation is a case of "a rule determining the application of a rule" (PI § 84). If the rule that is used to interpret another rule is still in need of another interpretation, then it will result in infinite regress: "any interpretation [of a rule] still hangs in the air along with what it interprets, and cannot give it any support" (PI § 198). But the regress is generated, precisely speaking, not by the multiplicity of interpretations per se, but by the Platonic assumption that what guides is something that can be come before the mind, isolable from any context

---

① In the following, by the end of this section, in stating my interpretation of Wittgenstein, I have been largely indebted to Meredith Williams' formulation in Williams (1999), *Wittgenstein, Mind and Meaning* (London: Routledge), chapter 6, since I find that her position is much closer to mine in this regard, and so it is convenient to make some reference to her.

and history of use. We can always conceive infinitely many applications of a given word or expression. It follows that if meaning or understanding is determined by interpretation, that is, by something that can be grasped in a flash in the mind, then paradox results. Wittgenstein neatly describes the paradox as follows:

> This was our paradox: no course of action could be determined by a rule, because every course of action can be made out to accord with the rule. The answer was [this]: if everything can be made out to accord with the rule, then it can also be made out to conflict with it. And so there would neither accord nor conflict here (PI § 201).

The infinite regress argument has more radical implications because it shows, if sound, that the realist picture of rules that is alleged to give the best account of normativity turns out to eliminate all space for normativity. Accordingly, nothing in the application of objectified meaning can serve to decide upon whether any action can accord with a rule or not. Kripke characterizes the paradox as "skeptical" in the Humean sense that the conclusion established by the argument is obviously unacceptable from a 'common-sense' point of view.① Kripke reconstructs the argument by

---

① The dispute is that some commentators do not think that the argument in question, as Kripke claims, results in a *skeptical* paradox. For Wittgenstein, they emphasize, immediately notices that "there is a misunderstanding here from the mere fact that in the course of our argument we give one interpretation after another." The air of paradox can be removed because "there is a way of grasping a rule which is *not* an *interpretation*, but which is exhibited in what we call 'obeying the rule' and 'going against it' in actual cases" (PI § 201). My understanding is that whether this is a skeptical paradox or not, Kripke does attempt to solve the paradox in the way that is substantively similar to the one Wittgenstein himself has suggested here. I shall thus avoid the dispute in question.

using a more impressive example. More precisely, Kripke argues that there are no facts about me that determine whether I am meaning 'addition' or 'quaddition' when I use the symbol '+' on the following reasons. First, my actual computations involving '+' do not suffice to determine that I meant addition, since these are logically compatible with my having meant some other function which agrees with addition for just the numbers on which I have performed computations with '+' but diverges thereafter. Second, my past inner states of consciousness cannot determine what I meant because they admit of various interpretations or applications. Third, even my past dispositions to use '+' rightly do not suffice to determine whether I will be rightly using '+' in the future. For dispositions to use are finite while addition is a function with infinite many arithmetical consequences.① Accordingly, Kripke concludes:

> This, then, is the sceptical paradox. When I respond in one way rather than another to such a problem as '68+57', I can have no justification for one response rather than another. Since the sceptic who supposes that I meant question cannot be answered, there is no fact about me that distinguishes between my meaning plus and my meaning quus. Indeed, there is no fact about me that distinguishes my meaning a definite function by 'plus' (which determines my responses in new cases) and my meaning nothing at all (WRPL, p. 21).

The challenge is then a challenge to normativity because it says that no fact about me, the subject, can determine whether I am meaning some-

---

① But we must be careful with regard to the dispositional interpretation. For, as it will become clear, the solution Kripke proposes to the paradox is in fact importantly relevant to the notion of a disposition, although he uses it in a different way, namely, by associating it to the thesis of public checkability.

thing or following a rule rightly or not. The challenge leads to a *skeptical* paradox because of the following grounds. From an ordinary standpoint, it seems that there is really something that distinguishes my meaning something one way rather than another way, when the argument tells us otherwise. The problem is then to find out a way out of the paradox.

For Kripke, the solution to the paradox is then 'skeptical' rather than 'straight'. A straight solution is to show that on closer examination the skepticism in question turns out to be unwarranted. But the paradox appears to exhibit itself otherwise: the related argument seems unquestionable. A skeptical solution is then to begin "by conceding that the sceptic's negative assertions are unanswerable", exactly in the way in which Hume dissolves the skepticism about causation and induction.[1] The 'skeptical' solution Kripke provides to the paradox can then be seen comprising three stages.

To begin with, Wittgenstein has noticed that the paradox arises simply because the notion of following a rule is understood in an intellectualist manner: instead of viewing 'obeying a rule' as a practice, it is seen as grasped in or by an interpretation or a set of interpretations. Furthermore, as Kripke has made it explicit, it is only that there is no fact about the individual that determines what she means. It may not be that there is nothing that can determine what she means. In fact, according to Kripke, we can decide whether a person is justified in asserting that she is obeying a rule correctly. If she follows her confident inclination to obey a rule, for example, to give answer for any two given number in using the function '+', and if we all agree to the answer she gives, then she can be said to have mastered the notion of 'plus' rightly. Kripke thus holds that to

---

[1] I shall come back to this point in the third section.

solve the paradox, we must first of all reform our intuitive conception of meaning, replacing the notion of truth-conditions with some notion like that of justification conditions. Having been determined to construct our theory of meaning in terms of assertability conditions, we then apply that theory to our meaning assertions. It is "the 'assertability conditions' that licenses an individual to say that, on a given occasion, he ought to follow his rule this way rather than that, are, ultimately, that he does what he is inclined to do" (WRPL, p. 88). The 'ought' arises from the *practical necessity* of responding in a certain way. This idea, as I shall explicate in some detail later on, is essential to the Humean understanding of normativity.

For Kripke, the introduction of assertability conditions in replacement of truth conditions is not the whole story yet, though it is the crucial part. For our ordinary conception of following a rule permits us to distinguish between an individual who thinks he is following a rule even though he actually is not and an individual who is correctly following the rule. When Wittgenstein contends that "to *think* one is obeying a rule is not to obey a rule" (PI § 202), he is not merely denying that obeying a rule consists in some mental state or process. But he is also saying that it does not make sensible sense for an individual who lives in isolation and has nothing to do with any human community to say that he is (rightly) obeying a rule. The normativity of rule-following, Kripke holds, requires regarding the individual's assertion as publicly checkable. The solution to the skeptical challenge "turns on the idea that each person who claims to be following a rule can be checked by others" (WRPL, p. 101). We must make sense of the conditions under which we affirm our statements in terms of their use to record acceptance of individuals into the linguistic community. Furthermore, the community's shared judgment is a brute fact about the community that cannot be further questioned without falling into circularity. In a word, on Kripke's view, the normativity of following a rule is guaranteed by a mutual policing relationship to each other in a given community. I am justified in asserting that I am correctly following a rule insofar as I do what I am inclined to do and what I am inclined to do conforms with what everyone else in my community does. If my inclination to respond to, for example, a computation or some color is not fully compatible with the inclinations of all other members in some community to respond to the same thing, it turns out that I have not learnt to obey the related rule. Furthermore, if all my responses did not accord with those of the community in enough cases, then I would perhaps not be accepted into the community. Normativity is then related to the agreement in mutual expectations with regard to a certain pattern to behave.

It is thus clear that even if some commentators have objected that Kripke's interpretation of Wittgenstein has not done justice to Wittgenstein, the skeptical solution Kripke proposes considerably draws on Wittgenstein's argument against private language. In judging whether an individual is said to be obeying a given rule, we examine his responses and compare them with those we would normally on a given occasion. The individual is then justified in claiming that he is obeying a rule if his responses are fully in accordance with ours. Thus, the notion of following a give rule is not to be analyzed "simply in terms of facts about the rule follower and the rule follower alone, without reference to his membership in a wider community" (WRPL, p. 109). But this also shows that it is not that there is nothing that determines the normativity of rule-following.① While

---

① This raises the question of whether the paradox Kripke is advancing is really a *skeptical* one. I shall return to this issue in the final section.

Kripke makes it clear that the normativity in question is determined by facts about the community, further questions arise about the nature of rules and the adequacy of Kripke's community view. I shall now turn to these issues.

2. Objections and Responses

Earlier I said that I would not concern myself with the question of whether Kripke's exegesis of Wittgenstein is right. For even if Kripke has not done justice to Wittgenstein, the issues Kripke poses in his interpretation of Wittgenstein are important in their own right. In particular, an investigation of these issues will help to show where the sources of normative lie, which particularly interests me. In the present section, I shall then examine and answer some objections to the community view Kripke advances so as to give a further understanding and defense of this view. Basically speaking, these objections can be divided into two types. The first type of objections says that the appeal to a community would not fare better than the view Kripke attempts to replace. For if there is no fact of matter about me on the basis of which it can be decided whether my application of a rule is correct or not, then the skeptic's worry can be equally extended to the case of community.[①] The second type of objections is more radical than the first type in that it is intended to deny the correctness of the community approach, and sustain an individualist interpretation of rule-following.[②]

---

① Simon Blackburn (1985), "The Individual Strikes Back", reprinted in Blacknurn (1993), *Essays in Quasi-Realism* (New York: Oxford University Press), pp. 213—228.
② This is typically reflected in Colin McGinn(1984), *Wittgenstein on Meaning*(Oxford: Basil Blackwell). But similar claims can be also found in G. P. Baker and P. M. S. Hacker(1984), *Scepticism, Rule and Language* (Oxford: Basil Blackwell).

Let me begin with the first type of objections. The argument for the 'skeptical' paradox, it is recalled, is crucially based on the claim that there is no fact of the matter about me, behavioral, dispositional or experiential, that can show whether I have correctly followed a rule. But there is really something that enables us to judge whether a person is justifiable in thinking he is obeying a given rule. This kind of things, as Kripke himself is clear, is concerned with "the brute empirical fact that we agree with each other in our responses" (WRPL, p. 109). I will not discuss, at the present, whether this will mean that there is after all fact of the matter in the judgment of whether or not a person is obeying a rule. But the objection says that the appeal to community would not fare better if there is no fact of matter *about me* on the basis of which it can be decided whether my application of a rule is correct or not. Note that my application of 'plus' is judged to be correct simply because the community confirms the application. *We*, the community, have justification conditions for the use of 'plus' with regard to any individual case. The community can confirm my use of a rule solely because each competent member in the community knows what it is to see me as obeying a rule. But what if its members failed to see each other this way? Therefore, if the dispositional account of rule-following in the case of the individual cannot meet the skeptical challenge, neither can it in the case of the community. If this is right, it follows that mention of the community is no good. This is so, especially because "we can imagine what we might call a 'thoroughly Goodmanned community' in which people take explanations and exposure to small samples—yesterday's applications—in different ways."[1]

Yet the objection is, in my view, impotent because it is based on

---

[1] Blackburn(1993), *Essays in Quasi-Realism*, pp. 223—224.

some misunderstandings of the community view as well as Wittgenstein's own views on a form of life. Recall the very point of the community view is that a person can be said to be obeying a rule only if he agrees in his responses with the responses produced by the members of that community with regard to the given rule. Wittgenstein as well as Kripke allows the possibility that there may be some other community in which their application of the function symbol '+', for example, is different from ours. In that case, we would say that they had another form of life that was different from ours and even incomprehensible to us. The same can be said of a community in which people somehow "take explanations and exposure to small samples" in different ways. This is particularly true of a liberal society wherein different comprehensive religious convictions can (be permitted to) exist. The existence of a Goodmanned community then only suggests the differentiation of that community on its original basis. As a result, the people in that community may begin to diverge in some 'secondary' forms of life.[①] But if the divergences between them would be ultimate, for example, if some people would use basic ethical concepts in ways that are completely different from the ones some other people used them, then we have reason to think that the original community would be divided by different forms of life of a ultimate kind. The fact, however, does nothing to undermine the view that whether an individual can be said to be obeying a rule is still determined by certain facts about the community. Moreover, we should notice that some people are committed to some form of life, or more precisely, to follow the rules or conventions consti-

---

① Their divergences are in 'secondary' forms of life as long as they continue to share and are willing to share the most fundamental convictions, for example, certain liberal principles, that will tie them together despite of the differences in some other convictions of their.

tutive of that form of life, essentially in virtue of its utility. ① The notion of normativity makes sense intuitively because it makes a difference to an individual whether he is justified in responding to some given situation in one way rather than another way. If nothing can be significant said of an individual's behavior, then the notion of normativity does not apply to him. But if it can be said, then it must be said from a communal point of view. In the sense, it is the existence of a community that makes normative judgments both possible and intelligible.

This brings us to the second type of objections. As I just mentioned, the normativity of our judgments and actions lies in their defeasibility: we can go wrong with regard to them. The fact suggests that the notion of normativity require a communal point of view. But it may be said that a community is merely, so to speak, the *bearer* of normative judgments, and that it is not, or cannot be, what *grounds* such judgments. For it must be because there is something in the first place that we can judge that an individual rightly follows a rule when his responses accord with ours. That is to say, there must be something deeper that accounts for how we can be in agreement with each other in responding to some given situation. Then, the judgment as to whether I correctly follow a rule should not merely depend on community agreement as such. Rather what is indispensable for correct or appropriate judgment is that there *is* concord, not that each individual justifies his (or anyone else's) judgment by appeal to its harmony with the judgment of others. ②

---

① I shall say more about this in the following section. But it is enough to imagine the troubles facing an individual who, when actually living in our community, nevertheless uses '+' as defined not in term of 'addition' but in light of 'quaddition'.

② These critics are not disposed to put the objection in the way I do it here. But I think that this is the most plausible way if the objection in question is to have any power.

Put in this way, this objection can be regarded as aimed to deliver two ideas. In the first place, it says that the relation between a rule and the instances of its application should be stronger than the one Kripke conceives between an individual's responses and our responses. The relation is, in Baker and Hacker's words, an internal one. By this they mean that the capacity to grasp a rule is not *separately* decided by the agreement in responses among the members of a community. Instead the capacity to judge that such and such accords with the rule and the capacity to judge the agreement in question are the same thing. Whereas acting in conformity with a rule is merely expressive of understanding the rule, what determines whether an individual is rightly obeying a rule is something *internal to* the rule. This means, on their view, that "an individual's behavior is merely inductive or quasi-inductive evidence for his understanding a rule-formulation."① When Kripke thinks that normativity is to be decided in terms of certain facts about the community, he is then treating rules or interpretations of rules as empirical generalizations or hypotheses for which behavior is either evidence for their truth or instances of their operation. But grammar is, they hold, autonomous.

Obviously, it is unclear whether this constitutes a *general* objection to the community view. For even if we believe that linguistic competence is, according to Chomsky, grounded in some kind of universal grammar, it cannot be that all rules are of this kind. But to be charitable, we may interpret the objection as advocating an individualist notion of rule-following at least to the extent that it is partly aimed to show that an isolated individual can be adequately said to follow rules. There is no reason to doubt, for example, that Robinson Crusoe could follow linguistic rules

---

① Baker and Hacker (1984), *Scepticism, Rule and Language*, p. 103.

even if he lived in an entirely isolated island.

But there are serious problems in the argument for an individualist interpretation of rule-following. First of all, Kripke does not deny at all that a *physically* isolated individual can be a competent rule-follower. What he denies is that an individual, *considered in isolation*, can be said to follow rules. The same idea is argued and accepted by Wittgenstein himself. Baker and Hacker have championed a regularity interpretation of rule-governed activity. On their view, what is needed for normativity is "regularities of action of sufficient complexity."① But this view appears to be inconsistent with Wittgenstein's positions on this matter. Wittgenstein had made it plainly clear that a solitary individual could not be said to be obeying a rule when he produced regular sequences of marks for himself. This is because "the words 'language', 'proposition', 'order', 'rule', 'calculation', 'experiment', 'following a rule' relate to a technique or custom."② A technique or custom is, however, a practice. This is not to deny that the invention of an individual can be related to the emergence of a rule. But it becomes possible only if anther individual can put an *interest* in that invention, for example, a game, in such a way that it makes sense to say whether the individual in question is justified in responding to something internal to that game. This is why Wittgenstein says that it is "a typical kind of reaction to a rule" that "[w]hen someone, whom we fear to disobey, orders us to follow the rule… which we understand, we shall write down number after number without hesitation" (RFM, VI, 47). In spelling out this point Wittgenstein is saying that we can properly call some activity a rule-following activity only if it makes a difference to

---

① Baker and Hacker (1984), *Scepticism, Rule and Language*, p. 42.
② Wittgenstein, *Remarks on the Foundation of Mathematics* (Cambridge: The MIT Press, 1996), VI, 43.

an individual or the community or both whether the individual acts in the specified way. The notion of normativity is then intrinsically bound up with the idea that no acting in some expected manner, or acting in some other way, makes sense. It thus presupposes the notion of a community, i.e., the notion that correctness or incorrectness can be legitimately asserted of any individual act from a public point of view. The defeasibility of our actions and judgments can get a hold only in and by the fact that we can compare the actions and judgments of any particular individual with those of the community.

But this may still be insufficient to support the community view. For it is a very possibility that the grounds on which the community makes judgment about the correctness or incorrectness of rule-following may not be derived from the community as such. As we just saw, Baker and Hacker purport to make the claim in arguing that the relation between a rule and the instances of its application is internal. Wittgenstein, of course, denies that there is anything transcendental or superlative which we can invoke to decide whether the rules, to which we appeal to decide the correctness of particular calculations, inferences, and the like, are themselves correct. For, on his view, to ask whether our human practices or forms of life themselves are 'correct' or 'justified' is to ask whether we are 'correct' or 'justified' in being the sorts of things we are, which does not make sensible sense. But it may be that there is really something which is antecedent to the establishment of any community and which nevertheless contributes to the judgment of whether an individual is obeying a rule rightly. If it turns out to be the case, then the community view cannot be, at the very least, the whole truth.

This is actually what Colin McGinn wants to express when he attempts to save the individualist interpretation of rule-following by ascribing a 'naturalist' view to Wittgenstein. The ascription, no doubt, does have some rationale in Wittgenstein's argument against private language. Wittgenstein's reflection on the skeptical paradox has led him to conclude that there must be some way of grasping a rule which is not a matter of interpretation, "but which is exhibited in what we call 'obeying the rule' and 'going against it' in actual cases" (PI § 201). Yet when we examine these actual cases what we find is that the person who follows a given rule has been trained to respond in a certain way. Wittgenstein then seems to rest on the consideration to reject the very possibility of a private language, i.e., a language whose individual words "are to refer to what can only be known to the person speaking" (PI § 243). But if to follow a rule is to be trained to react in a certain way, it follows that no such language is possible. For the possibility of following a rule at least assumes that someone else can know the language. At this juncture, it may be asked this: How can a person teach someone else to follow a rule if not because there has been something that ground the capacity?① If it is true, then at least facts about meaning and rule-following may be prior to the existence of a community.

This is one point of McGinn's objection to the Kripkean interpretation. McGinn is indeed right in holding that the fact that interpretations do not determine meaning and understanding does not mean that there is nothing that can determine meaning and understanding. For "Wittgenstein *does* suggest that understanding consists in a fact, the fact of having an ability to use signs."② But this does not help much if we can call a 'fact'

---

① Of course, a person does not have to be able to do something in order to teach someone else to do that. But in any event he must have knowledge of that thing. So the fact in question does not undermine the question we are considering.

② Colin McGinn (1984), *Wittgenstein on Meaning*, p. 71.

whatever happens in time-space. In the sense, having an ability to use signs is of course a fact. What is at stake is that what kind of a fact the ability in question is. McGinn, somewhat like Baker and Hacker, suggests that the ability is the capacity to see certain objects as falling under a concept.① If grasping the meaning of the term 'red' consists in rightly applying it to red things, then it seems that normativity is determined by the nature of meaning as much as what is right to do is determined by the nature of moral values.② But this is a trick. For not only can the proposal not answer to the challenge of Kripke's skeptic but it also seriously misconceives the nature of normativity. Let me explain.

We need not deny that following a rule is indeed a matter of capacity, that is, a matter of being able to respond to a given situation in a certain way. But we must ask what it is to respond 'rightly'. I can be said to have understood the term 'red' when I apply it to a red tomato, for instance. This gives rise to an illusion as if correct use was determined by meaning.③ I said it was an illusion because we could conceive, as Kripke's skeptic does, that our conventional use of the term 'red' had changed. If some event happening in the universe had somehow changed the structure of our perceptual system, it might be possible that we would no longer apply that term to what we initially perceived as red. In actual cases the meaning of the term 'red' is said to determine our use of it only because

---

① McGinn writes: "Suppose someone understands 'red', and suppose that the correct use of 'red' consists (in part) in applying 'red' to red things. Then the ability suggestion makes a direct connection between understanding and use in just this way: to understand 'red' is (akin to) having the ability to apply 'red' to red things — the correct use is thus built into the specification of the ability." McGinn (1984), *Wittgenstein on Meaning*, p. 32, note 33.

② Cf. McGinn (1984), *Wittgenstein on Meaning*, p. 163, note 31.

③ Quite surprisingly and in fact contrary to Wittgenstein, McGinn holds that meaning determines use.

we have been determined to subsumed under that notion all things that are perceived as some color, which we conventionally call 'red', to a normal human agent under normal lighting conditions. Nothing can be significantly said of an individual who had not participated in the practice of the naming and classifying of colors with regard to whether he could be said to have rightly captured the meaning of the term 'red'. Similarly, I exercise the concept of *addition* rather than the concept of *quaddition* when I do computations involving '+' simply because 'addition', not 'quaddition', is what we mean by '+' in *our* practice. The agreement we have reached in that point is, in Wittgenstein's words, "not agreement in opinions but in form of life" (PI, § 241).

McGinn, of course, is not wrong in thinking of rule-following as a matter of capacity. Nor is he wrong in "taking capacity concepts as primitive"[①] if by this he means that such capacity lies in participation in a form of life. Then, when McGinn ascribes an epistemological naturalist position to Wittgenstein by saying that "in the case of rule-following our natural ways of acting with signs provide an adequate basis for the epistemic claims we make about the correctness of what we do",[②] he is endorsing the Wittgensteinian view that rule-governed activity is a form of action rather than a form of thought. But the endorsement, together with the seemingly right claim that the basis of the normative is the natural, has not directly shown that the community view is wrong. For even if we suppose that there are certain 'natural' dispositions in human nature that underlie the establishment and use of rules, it does not follow that the community can be dispensed with in the practice of normative judgment. In

---

① McGinn (1984), *Wittgenstein on Meaning*, p. 173.
② McGinn (1984), *Wittgenstein on Meaning*, pp. 25—26.

fact, the community is not required in order to police the actions and judgments, but in order to sustain the articulated structure within which understanding and judging can occur and against which error and mistake can be discerned. That is to say, when the *ground* of normative judgment may be thought to exist prior to the agreement reached in the community with regard to any individual act of rule-following, the community is required to sustain the practice of normative judgment — in fact, it is that which makes the latter both necessary and possible. This understanding, I believe, well accommodates some apparently plausible ideas presented in the critics of Kripke. But the understanding can be most fully appreciated and substantiated only by introducing and examining Hume's own investigation of normativity in general and convention in particular, to which I now turn.

3. Community, Convention and Normativity:

A Humean View

Despite their common commitment to naturalism, any attempt to 'appropriate' Hume to illuminate Wittgenstein (or for that matter, Kripke) will have to deal with, in the first place, an apparent tension between Hume and Wittgenstein. The tension would almost automatically disappear if naturalism were shown to be the most dominant ingredient in Hume's philosophy, as Kemp Smith had powerfully illustrated. ① But we will have to be cautious since Hume's philosophy itself presents a complex structure and since interpretations of Hume have been strongly controversial. In particular, in recognizing and acknowledging the importance of natural-

---

① Cf. Norman Kemp Smith (1941), *The Philosophy of David Hume* (London: Macmillan).

ism in Hume's philosophy, some commentators have also emphasized that the more conventional empiricist interpretation of Hume should not be neglected.① But if Hume is still committed to empiricism at least to some extent, then there is an obstacle to a Humean solution to the 'skeptical' paradox. For the empiricism in question is distinctively characterized by the principle that all ideas are derived from impressions, which has been seen as the first principle of Hume's philosophy. The principle, according to some commentators on Hume,② commits Hume to a theory of language, completely unacceptable to Wittgenstein, according to which public language must somehow be constructed out of private language. We must then make clear whether Hume's commitment to the principle constitutes a genuine obstacle to making use of him to cast light on Wittgenstein or Kripke in this regard. In fact, getting clear about the status of the first principle is, as we will see, itself essential to seeing how Hume holds a doctrine about language and language understanding that bears substantive similarities to Wittgenstein's.③

---

① See, for example, H. O. Mounce (1999), *Hume's Naturalism* (London: Routledge). In this book, Mounce provides us with a quite clear view of what are essentials of Hume's naturalism. Yet he also emphasizes that Hume's philosophy "cannot be fully understood unless we recognizes, first, that it contains incompatible elements, and second, that in its profounder elements it differs fundamentally from a later doctrine which superficially resembles it [i. e., 'scientific' naturalism]" (pp. 13—14). The author argues that Kemp Smith helps us to recognize the second point, but he himself hardly appreciates the first point.

② Jonathan Bennett and Antony Flew are typical of those who ascribe the view to Hume by thinking about Hume's views on ideas in a completely Lockean way. See Bennett (1971), *Locke, Berkeley and Hume* (Oxford: Clarendon Press), and Flew (1961), *Hume's Philosophy of Belief* (Bristol: Thoemmes Press, 1997), pp. 18—52.

③ In making this point, I have been greatly indebted to Livingston. See Donald W. Livingston (1984), *Hume's Philosophy of Common Life* (Chicago: The University of Chicago Press), especially chapter 3.

The first thing we need to do is to make clear the status of the principle in Hume's philosophy. Hume's theory of the derivation of ideas from impressions is designed to answer two questions: "What ideas may we legitimately have?" and "What may we legitimately believe?" While this is certain, whether Hume's empiricist account of the derivation of ideas from impressions directly corresponds to an empiricist account of the way in which words get their meanings from things to which they are applied is typically unclear, or at least in dispute. Indeed, Hume does say that an idea would be spurious if it is not derived from impressions either directly by copying a single impression or indirectly by combining ideas that are themselves direct copies of impressions. In this regard, the theory of derivation is much like an empiricist account of the way in which a word gets it meaning, especially, like Russell's theory of knowledge by acquaintance.① But the identification is not straightforward. For even if there is some reason to believe that Hume does hold that the theory of derivation is relevant to an account of how we understand a concept, the connection between having a concept and having an image is, as Hume himself conceives, complex. For one thing, Hume quite explicitly thinks that images can occur in ways that have nothing to do with meaning, for example, as mere data. In addition, one might get an image of, for example, a strawberry, before one acquired the ability to recognize it, or anything else, as red. Thus, it seems that Hume does not directly treat his account of the derivation of ideas as an account of how words get their meanings, even though he does, as we will see, regard the principle in question as a rule of implementing a paradigm of what it is to have a concept of something.

---

① For an explicit reference to the analogy, see David Pears (1990), *Hume's System* (New York: Oxford University Press), pp. 1—2.

Furthermore, the Lockean view that to understand a word is to associate it with a kind of 'idea', which is for Locke a quasi-sensory state, cannot be ascribed to Hume for two reasons. First, the ascription requires interpreting Hume as a phenomenalist. But this cannot be true of Hume.① Even if Hume maintains that ideas must somehow be linked to impressions if they are to be legitimate, he does not think of ideas as logically private mental images. For Hume, the perceptions of the mind are not private existences because it is not possible to have a concept of oneself that does not make reference to public objects. Ideas are then internal to the public world of common life. Second, as we will see, Hume does not directly identify the meaning of a word with its related idea(s).

In fact, Hume did not explicitly and officially lay down a theory of meaning (to ascribe him this intention is to see him from a twentieth century view). Instead his understanding of how words have meaning is implicit in his account of the nature of language. One effective way to see this point is by examining Hume's account of how some words that are not immediately related to our experience have meaning. For something that is the object of our immediate experience, having a concept of it seems closely related to having an image of it. This is one reason why the theory of derivation of ideas is easily seen as also a theory of meaning. However, how do we understand such sentences as "I have a right to X" as opposed to "I want X", or "I promise you" as opposed to "I make you feel painful"? The way to capture the concept of a right or promise is in some important aspects different from the way to grasp the concept of pain. There is no problem that in both cases, a person can be said to

---

① For Hume's explicit rejection of phenomenalism, see David Hume, *A Treatise on Human Nature* (T, for short) (edited by L. A. Selby-Bigge, Oxford: Clarendon Press, 1978), pp. 225—231.

rightly capture the concept in question, or understand its meaning, if he can apply it to respond to a given situation or some features of it in the way in which we judge that his responses are appropriate. But these concepts occur in significantly different ways. In the case of pain, if we have conventionally employed the concept 'pain' to describe or pick out a certain pattern of behavior, then every individual can be said to have rightly used the concept when he applies that concept to that pattern of behavior. In this case, convention appears between a pattern of behavior and its naming. But for the concept of a right or promise, things become different and complicated. The differences can be explicated as follows.

When a person says "I pain" and yet he is not actually in that state, we can hold that he is either misusing the concept or simply pretending it for whatever purpose. But if a person says, "I have a right to X", when it is obvious that he merely wants X, something more will happen. Indeed, it is still possible that he does not know how to apply the predicate 'right' and 'want'. But if he claims that he actually knows how to distinguish between them, then a conflict in communication will occur. For the concept of a right means that there must be someone or some institution who or that is to be responsible for the right-claim of that person. A conflict in communication will occur because the person does not actually have a right to X when he claims so. The very possibility of communication by language lies first of all in the ability to recognize intentional behavior in others and ourselves. But this is not enough: there must be also a public world by reference to which linguistic utterances are meaningful. For Hume, some linguistic utterances have meaning only by means of human conventions. This is because some concepts occur as the result of those conventions. Now such conventions occur not between things (or their features) and their naming, but in certain patterns of human activity in themselves. The expression "I promise" cannot be taken to refer to any act of the mind in the sense in which "pain" expresses or refers to a state of the mind. For there is nothing else which it could refer to, that is to say, there is no impression from which the purported idea of the term could be derived. But it does not mean that the expression "I promise" would have no meaning. Instead its meaning issues from its use in the convention of promise-keeping. And the convention in question is itself originated in some principles of human nature, for example, those concerning conflicting interests and limited human benevolence. "I promise" makes sense because, in saying that, the agent expresses a resolution of performing it. The meaning of the expression "I promise" is then constituted by the act of properly using that expression. Hume is among those who first recognize the 'performative' use of language as opposed to its descriptive use. But such use rests on and assumes some forms of human activity. Without them we would never understand such terms as "promise", "right", "negotiation", or even "transubstantiation". It follows that for Hume, the meanings of words are not private mental images at all, because even the meaning of a referential expression like 'red' is determined by the rules for its application in a linguistic convention.

Hume can then be said to have a Wittgensteinian idea, namely, that understanding an expression consists in correctly using the rules for its application in a linguistic convention. Such rules, for Hume, are determined by such a convention itself. I will later on analyze the nature of a Humean convention. But now let me call our attention to the status of the principle of the derivation of ideas from impression in Hume's philosophy. It has been clear that Hume holds that some words or expressions have meaning even if we do not have adequate images of them. Basically speaking, for Hume, meaning is correlated to a significant pattern of human activity.

This is why we can capture the meaning of something even if we have no mental imagery related to it. Hume can thus talk about an *idea* of something in an indirect or derivative sense: we can have an idea of something as the result to comprehending it in some way even if we do not have immediate image of it. An 'idea' in the Humean sense is probably equal to a 'sense' or 'conception' in our ordinary sense. That is to say, in the sense, to have an idea is to follow a rule in a linguistic convention. If we have mastered the public criteria for applying a term by correctly following the rule for its application, then we have avoided talking about nonsense — we have, that is to say, acquired what are necessary for meaningful discourse. But although we can capture a sense of something by mastering the public criteria for applying it, we do not, according to Hume, thus acquire a 'just' or 'adequate' idea of it. We have such an idea only if we have immediate experience of that thing. We do not have a 'just' or 'adequate' idea of a pineapple when we only correctly apply the expression "taste of pineapple" in all contexts but have never actually tasted the fruit. Hume insists that in order to have a 'just' or 'adequate' concept of X we must, in addition, understand what it means to apply 'X' to our own experience. Hume's first principle, then, is made to reflect his stress on the importance of an interior understanding of concepts rather than deliver the view that meaning is identified with, or at least related to, private mental images. When Hume insists that in order to understand a concept we must not only master the public criteria for its application but also achieve an internal imagery of it by learning how to apply it to ourselves, we can take him to imply that, in Wittgenstein's words, participation in a form of life is itself essential to understanding. For it means that we are not merely *formally* following the rule for applying a term or concept. This is important because many concepts do require an internal understanding for their full comprehension.

A typical example of this kind appears in Hume's analysis of causation. Hume has dismissed the view that we can be said to have an impression of causation. For Hume, the idea of causal necessity is not derived from any external impression of causal power: we simply have no impression of this kind. Nor can we explain the idea of causal necessity in terms of such concepts as efficacy, agency, power, energy, and productive quality since all these concepts are conceptually synonymous and reciprocal. But this does not prevent him from thinking that we can meaningfully talk about the expression 'A causes B'. Simply put, Hume analyzes 'A causes B' in terms of two things: (1) A and B are constantly conjoined and (2) the mind upon the appearance of A is psychologically determined to expect B. Statement (1) picks out an objective condition for applying the concept of cause, and so helps us to understand that concept. But this is not enough. Our concept of causation is, let us bear in mind, actually a belief. Belief occurs exactly because, in inferring one event from another one, I take a step *beyond* my experience of their constant conjunction. But a belief is different from a mere idea precisely because the liveliness of the idea as the content of a belief is transferred to the mind from a present sense-impression along the track formed by causal inference. Enough past experience sets up associations of ideas that cause us to come to have unreflective beliefs about a familiar object's future behavior. This is a form of causal reasoning. But it is not based on reason, but through custom and habit. Central to the concept of causation is the fact that having repeatedly experienced some constant conjunction, the mind is determined to infer how the second kind of events behaves whenever it is exposed to the first kind of events. Statement (2) is aimed to capture the fact. It shows how we can have an internal understanding of such expressions as 'If A occurs, B must follow.' This means that the idea of causal necessity arises from the (internal) impression of the mind to be inevitably determined to make causal inferences.① The fact that we cannot help believing causal necessity then means that Hume may be a skeptical realist: realist with regard to causal power, skeptical with respect to the rational warrant of the belief in causal necessity.②

So far I hope I have cleared away the obstacles to illuminate Kripke's Wittgenstein from a genuinely Humean point of view. But the work we have done thus far is basically negative. Recall my purpose to make an appeal to Hume is to show how Kripke's community view can accommodate the challenges from his critics. These challenges must be met not only because it is necessary for sustaining the community view but also because, in my view, there are really plausible ideas implicit in those challenges. In particular, we must show why it seems plausible to say that the ground of normative judgment does not initially lie in the agreement (or disagreement) reached within a community. Hume's investigation of the nature of human conventions sheds much light on an adequate answer to the ques-

---

① This is why Hume's two definitions of cause actually come to the same thing. Here, it is important to notice that even if Hume can be taken to treat causal necessity as projection the mind makes by virtue of the impression of being inevitably determined, he is simply agnostic about the *nature* of empirically observed constant conjunctions. Nature is, Hume holds, deep and secretive, and our knowledge of it so superficial, that we simply cannot connect the sensible qualities of the objects we experience with any of the real and hidden powers of these objects (see, for example, T 168—169, E 36—39). This means that Hume allows that we have an understanding of the hypothesis that objects have causal power, although he may deny that we have any way of discovering them. The point is important because it is relevant to our following discussion of the nature of normativity.

② For the proposed interpretation of Hume in this point, see Galen Strawson (1989), *The Secret Connexion: Causation, Realism and David Hume* (Oxford: Clarendon Press), and John P. Wright (1983), *The Sceptical Realism of David Hume* (Minneapolis: University of Minnesota Press).

tion.

Hume's views on normativity are most explicitly articulated in his analysis of what he calls 'artificial virtues' like justice and promise. Just as Kripke's skeptic keeps asking for the fact that constitutes meaning addition, Hume's trouble-maker wants to know what the fact of 'having to' pay back his loan consists in: "What reason or motive have I to restore the money?"(T 479) An obvious answer to the question is that he should return the money out of a 'regard to justice'. But for Hume, as well as for Wittgenstein, the matter does not rest there. For, if we can take a 'regard to justice' to capture a sense of obligation, we can likewise ask this: what is the fact of the matter that constitutes obligation? Hume's answer, simply put, is this. Firstly, Hume thinks that the idea of obligation can never be generated by an isolated individual's act of willing or resolving. It makes nonsense to say that we impose an obligation on ourselves independent of our relations to others. This is really similar to the part of Kripke's skeptical paradox that no fact about me will constitute my meaning of addition. Having recognized that moral obligation cannot exist in a state where each individual can only rely on and mobilize their own individual resources, Hume concludes that they can be originated solely in social conventions. Yet it is remarkable that Hume never understands the nature of such conventions in terms of the concept of a contract. For, on his view, the convention that grounds or explicates the obligation of promise turns out to be, or to come from, the pattern of coordinated and reciprocal behavior, which is naturally formed on the basis of our interest and our inductive capacity to frame reasonably well-formed expectations about the behavior and reactions of others. Once the convention is established this way, we *keep* a promise exactly because we are under a moral obligation to keep it. While such a convention does 'create' some new socially structured relationship in a characteristic fashion, the emergence of the sense of morality to keep the convention is a completely natural process. ①

The same things are true of justice. We do not have the sense of justice or injustice before the convention of justice is established. But the convention in question has its basis in the human condition, for example, in a scarcity of goods and limited human benevolence. Given that, men come to through painful experience discover the advantages of society and, with this, rules for governing the transference of goods. These rules are not the result of conscious reflection or of a promise. For society could not have arisen *because* men calculated its benefits in that those benefits could be known only by those who already knew society. Instead they arise gradually over time as men insensibly discover the disadvantages of deviating from them. Once men came to find out that certain ways to transfer and distribute goods were advantageous, they would conventionally set up certain rules to sustain those ways of transference and distribution. For Hume, Human conventions are then natural processes whereby social rules are hammered out unreflectively over time, yielding "a sense of common interest; which sense each man feels in his own breast, which he marks in his fellows, and which carries him, in concurrence with others, into a general plan or system of actions, which tend to public utility." ②

The idea that general rules tend to social or public utility is then essential to Hume's account of normativity. As has been clear, for Hume, the

---

① Of course, Hume is explicitly aware that the new luster of sentiments attached to conventions can obscure the underlying interests and calculations from our view when we have come to act purely out of a sense of duty (cf. T 523).

② David Hume, *Enquiries concerning Human Understanding and concerning the Principles of Morals* (ed. P. H. Nidditch, Oxford: Clarendon Press, 1975), p. 306.

normative 'ought' is derived from the practical necessity of conducting oneself in a certain way. To shape some stead and general points of view and act in conformity with them are essential to the undertaking of communication and the avoidance of conflicts as well. In general, to obey a rule is always advantageous to the agent as well as to the society. The recognition of the necessity of obeying a rule will, all things considered, motivate the agent to obey it as long as he is rational in some sense, although the *obligation* to obey it depends on something more complex, for example, whether others also comply with the rule.① For Hume, then, the notion of obeying a rule can make sensible sense only *after* certain human conventions have been established, even if the pattern or form of human activity a rule is made to reflect or express may have its practical necessity before the establishment of those conventions. This is because the normativity of obeying a rule arises with related human conventions. The fact that general rules tend to public utility means that rule-following is partly a matter of mutual expectation. Even if I see acting in a certain way as advantageous to both you and me in an activity of some form that relates to both of us,② it does not impose an obligation on me unless we have arrived at a convention on the basis of, for example, consideration of our respective long-term self-interest. Obligations are generated by social conventions. This is why Hume says that "a man, unacquainted with society, could never enter into engagement with another, even tho' they could perceive each other's thoughts by intuition" (T, 516). We can sensibly ascribe our judgment as

---

① Hume himself is quite clearly aware of the complexity in question in his analysis of the obligation to justice as well as in his responses to the sensible knave. For the limits of space, I will not discuss this.
② For example, consider Hume's example about how two people are committed to help each other to gather corn (T, 520—521).

to whether an individual is rightly obeying a rule to the individual, then, only if he has entered (or been committed to enter) into the related conventions. But entering into such conventions is itself constitutive of the formation of a community or society. It follows that normative judgment can be sensibly made only within and through a community, even though the ground for following a rule may not initially reside in the community. But it is also proper to say that a community is constituted on some normative basis.

From the point of view, it is unsurprising that we check whether our dispositions to respond to something are correct only by learning to respond in proper ways to what constitutes the related practice. The same is true of Wittgenstein: being trained into a social practice is the way in which we come to follow a rule. It is because meaning is essentially social that no isolable state of mind (or formula, or interpretation) can be reasonably posited as the objectified and so constraining meaning. The 'skeptical' paradox arises precisely because grasping a rule is seen as a matter of *interpretation* in terms of some other interpretation. There is no problem that after having been trained into the practice of rule-following, I am able, when asked, to give some reasons to explain whether I am correctly following a rule or not. However, as Wittgenstein tells us, "my reasons will soon give out. And then I shall act without reasons" (PI § 211). But "if I have exhausted the justification" and thus "I have reached bedrock," then I would not be unjustified in claiming: "This is simply what I do" (PI § 217). I am not unjustified because what I am doing is just what I should do *as I am constituted this way*. The justification in question is reached not by any rationalizing argument. But rather it is manifested in or by the fact that what I do conforms to the deepest level of practical necessity which I feel as a member of the community. I can then judge whether I have followed a rule correctly by seeing whether my dispositions to behave fully conforms to some regularity that prevails in the community and finds its expression in agreement in action and judgment. The appeal to shared judgments reached within a community becomes necessary because it is always possible that an individual may not follow a rule, or may be mistaken in holding that he follows a rule.

We are now in a position to see why the community view, as we reconsider it from a Humean point of view, can accommodate the challenge to the effect that the connection between actions and rules is essentially 'internal'. If I am right, the challenge is to say that the judgment as to whether an individual is following a rule correctly is not determined by the mere agreement reached within a community because there must be something in the first place that underlies the agreement in question. Yet construed in this way, the internal connection claim, as we may call it so, is not incompatible with the community view. As we have just seen, normative issues arise only when conventions have been established, even if they are merely made to express our attitude towards certain naturally formed patterns of coordinated behavior. Insofar as a community or society is substantively constituted by such conventions, there would be no normativity without such a community or society formed. For a community or society is ultimately instituted to sustain what are presented as practically necessary. When a community or society has been set, a rule is made to reflect or express a practical necessity.

However, there is no reason to assume that what is practically necessary must be also a priori necessary. It is conceivable that if our natural history had been otherwise, we would probably have had or chosen different kinds of rules from we hold right now. This, of course, is compatible with the claim that, given that our natural history had been what it is, all rules that emerge with the natural history are practically necessary and objectively valid to any particular individual.[①] Moreover, if there is no reason to suppose that most rules are innate (even if we can see the capacity to acquire grammatical rules as innate with regard to human species), then it is more plausible to view the connection between actions and rules as at best a posteriori necessary. The connection is psychologically established by making each individual feel the practical necessity to follow rules, even if those rules have been practically necessary in some first-order sense. But their *normative* necessity does not occur until conventions have been introduced. For even if we can regard rules as rooted in certain natural propensities insofar as their origins are concerned, they may not be necessitated by those propensities. Instead certain historically contingent elements can play a role in their formation. This is one reason why we could no longer follow a rule we had ever followed. This fact also provides a reason for explaining why we can be fallible in having epistemic access to a rule. If the *a posteriori* necessity of the connection in question holds only under certain favorable conditions, we must assume that we are not always able to recognize or identify those conditions in advance. In a word, the connection under consideration must be treated as at best a posteriori because, as Wittgenstein puts it, even bedrock practices are rooted merely in "the common behavior of mankind" (PI § 206). We must acknowledge

---

[①] A pertinent discussion of this point can be found in Lear's account of 'other-mindedness.' See Jonathan Lear (1983), "Ethics, Mathematics and Relativism", *Mind* 92: 38—60, and (1986), "Transcendental Anthropology", reprinted in Lear (1998), *Open Minded* (Cambridge: Harvard University Press), 247—281.

that sometimes we simply have no *rational* justification of why things are what they are. ① The very idea of normativity, as well as the structure within which the distinction between the correct and incorrect is drawn, cannot get a foothold unless the practice of rule-following is a social one. We must then suppose that both rules and their applications must be dependent for their correctness on a collective and historical deliberation. It is for this reason that there are no a priori and clear-cut boundaries to be drawn between the internal and the external.

It is true that the way to capture the nature of rule-following by appealing to the community view introduces a relativist element into the domain of normative discourse. Normativity, we must keep in mind, is originated in two things. Firstly, it requires the agreement that creates the place for standards. Secondly, it requires the possibility of deviation from the actions of the community that sustain the standards in place. Normativity does not appear in the state of nature, nor does it appear in the case of an isolated individual, despite the fact that even there are regular patterns of behavior in the state of nature or in the case of the individual. Normativity arises only when we have, *by explicit convention*, begun to approve or disapprove of an individual with regard to her actions or dispositions to behave. Before social interaction had become necessary and been introduced, we had no resources for explaining the normativity of such ac-

---

① How Wittgenstein opposes his own theological naturalism or voluntarism to theological naturalism is clear from the passage: "Schlick says that theological ethics contains two conceptions of the essence of the Good. According to the more superficial interpretation, the Good is good because God wills it; according to the deeper interpretation, God wills the Good because it is good. I think that the first conception is the deeper one: Good is what God orders. For this cuts off the path to any and every explanation 'why' it is good, while the second conception is precisely the superficial, the rationalistic one, which proceeds as if what is good could still be given some foundation." "Wittgenstein's Lecture on Ethics", *Philosophical Review* 74 (1965), p. 15.

tivities as meaning, understanding and rule-following. Thus, the necessity of following a rule, as Wittgenstein can agree, lies in cultivating or establishing a second nature of a man (PI 238). Normativity makes sense only relative to a given community that has somehow had the authority of judging the actions of its members in the way in which substantive agreement can be reached among those members with regard to that judgment. An individual who lacked the requisite second nature would either have no capacity to follow a rule or simply have no intention to follow it. But if he does have an intention to do so and he can be fallible in doing so, then the appeal to the community makes sense.

4. Is the Paradox still a Skeptical One?

So far I have argued, mainly from a Humean point of view, in defense of the community view, on the basis of which Kripke attempts to provide a solution to the paradox under discussion. Kripke explicitly thinks of the solution he offers as 'skeptical' to the extent that it is worked out by an analogy to Hume's solution to skepticism about causation and induction. But my analysis of Hume's positions on normativity shows that Hume seems to think that there is the fact of matter that underlies normativity (and, of course, meaning if it is a normative undertaking). In the final section, I shall briefly explore whether the paradox in question is actually a 'skeptical' one. This is relevant because some critics, Colin McGinn and John McDowell, among others, have argued that Kripke is simply wrong in holding that there is a *skeptical* paradox in Wittgenstein's account of meaning and understanding.

What is at stake in the dispute is of course the question whether there is no fact of the matter to judge whether a term is rule-governed or not. As has been clear, both Kripke and Hume maintain that there is really something on which we can decide whether an individual is following a rule correctly. The problem is then this: if it is true, how, or in what sense, can Kripke be said to provide a 'skeptical' solution to the paradox under discussion? Insofar as Kripke thinks of his solution to the paradox as modeled on Hume's skeptical solution of the skeptical doubts he addresses, it is natural to make clear in the first place in what sense Hume is said to develop a 'skeptical' solution.

This will first involve an understanding of Hume's attitude towards skepticism. I have no space to discuss the issue in any detail here.① Simply put, I am disposed to believe that Hume's skepticism is both instrumental and intrinsic to his philosophy. It is instrumental because it is through skepticism that Hume displays the appeal of naturalism. And it is intrinsic because mitigated skepticism is essential to what Hume calls a 'true' philosophy.② Moreover, I believe it is also proper to hold that Hume's skepticism is mainly directed toward rationalism, in particular, the rationalist notion of reason. Hume's negative account of probable reasoning is aimed to produce a *reductio* of the rationalist model of the mind by showing that if that model were correct, then not only would we, as rationally reflective agents, know nothing, but also we would unable to form any belief at all. This is really a skeptical conclusion since we do in fact believe something, for example, the existence of the external world and causal connections between things. The conclusion in question is then

---

① For some relevant discussions of the nature of Hume's skepticism and its place in Hume's philosophy, see David Fate Norton (1982), *David Hume: Common-Sense Moralist, Sceptical Metaphysician* (Princeton: Princeton University Press), and John P. Wright (1983), *The Sceptical Realism of David Hume*.

② For a wonderful investigation of this, see Donald W. Livingston (1998), *Philosophical Melancholy and Delirium* (Chicago: The University of Chicago Press), especially chapter 2.

unacceptable from the point of view of our common-sense life. Hume thus attempts to give a 'skeptical' solution to the paradox. The solution is conceivably to show that belief and probable reasoning cannot be treated as a matter of calculation. Abstract arguments, as Hume has at pains shown, produce ideas that lack sufficient vivacity to have much influence on us (T 153). Alternatively, Hume sets out his own account, which is focused on showing how an idea at the end of a chain of ideas is enlivened, typically, by its association with an impression. In making causal inferences we take a step beyond what we immediately perceive. Yet what makes us "make a transition from the idea of one object to that of its usual attendant" (T 170) cannot be explained in the way the rationalist assumes. Instead it is by means of custom that the mind is determined to make such inferential transition. But the inferential custom is what we *feel* under appropriate conditions, not what we reach by reasoning. That we have certain beliefs depends on the ways in which we interact with the world, and is a result of our feeling some necessary effects of the world on us. In an important sense, it is the attuned adjustment between the mind and the world, which is itself a causal process, that lays down the inferential custom. For Hume, then, whereas there is no ultimate or metaphysical explanation of the nature of causality itself, a naturalist explanation of how we can come to have causal beliefs is in place. The idea of causal necessity, in particular, arises through instinctive or natural workings of the mind and not through any rational insight into the objective process. This is why Hume finally thinks "that all our reasonings concerning causes and effects are deriv'd from nothing but custom; and that belief is more properly an act of the *sensitive*, than of the cogitative part of our nature" (T § 183, Hume's own emphasis omitted, my emphasis added).

Therefore, even if Hume did not regard causal inference as warranted by reason, he did seem to hold that causal inference could be said to be reasonable or proper in the naturalist sense that causal inference and causal belief are necessary to "the subsistence of our species, and the regulation of our conduct." If reason can be said to have any role in the formation of our causal beliefs, then it has such role, according to Hume, only as a set of properties (or principles) of the imagination.① But even considered as a set of properties of the imagination, reason undermines itself.② When reason acts alone, it is simply prey to the argument of reiterative probability diminution. This means that reason is not an independent faculty, having its own rules to follow. Instead, the beliefs we form as the result of reasoning are formed only when enough vivacity is communicated to the last idea in the chain. Without the sensitive side of our natures beliefs could not be formed. Moreover, even if beliefs could be counterfactually formed by reason in isolation from the sensitive side of our natures, they would not survive skeptical arguments. This is why Hume concludes that "[to] consider the matter aright, reason is nothing but a wonderful and unintelligible instinct in our souls, which carries us along a certain train of ideas, and endows them with particular qualities, according to their particular situations and relations"(T 179). Reason cannot properly

---

① See especially I. III. 8, "Of unphilosophical probability".

② This is illustrated in T I. IV. 1. The importance Hume attaches to his argument in I. IV. 1 I can be seen from the fact that Hume repeatedly refers to the argument thereafter. The most famous reference may occur in Conclusion of this book: "For I have already shewn, that the understanding, when it acts alone, and according to its most general principles, entirely subverts itself, and leaves not the lowest degree of evidence in any proposition, either in philosophy or common life. We save ourselves from this total scepticism only by means of that singular and seemingly trivial property of fancy, by which we enter with difficulty into remote views of things, and are not able to accompany them with so sensible an impression, as we do those, which are more easy and natural" (T 267—268).

work apart from habit, which is "nothing but one of the principles of nature, and derives all its force from that origin" (T 179). It is thus clear that Hume's ultimate intention to construct skepticism with regard to reason is not to establish skepticism *per se*, but to destroy pretensions of reason. Reason can properly work only within the limits which nature delineates for it. "Where reason is lively, and mixes itself with some propensity, it ought to be assented to. Where it does not, it never can have any title to operate upon us" (T 270).

If Hume can be said to present a skepticism about the rationalist treatment of causation, then it is proper to say that the paradox Kripke is putting forward in the name of Wittgenstein is skeptical as well. The analogy Kripke makes between the two cases is actually in place. For Wittgenstein's point that interpretation does not ultimately determine meaning and understanding is closely parallel to Hume's point that belief is not, fundamentally speaking, a matter of reasoning. Skepticism, we should notice, does not unconditionally occur. Instead, skepticism is always relative to, or directed towards, some philosophically committed way to look at and make sense of things. Skepticism does not have to be totally and exclusively destructive. To the contrary, it is often employed to reveal something positive. Skepticism is undermined not by any further theoretical speculation but by a practical attitude of some kind. This is why Hume's skepticism is particularly aimed to exhibit the power of naturalism by showing that reason, as well as its functions, cannot be properly understood unless it is itself viewed as part of nature. The exercise of skepticism enables us to see how some ways of theoretical understanding or philosophizing are inherently flawed. It invites us to transform ways of conceptualizing things. In this regard, Wittgenstein is actually similar to Hume in that he purports to show that some ways to conceptualize language, meaning and understanding must be wrong by making some paradoxical cases for those ways. His attack on the Augustinian picture of language understanding bears substantive similarities to Hume's attack on the rationalist notion of reason.

It is thus not true that one way of thinking would no longer be skeptical if it turned out that we could in fact think otherwise. It cannot be that Pyrrhonian philosophers were not exercising a form of skepticism only because they finally found out the importance of common-sense life, that is, arrived at some positive understanding of how to live. In fact, even in discussing 'skeptical solution of skeptical doubts', Hume himself is clear that there must be matter of fact to distinguish between belief and mere fiction. For "if we proceed not upon some fact, present to the memory or senses, our reasonings would be merely hypothetical, [and, as a result], the whole chain of inferences would have nothing to support it, nor could we ever, by its means, arrive at the knowledge of any real existence" (E 46). The rationalist notion of reason is susceptible of skeptical doubt simply because rationalist philosophers think of reason as independently autonomous, insulating it from nature to which it should be linked were it to function properly. Even if we can on the basis of some reasons distinguish between belief and mere fiction, on the one hand, and between legitimate and illegitimate belief, on the other, such reasons, Hume insists, "must at last terminate in some fact, which is present to your memory or senses; or must allow your belief is entirely without foundation"(E 46). No further rational considerations can be invoked to account for a natural belief because we have such beliefs as a result of our being so constituted. Naturalism thus defeats radical, i. e., unmitigated, skepticism at the most fundamental level. But the very point of Hume's naturalism is its insistence on the primacy of the practical to the theoretical or speculative. Wittgenstein joins Hume in this regard in that he, like Hume, puts a great deal of stress on the practical primacy and normative irreducibility of a form of life.

Therefore, the paradox Kripke poses is still a skeptical one even if his solution to the paradox requires us to reinterpret some kind of fact. The move Kripke makes is, in Blackburn's words,① to "lower the truth-conditions". I will not further inquire here whether Kripke is actually justified in replacing the notion of truth-conditions with that of assertability—conditions in his solution to the paradox. However, at the very least, I believe that in the domain of normative discourse like ethics we have no transcendental notion of truth-conditions. If we must talk about the truth of a normative proposition, then the only sensible way is in terms of the convergence of our opinions on that proposition. Of course, if there is something that makes us think and act in the way in which we actually think and act, as Hume does seem to suggest, then it makes sense to say that there are objective normative truths. But we must bear in mind that any such truth is always relative to some given form of life, although we have no a priori reason to assert that different human communities cannot (somehow) share a certain form of life, or some elements internal to such a form of life. We actually believe that '+' meaning 'addition' rather than 'quaddition' is unique to our human beings. But there is no a priori guarantee that our language game would perhaps be otherwise. It is more suitable for the fact of human nature to talk about what we can reasonably assert than what is true independent of our sensibilities or sentiments.②

(作者系北京大学哲学系副教授)

---

① Simon Blackburn (1993), *Essays in Quasi-Realism*, p. 215.

② An earlier version of this article was presented in the annual conference of American Philosophical Association, Eastern Division, December 2000, New York. Thanks are to Philip Pettit for the valuable comments he made on another occasion.

Idealization: Getting Scientific Laws by Carving Nature at its Joints

刘 闯

Most laws in science are idealized laws. To offer a proper understanding of such laws, I first analyze the notion of idealization — giving first a critique of the traditional conception of idealization as either neglecting the negligibles or approbating approximations, and then an account of an alternative theory which characterizes idealization as 'carving nature at its joints' (taking a cue from Zhuang Zi) —an essential tool in science for building models and formulating laws of nature. For the latter purpose, I give an account of laws of nature that implies a new interpretation for *ceteris paribus* laws.

庖丁释刀对曰：……始臣之解牛之时，所见无非全牛者。三年之后，未尝见全牛也。方今之时，臣以神遇而不以目视，官知止而神欲行。依乎天理，批大郤，导大窾，因其固然。技经肯綮之未尝，而况大軱乎！

——庄子

We seem to trace [in *King Lear*] ... the tendency of imagination to analyse and abstract, to decompose human nature into its constituent factors, and then to construct beings in whom one or more of these factors is absent or atrophied or only incipient.

——A. C. Bradley, *Shakespearean Tragedy*, p. 264.

I

The central challenge of modern science is to discover invariant laws of nature in a sea of ephemeral phenomena. I say 'modern science' because ancient astronomers were not dealing with the ephemera among the starry spheres, and by 'invariant', instead of 'universal', I mean laws that apply in diverse circumstances. This is especially true ever since the kinetic theory of gas dawned the search for invariants in the murky realm of thermo-statistical phenomena. Just as experimental design or control is essential to experimental sciences, idealization — the counterpart of that — is indispensable for theory construction.

Idealization is usually meant as acts of theorizing by which *ideal-condition claims* are stipulated and *idealized claims* obtained as a result, where ideal-condition claims are of physically possible but non-actual conditions and idealized claims are some kind of conditional (to be made precise later), where the antecedent expresses the ideal-condition and the consequence a law. The existing theories (or conceptions) of idealization further take such acts to be ones which either *neglect the negligibles* — the ideal-condition claims are approximately true — or *approbate approximation* — when the ideal-condition claims are relaxed towards the truth, the lawlike statements become more and more approximately true. Here, p is *approximately true* if the possible world in which it is true is *factually close* to our world. The factual distance may be most simply defined as a metric in a predicate space that gives exhaustive description of all the possible relevant states of affairs (cf. Hilpinen 1976; Niiniluoto 1984).

To make the above idea more precise, two theories of idealization stand out. Here is a brief summary of them and an account of how one may fit the other. Extracting from Laymon's (1980, 1985, 1989) comprehensive theory of confirmation, idealization, approximation and realism the part about idealization, we have roughly the following. Suppose that we have a generic theory T, and a set of n ideal-condition claims: $I=\{I_i|i=1,\ldots,n\}$, such that I_j is less idealized (or more realistic) than I_i, if $j > i$. For all I_i's, we have $I_i: T \Rightarrow T_i$, and $T_i|=P_i$, where $P=\{P_i|i=1,\ldots,n\}$ is a set of predictions. Suppose again that the non-idealized theory, T^U, predicts the true P^U. And let $\Delta^- I = |I_j - I_i|$ and $\Delta^+ P = |P_j - P_i|$ (where $j > i$) denote the factual distance between two idealized conditions and two predicted states of affairs, we then have,

[A]   T is confirmed (and therefore a good idealized theory) if it is always true that

$T: \Delta^- I \Rightarrow \Delta^+ P$; otherwise, it is not confirmed (or not a good idealized theory). In other words, when $I \to 0$, we have $T \to T^U$ and $P \to P^U$, if T is a good idealized theory. Nowak's (1972, 1980) theory takes all idealized theories to be of the following standard form:

(1) $\forall x[Cx \supset h_1(x) = g_k(h_2(x),\ldots,h_n(x);w_1(x),\ldots,w_k(x))]$,

where C is the background, $h_i(x)$'s are variables, and $w_i(x)$'s are claims which have non-zero values to begin with and become ideal-condition claims when their values are set to zero. With the following identification, the two theories can be fit together. Let our set of ideal-condition claims be

$I=\{I_i | I_i = [w_i(x)=0 \& w_{i+1}(x)=0 \&,\ldots,\& w_k(x)=0]; i=1,\ldots,k\}$,

and our theories

$T=\{T_i | T_i = T^U \& I_i\}$, where $T^U = [(1)$ without any $I_i]$,

and our predictions

$P=\{P_i | P_i = T_i[x/\alpha]\}$, where $P^U = T^U[x/\alpha]$.

Moving from T_1 to T^U via the T_i's is called *concretization*, and if the P_i's approach monotonically to the true P^U, which means that T or I is approximation improving, then the idealized theory is good. And this is taken by the advocates of both theories to lend strong support for scientific realism. The realness and truth of our scientific laws give the best explanation for their success in yielding ever more approximate predictions. Therefore, while the widespread use of idealized theories seems to pose a problem for realism, the problem is never there as long as those theories approbate approximation, and no idealizations are justified unless they produce approximation improving theories.

II

The theories sketched above and their variations are not so much wrong as are too simplistic in their depiction of idealizations. For some limited domain of applications, Laymon's and even Nowak's theory is just right, but if one looks at the whole range of things for which idealizations are needed — a major portion of the enterprise of discovering scientific laws via the construction of models — one should realize that approximation approbation could not be its defining feature. To show this I here give one example (see Liu 1999 for more).

Suppose that we are in Newtonian regime so that Newton's law of gravity is the law, i.e. $F=G(mM)/r^2$ for two objects with masses, m and M, and separated by a distance of r. Let us see which of the following is more approximate.

[B]   It is a law that I and $F=G(mM)/r^2+a$;
and
[C]   It is a law that I' and $F'=G(mM)/r^2+bsin(\omega r)$, where $|b|<|a|$ and ω is a frequency term.

If factual closeness — approximation approbation — is the measure, [C] is a better fit than [B], especially if the frequency term, ω, is large. While [B] consistently misses the law by $|a|$, [C] not only misses less — $|b|<|a|$ — but also has frequent 'hits' on the correct values because of $sin(\omega r)$. Hence, F'given I'is a better idealized theory than F given I. But we all know that [B] is a better 'approximate' *qua law* of Newton's law even though it is not so *qua facts*.

Idealization, as mentioned earlier, is too complex a notion of theory construction to be captured in a single logical formulation — as in Nowak's — or by a simple connection to approximation production — as in Laymon's. To see a few of its diverse applications we note, first, many acts of idealization are indeed for neglecting the negligible; for instance, making $sin\theta=\theta$, when the swing angle θ of a pendulum is very small, or taking some edge of a solid to be a continuous line.[1] Second, idealizations play a big role in experimental data collection and analysis. Here, the idealized curves drawn among the data points, for instance, are the result of combined considerations of approximation and optimal statistical regularities. The third kind is in some respects the largest and most important category of idealizations whose sole purpose is, to use a catchy phrase, *to carve nature at its joints*. What scientists would like to do with nature in their theories is what that fabled butcher in Zhuang Zi can do with an ox: he can cut up (all the joints of), and so kill, an ox without anybody around him realizing it; not even the ox itself! (If someone but touches the ox, it will then collapse to the ground with all the parts in perfectly clean separation.)

---

[1] Note that in the former we *subtract* something, i. e. $\delta=sin\theta-\theta$, while in the latter we actually *add* something to the edge to make it continuous; but for convenience I shall call both types of idealization neglecting the negligible since adding is nothing but removing the vacancy the added is to fill out.

III

Let me now leave the metaphor and begin to sketch a theory for idealization. First, it seems better to call those abstractions which do nothing but to neglect the negligibles acts of approximation rather than of idealization. They are in fact called so by scientists. Then, our questions are what idealization is, why it is indispensable, and how it is justified. To approach these questions we must first investigate that which idealization is allegedly used to obtain in the practice of theory construction. There are many competing theories of laws of nature, whose details and many controversies are beyond this paper. I shall take laws to be necessary but contingent — physically necessary — relations among properties and are of the following two general forms (Armstrong 1983):

(2) It is a law that all Fs are Gs, or $N(F,G)$, and

(3) It is a law that for all the values in P's domain and all the values in Q's range, all Ps are Qs where $Q=f(P)$, or $N[P,Q|Q=f(P)]$

(3) is what Armstrong call the form of functional laws, which is the form the majority of lawlike statements in exact sciences take.

If there are laws in nature, only certain properties are related by them[1]. And what those properties — and laws — are is ultimately for science (or empirical inquiries) to determine. But some general questions may be settled independently of particular scientific inquiries (see also Lewis 1983). Some (e. g. Armstrong and Lewis) want to rule out disposi-

---

[1] I take a rather generous view of properties. Any predicate whose extension is NOT determinable only by a list of names of its elements denotes a property (from Gene Witmer in private exchange). Hence, those properties which are related by laws — Armstrong's universals — form a special proper subset.

tions and only allow categorical properties. I find the restriction difficult to defend. The categorists seem to take the fundamental magnitudes — positions and momenta — which uniquely determine the states of a system of particles to be categorical. But are they? Could the instantaneous velocity of a non-uniformly moving particle be considered a categorical property? Obviously not! What the particle has at a moment is precisely the *tendency* of moving with the velocity it possesses at that time but not actually *moving* with that velocity. The latter is a categorical property which it does not have, and the former — which it does — is a *bona fide* disposition. Therefore, I shall admit dispositions (and propensities) in my ontology. But not all properties are universals even if they make some universal claims true, e. g. 'all the coins in my pocket on February 29, 1996 are dimes.' But the coins in my pocket at that time got there by accident; and therefore, one may infer, it is not an universal. However, isn't this circular since 'by accident', if not a primitive notion, may only be definable by 'not by law'? Nor is Armstrong's characterization of universals — properties admissible to laws — as properties which keep their *identity* in all their instantiations tenable: how could all the instantiations of 'being a coin in my pocket on February 29, 1996' anything but be identical? This shows in part the difficulty of an *a priori* settlement and hence suggests giving it over to common sense and science.

In fact, the conception of idealization I develop below shall show why picking out universals is one of the chief tasks of scientific research. Without lost of generality, we may take idealized lawlike statements to be of the form:

(4) $N(I \& F, G)$, where I is the ideal-condition claim.

(And for the functional laws, we similarly have, $N[I \& P, Q | Q = f(P)]$.) One might think that it should have the form: given I, $N(F, G)$, but that's not right. It says if I is true in the actual world, then in every physically possible world, if F then G (i.e. trivially true); whereas an idealized lawlike statement should say that in every physically possible world, if I holds then so does G if F, which is what (4) says. It is still trivially true in the actual world, but in all those worlds where I hold, it is no trivial matter that if F then G. I separate I from F because I think — following Armstrong — there are good reasons to believe that universals are fully instantiated in actual particulars (excepting the cases where missing values are involved in functional laws). Therefore, for $N(I \& F, G)$ to be lawlike Fs and Gs must refer to actual particulars but not I s. Moreover, it is not required at all that I express a universal since it refers to a condition under which the real law $N(F,G)$, if it is one, holds.

We can now begin to see what idealized lawlike statements express. Without I, we have lawlike statements in the form of (2) which tells us that in every physically possible world all Fs are Gs. There are plenty of such statements which if true are laws. 'All human are mortal', 'all objects have mass (including of zero mass)', and 'whenever a force is applied the affected object's behavior is altered in one way or another (including of zero alteration)', and …; all these if true are said to express *exceptionless* or *covering* laws. What then is the case for the following example:

(5) It's a law that all objects move uniformly on rectilinear trajectories? The conventional wisdom says that it is not true in the actual world and therefore is not lawlike unless it is fitted with a clause which says 'given they are not affected in any way'. Then it expresses a *ceteris paribus* law or what Armstrong (1983) calls an oaken law, a law that is only true with the provided condition; and the condition is an ideal condition because it does not obtain in the actual world (cf. Cartwright 1983, 1989).

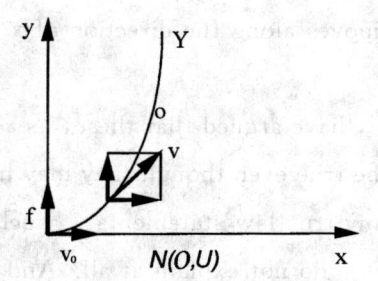

Idealization: Getting Scientific Laws by Carving Nature at its Joints 259

(a): O = being an object with an initial velocity, $\mathbf{v}_0$, at $t=0$;
U = moving with that velocity along the x-axis.

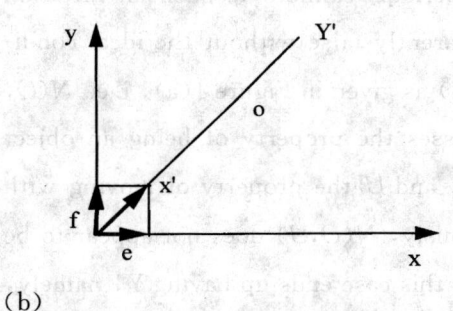

(b)

Figure 1: (a): a situation for (4), (b): a situation for (5).

Figure 1(a) gives a possible situation in which (5) is not true. ① There, the inertial motion of an object, o, with initial velocity $\mathbf{v}_0$, is affected by a force, $\mathbf{f}$, so that it ends up having Y (= a curved trajectory). The following seems another example of the same kind:

(6) It's a law that whenever an object of a mass, m, is acted upon by a force, $\mathbf{f}=m\mathbf{g}$, moves with an acceleration, $\mathbf{g}$.

Similarly, this is said to be true only to an object under the condition that no other forces affect it. Figure 1(b) gives a possible situation in which (6) is not true. When another force, $\mathbf{e}=\dfrac{m}{e}\mathbf{a}$, is also acting on o, it fails to

---

① Here, the law of inertial in (5) should be understood in its more precise formulation: it is law that for any object, if it is initially in a state of motion with $\mathbf{v}_0$, it will remain in that state.

move in the direction of **g**. Instead, it moves along the direction of **x** (or ends up having Y').

Some, such as Cartwright (1983)[①], have argued that these, as *ceteris paribus* lawlike statements, cannot be true even though they may have enormous explanatory power, while many true law statements — such as the exceptionless ones mentioned above — do not explain at all. And yet one cannot deny that our intuition strongly suggest that (6) can be true without the idealization while (5) perhaps cannot. Is such an intuition simply false? Now, why is (5) apparently false without the ideal condition? Because if so, an instance of (5) as given in Figure 1(a), i.e. $N(O, U)$, would be true, where O expresses the property of being an object with an initial velocity, $\mathbf{v}_0$, at $t=0$, and U the property of moving with that velocity along the x-axis. Obviously, $N(O, U)$ does not appear to be true since any object possessing O in this case ends up having Y, namely, tracing out a curved trajectory as shown. One may say that for essentially the same reason (6) is also false in the situation of Figure 1(b). However, there is a difference between.

(7) the property of having described a trajectory of a certain shape,

and

(8) the property of moving at t with a v towards a certain direction.

(7) and its likes are full-bodied categorical properties while (8) and its likes can be seen as dispositions. If (6) is understood as a law which relates the actions of forces to dispositions of motion, it is possible to regard (6) as true in Figure 1(b): at every moment of its motion, the object, being acted upon by **f** (and also by **e**), has the disposition of moving with **g**.

[①] For criticisms of this view of Cartwright's, see Creary 1981 and Kline & Matheson 1986, and for Cartwright's response, see Cartwright 1983, pp. 54—73.

It is only when one demands that the admissible properties, at least in such cases as regarding an object's motion, be categorical do we run into the problem, and such laws as (6) become false without the ideal-condition.

How should we understand the case for (5) then in this light? I shall return to this question in a moment; but first let us see another case of coinstantiated properties where it is clear that no relevant *ceteris paribus* clauses are needed.

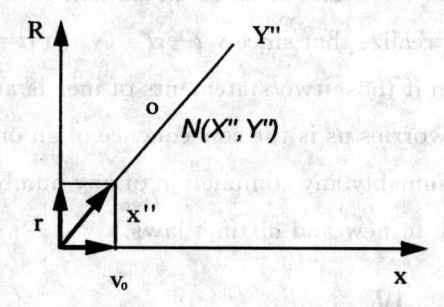

Figure 2: A hot body moving and radiating energy at the same time. $X''=$ being moving with v_0, at $t=0$ *and* hot with r; $Y''=$ having moved a distance of $v_0 t$ *and* having radiated an amount of energy $R=rt$, for some $t>0$.

In Figure 2, we have a hot body moving inertially along the x-axis and radiating heat energy at the rate of r. Suppose that two laws govern the behavior of such objects: one is (5), and the other a law: $R=rt$. Supposing again that uniform motion and heat radiation do not affect each other, we should have no qualm in asserting that the two laws are true in this situation and true with no exception. By the end of a time interval, the object describes a certain distance along x-axis and radiates a certain amount, R, of heat energy. If we compare this case with the case of (6) in Figure 1(b), we could not help making the following observation. If there is a law in Figure 1(b) which is obviously true without exception among the relevant factors, it should be $N(X',Y')$ where X' = being acted upon be a force, $\mathbf{x}'$. For this law, whether one use Y' — which is categorical — or an dispositional equivalent, the law is true without exception. However, it seems odd to think that there is an exceptionless law, $N(X'',Y'')$, in the case of Figure 2, where X'' = being moving with $\mathbf{v}_0$ and hot with $\mathbf{r}$ at $t=0$, and Y'' = having moved a distance of $\mathbf{v}_0 t$ and radiated an amount of energy $R=\mathbf{r}t$, for some $t>0$. One must realize that since $\mathbf{v}_0 t + \mathbf{r}t = (\mathbf{v}_0 + \mathbf{r})t = \mathbf{x}''t$, $N(X'',Y'')$ is a true generalization if those two statements of inertia and of radiation are, separately. What worries us is the consequence of an unnecessary proliferation of laws: presumably any conjunction of any number of co-instantiated laws will give rise to new and distinct laws.

IV

Let us now try to generalize the above discussion. For that I first add a few precepts concerning *properties* and their *instantiations*, besides what I have already said about them. Properties admissible to laws (or universals à la Armstrong et al) must be instantiated in — or, equivalently, possessed by — actual particulars. Some such properties can be instantiated at the same time in a particular (hence, they are compatible) and some cannot (hence, incompatible): a object can be cold and blue, but not cold and hot, at the same time. Properties may be simple or complex: being at a certain instant in time is simple while being water certainly is not. All the constituent properties of a complex property are instantiated whenever the property is instantiated: an object cannot be water without at the same time being odorless, colorless, transparent, in a liquid state, etc. (albeit not *vice versa*, *sec*. Kripke); and all the constituent properties must be compatible if the property they comprise is a universal[①]. Universals include both categorical and dispositional properties (as I have argued in section II), and the instantiations of a disposition are entirely different from its displays; for instance, the disposition, being fragile, is instantiated whenever a fragile vase is made, but it won't be displayed until, for instance, the vase is shattered. Saying that the property of an object changes over time is equivalent to saying that different properties are instantiated in the object at different times. I believe that these precepts are immune to many specific controversies over the concept of property (cf. Mellor & Oliver), except the one over the distinction between particulars and universals broached by Ramsey. Here I do assume that the distinction is unproblematic, and in the context of empirical scientific theories, my assumption appears to be relatively safe.

Let us now see what universals are instantiated in the three examples we discussed above. In Figure 2, every moment since $t=0$ sees the instantiation in the object, o, of the properties of being an object and of moving in its initial velocity and of being hot and of radiating energy. And any complex properties consisting some or all of these four properties are also instantiated in o at that moment. The two laws, one relating being an object and moving in its initial velocity and the other relating being hot and radiating energy, hold separately on o, because *each holds regardless of whether the other holds*. We can generalize this result to all laws that relate compatible categorical universals and to any number of their co-instantiations; the laws, if they hold, hold *without exception* in all

---

① This implies the acceptance of conjunctive properties into universals. Some disjunctive properties may be admissible although most of them are obviously not, while negative properties, if there are such, are most likely not admissible.

such circumstances. And for the discovery of such laws, idealization is rarely needed, even if approximation is unavoidable. Such laws include causal and non-causal laws; for the latter we have co-existence laws.

In Figure 1(b), every moment since $t=0$ sees the instantiation in o of the properties of being affected by a force $\mathbf{x}'$ and of moving with an acceleration, $\mathbf{c}=\mathbf{g}+\frac{e}{m}\mathbf{e}$. Since these two properties may be regarded as complex, the two pairs of properties — being acted on by an $\mathbf{f}$ *and* by an $\mathbf{e}$, and moving with an acceleration of $\mathbf{g}$ *and* of $\frac{e}{m}\mathbf{e}$ — are also instantiated. Even though one cannot say that after time $t>0$ o has in fact moved a distance of $\frac{1}{2}\mathbf{g}t^2$ *and* a distance of $\frac{e}{2m}\mathbf{e}t^2$, one can say that at each moment it moves with $\mathbf{g}$ *and* it moves with $\frac{e}{m}\mathbf{e}$, because it is indeed true that at that moment it has the disposition of moving with $\mathbf{g}$ (or with $\frac{e}{m}\mathbf{e}$) regardless of where and how the other force is directing it to move. Although the final 'categorical' results over time cannot be a combined display that is *decomposible* into individual displays, the dispositions are uniquely and exactly decomposible at each moment. Therefore, if the two force laws are taken as laws relating dispositional universals, they are equally exceptionless laws, just as the ones in Figure 2, and are both true in the circumstance. The result of this analysis agrees well with the scientific image of such causal laws. It would be extremely puzzling to physicists if they are told that every time a force acts on an object which is already acted upon by some other forces, the law of the force ceases to apply and is replaced by a new law which govern the behavior of the combined forces. In other words, there must be a different law for a different combination of any set of co-acting forces. We can certainly generalize this result to all laws that causally relate dispositions, at least when the causes and their joint effects are unambiguously decomposible. In this respect, there is no good reason to believe that such laws are fundamentally different from the previous kind. But now, idealization, unlike in the previous kind, becomes essential in the discovery of such laws through decomposition. It is only when other laws and the universals they relate are 'idealized away' can we find out the desired law in its full display.

In Figure 1(a), every moment since $t=0$ sees the instantiation on the object the properties of being a object that moves initially at v_0 and of being acted upon by a force f and of moving in a velocity v. After some time $t>0$ it also has the property of having moved a distance of Y''. The motion of the object at each moment is completely determined in this case by two dispositions: the inertial tendency to moving with v and the tendency to accelerate with g (which changes v through time). With them are instantiated two laws: the law of inertial (as in (5))① and the law of gravity (as in (6)), and each is true regardless of the other: if f is removed at some moment, the object will move with v from that moment on in accordance with (5), and the same is true if $v_0=0$, *mutatis mutandis*. This is an example of a kind in which co-instantiated universals

---

① I may be charged here with a gross equivocation between the law of inertial which governs objects that move under no influence and an intrinsic disposition—inertia—that all massed objects possess in resisting any changes of their states of motion. I take the point, which is what makes me uncertain of how exactly to categorize laws like (5). On the one hand, it is a law concerning the universal intrinsic disposition of change resistance that all massed objects have; but on the other hand, the traditional formulation of the law is about objects' being moving uniformly and rectilinearly unless being prevented from doing so. The latter cannot be true without the 'unless…' clause, while the former is true at every moment of every massed object with no conditions required. Since there are not many lawlike statements of this kind in scientific theories, I shall leave the analysis at this point.

change each other over time, so that even though there are unique decompositions into sets of the same *kind* of universals at each moment in the process, the universals change — i. e. having different universals at different times — over time.

A large number of laws in science — especially those that play an explanatory role — belong to the three categories discussed above. If by *ceteris paribus* laws we mean laws that are not true except under the ideal-conditions, then *they are not such laws*. In this respect, I disagree with Cartwright (1999, 25—26, 28—29) who consider such laws as typical *ceteris paribus* laws, namely, they are not true unless the *ceteris* are *paribus*. In the next section, I shall explain where the disagreement really lies. For the universals — in most cases as dispositions — the laws relate are instantiated fully in those non-ideal circumstances and thus the laws obtain. What is not always true for such laws when they are co-instantiated with other such laws — when the universals they relate are co-instantiated — is that they can show themselves in their full categorical display. Therefore, *ideal conditions are no more than stipulated circumstances under which the laws can show in their full categorical glory*. In a staged drama where imaginary situations 'occur', certain typical characters which daily drive all of us to commit certain kinds of acts show themselves in their 'true' — which means fully displayed — color. Modeling in science, whose essential means is idealization, does a similar job. The need of idealization and its difficulties increase when we go from those type of cases as in Figure 2 to those as in Figure 1(a). Little idealization if any is needed to discover the kind of laws operating in cases such as in Figure 2 because the antecedent and consequent universals, especially the latter, are separately instantiated categorical — and *separately observable* — properties. The situation is different in the case of Figure 1(b) and its likes. It would not be so absurd for someone to argue that the law operating in this situation is really not the one for **f** or for **e** but the one for **x′**; and one don't need any idealization — given these are the only two relevant forces — to discover this law. But one needs idealization to discover that in this case two laws are in operation and the result is a co-instantiation of the two. In other words, $N(X',Y')$ expresses a regularity between X' and Y' as a result of the two laws. One may be skeptical about this conclusion, but can be so only at the risk of doubting what most scientists have been doing for centuries (at least since Galileo's time when he inaugurated the method of idealization (cf. McMullin 1985)). It is precisely this kind of 'disentanglement' of invariant laws, whose co-instantiations in different combinations produce the great variety of empirical or phenomenological regularities we see in the actual world, that science aims to. And if one wants to know whether certain law is indeed operating in a mixture, one imagines ideal conditions in which the law operates relatively alone — not that nothing else co-instantiate but rather that the situation be like in Figure 2. Models are imagined in this fashion and experiments are often constructed to *approximate* the modeled circumstances. Here is the real connection between idealization and approximation. One must realize that not all good idealizations in science are directly approximatable; many have to be reduced via theoretical reasoning to some less abstract or more phenomenological situations where approximation in experiments are possible. We all know that whether a play reveals to us the true color of some characters does not depend on the verisimilitude of the circumstances designed to show them in the play (realistic plays are not necessarily the best ones). The merit of an idealization is rather measured in how well it offers the circumstances in which universals are easily separated and identified.

V

Before I summarize the theory of idealization I argued for above, let me recapitulate my analysis of laws of nature which underlies the theory by comparing it to accounts by Armstrong and Lewis and by Cartwright. The fundamental, and perhaps the only relevant, difference between my conception of laws and that of Armstrong's and Lewis's is that I admit noncategorical properties for universals whereas they do not. In this sense I am not a Humean; and I have already given one argument for why dispositional properties should be included (i. e. the case of the instantaneous momentum). Besides, if (Humean) categoricalism is to be adhered, many lawlike statements in science — especially in physical sciences — will have to be transformed into regularity-type statements among predicates for strictly occurrent properties. The results of such transformation (or translation) are most likely to be oaken, rather than invariant or exceptionless, lawlike statements (recall the examples in Figure 1). This is something science neither wants nor can afford to want. (I shall not belabor this point, but unless one can defend the existence of actual infinitesimals, all lawlike statements in the form of differential equations would have to be thrown out since what are connected by such equations are precisely dispositional properties, viz. rates and directions — tendencies — of change.)

Then, one may argue that I would be thus barred from using Armstrong's (and Lewis's) theory of laws since it seems that I have to give up one of the three basic assumptions of Armstrong's theory (Armstrong 1983, 7—9). For Armstrong's Actualism 'debars us from postulating such properties as dispositions and powers where these are conceived of as properties over and above the categorical properties of objects. (9)' Two observations on this point. First, a minor point, I should point out that Armstrong admits that this assumption is the weakest, and 'the most difficult and uncertain of [his] three assumptions. (9)' But second, and more importantly, I believe that one should distinguish dispositions (and propensities) — at least those ones which find frequent uses in physical sciences — from those modal properties which are pick out by predicates of mere possibilities. (Armstrong in (1983) at least does not make such a distinction.)

Prima facie, there should be a fundamental difference between a vase being fragile (a disposition) and Bill Clinton possibly being at present a British subject. The former seems to be just as good an actual property for the vase to have (whenever it is indeed fragile) as the property of its actual shape, while the latter clearly could not be actual for Bill Clinton. If one insists that being fragile supervenes on a set of categorical properties and that what obtain actually are in fact those properties, I shall again invoke instantaneous momentum, which clearly does not supervene on any set of categorical properties and which is actually instantiatable on an object that happens to possess it. Therefore, I do not differ from Armstrong by simply rejecting his assumption of Actualism, but rather I adopt his requirement of actual instantiation of universals (as is evident in my previous discussion) and only drop his exclusion of dispositions (and propensities).[①]

[①] See Mellor 1971 and 1974 for arguments on the legitimacy of dispositional properties in laws of nature. Mellor maintains that all properties are dispositional, which I do not share. I cannot see how one can make of the display of a dispositional property if one does not also have categorical properties. But dispositions can be possessed actually and nomic connections among them are no different from ordinary nomic connections, and dispositions (and propensities) may change through time in accordance with the laws which bind them (without ever being displayed), just like categorical properties do.

I have no space in this paper to say how in general dispositional properties (including propensities) are to be distinguished from modal properties which are the extensions of predicates expressing mere possibilities (logical or physical), except the above appeal to our intuition and the following brief observations. First, dispositions are only plausibly seen as modal properties if one characterize them in terms of their display: a vase's being fragile is modal in the sense that it implies what state the vase would be in if it were subject to a certain set of conditions. Both the possible state and the conditions are supposed to be determined be categorical properties. Since the vase is by assumption not actually in that state, the properties are had only as possible ones. Similarly, I have the modal property of being a lawyer even though I am in fact a philosopher. Had certain other conditions obtained earlier in my life, I would have become a lawyer instead of a philosopher. But no one should equate the vase's disposition — being fragile — with its display. If fragility is not a primitive property — which it is indeed not, the set of categorical properties it may be reduced to is certainly not the set by which the state that displays fragility is determined; it is rather the (microscopic) mechanism of the vase on which fragility supervene, if it does supervene on some such mechanisms. This feature of dispositions is certainly not shared by, for instance, my possibly being a lawyer. (There certainly are difficult borderline cases which will make this simple distinction hard to maintain, but I shall not entertain those here.) Second, it seems possible to dispense altogether with the use of modal properties, for it is possible to switch from viewing having modal properties as a particular's possession of a special kind of properties to viewing it as a special way or manner in which a normal property is instantiated in a particular. This possibility does not seem available for dispositions (and propensities) (again, detailed arguments for another occasion).

Cartwright (1983, 1989, 1999) also rejects this kind of Humeanism (i. e. there are laws but no dispositions) and argues that we should admit *capacities*. Capacities are an entirely different concept from dispositions (or propensities), according to Cartwright (1999, 59, 64), because while dispositions 'are tied one-to-one to law-like regularities (59)' or are 'identified with [some] particular manifestations, (64)', capacities are not. They are entirely general and 'can have endless manifestations of endless different varieties. (64)' And most important of all, they are not bound by laws of nature, which do bind dispositions. This distinction is crucially, as far as I can tell, dependent on Cartwright's conception of laws. For some reasons, which is not clear to me, Cartwright chooses to remain an actualist (á la Armstrong) when laws are concerned (cf. Cartwright 1999, 49—50), for she maintains that laws are regularities among occurrent (i. e. categorical) properties. This explains why she believes that most laws of nature are *ceteris paribus* laws in the strong sense that they are false when the *ceteris* are not *paribus*. Moreover, when the *ceteris* are not *paribus* and the laws are thus inoperative, capacities take over, or fill out, what is previously thought the role for laws. So, what happens when a situation as in Figure 1(b) arises? The law of gravity is no longer true there because of the interference of the electric force, but gravity as a capacity is still in operation since the object is indeed affected by it, and the tendency to move along **g** — if it can be regarded as a capacity — is also in operation since the object does tend to move that way at every instant when it is affected the gravity. But all these operations no longer obey the law of gravity!

What is it that connects the capacities so that they can be causally efficacious? Can such connections anything but nomic (= lawlike) ones?

They cannot be logical, nor can they be merely factual. In fact, I think Cartwright does consider them to be lawlike in some sense of the word, but not the sense she is using: 'We may ask, though, "Are not the laws for describing the capacities themselves just further regularity statements?" But we know from chapters 3 and 4 that the answer to this is "no". (1999, 142)' I couldn't agree more; and part of what I have been arguing is that there is no reason for a realist (at least concerning laws of nature) to so narrowly construe laws as regularities among occurrent properties. But perhaps this is not the right question to ask; the right question may be the one that Cartwright asks in her book (1999, 49), 'Where do laws of nature come from?' And a short answer comes down to: from the capacities and the nomological machines. Capacities are supposed to be natures of things (in the Aristotelian sense of the concept) which 'manifest' themselves in the nomological machines as laws of nature. To a great extent I think that this is right; but as I have explained earlier, there is a difference between when and how laws are displays and when and how laws operate (or are obeyed). Many laws of nature are indeed displayed in approximately ideal settings (i.e. in the nomological machines), but they do not *only* operate there.

In any case, this view, as I have argued earlier, is contrary to my construal of laws of nature, where I understand many important laws in science to be relations among dispositions, which are therefore not *ceteris paribus* laws and true exceptionlessly. It is also not clear to me whether Cartwright regards dispositions (and propensities) — in the restricted sense she gives them above — as respectable or important denizens of reality (I am certain that they do live in Cartwright's ontology). Capacities, it seems to me, may be looked at as a highly abstract or general kind of dispositional property; or at least, the difference between the restricted dispositions and capacities is a difference of degrees but not of kind as the difference between dispositions and categorical properties is. So, when I open the door for dispositions and propensities, there is no sound general philosophical reasons for barring capacities (or powers or some other kinds of dispositional properties). There may or may not be good empirical reasons — in terms of scientific practice — to exclude capacities, but I do not see how one could reject them on purely metaphysical grounds while including dispositions.

Therefore, the fundamental difference between Cartwright's theory of laws and mine — which obviously owes a great deal to hers — is that I no longer subscribe to the restriction that laws of nature be strictly relations among categorical properties. In fact, it is not clear to me whether it is even possible to hold such a stance once one lets into one's ontology dispositions of any kind. Wouldn't the connection be lawlike between a disposition and any of its possible (type of) displays when the right conditions obtain? Be that as it may, Cartwright's conception of nomological machines is entirely compatible with me view. In fact, this is exactly where idealization plays its true role in the practice of science, as I have already articulated earlier. However, as I argued above, devising models or designing nomological machines are not for the discovery of *ceteris paribus* laws — regularities among occurrent properties that only obtain in these models or machines — but rather they are for the isolation of universals or genuine properties among which scientific laws may obtain. Recall the simple example in [B] and [C]: to have the right lawlike statement, scientists must first figure out the right kind of predicates (e. g. magnitudes) which may figure in such statements. If one does not get those right, one may have one of those hypotheses which W. Pauli regards as 'not even false' (i. e. not having the right form of lawlikeness).

Now, do I deny the existence of any genuine *ceteris paribus* laws in science — i. e. laws that obtain only when the *ceteris* are *paribus*? No, I do not nor do I need to. My earlier argument simply aims at yielding the conclusion that those laws which do the most explaining in science — laws of the types given in Figure 1 (a) and (b) — are not *ceteris paribus* laws but are ones which are true and co-instantiated in situations where 'not all things are right'. As I argued earlier, whether one, in the case of Figure 1(b), takes the process to be governed by one 'law' $N(X',Y')$ (which would be a genuine *ceteris paribus* law) or by the co-instantiation of the laws of **f** and **e** (which are not) has important implications for one's metaphysical image of reality. The former seems to mandate an incredibly messy world — to every new actual combination of compatible universals a new law of nature, not to mention that to every new combination of universals a new universal which increases the combinatorial basis of laws. If generalizations such as $N(X',Y')$ and $N(X'',Y'')$ in Figure 2 are to be considered as genuine *ceteris paribus* lawlike statements, I would rather deny them the lawhood.

VI

Let me now give a summary of the main features of idealization which I have argued for in this paper. Again, the purpose of idealization is to carve nature at its joints. But nature's joints, we now realize, are not where nature's 'parts' meet but rather where compatible universals or genuine properties 'meet' (i. e. are co-instantiated), while such universals ground objective resemblance — across space and/or time — and bear causal or nomic or other relations which are instantiated and true in numerous possible combinations. *To cut nature at its joints*, to use another metaphor, *is to use idealization to unweave the rainbow*.

Which predicates denote such properties is a matter, sometimes, of common sense and, most of the times, of science. In science, it has a lot to do with *levels of description*, which corresponds in reality to the *stability* of phenomena at different levels (hence, there must be complex universals, such as the pressure of matter in bulk). Such predicates are definitely not to be identified with natural kind terms (as opposed to terms of artificial kinds), for they are not used to keep track of what 'Nature' has given us, but rather to make sense of such notions as possibilities, nomic and causal relations, counterfactuals, supervenience, determinism, etc. (cf. Lewis 1983). For example, in making sense of nomic relations, universals allows us to separate that which is lawlike but approximately true and that which is not lawlike and still (and perhaps more) approximately true (cf. [B] and [C] above). $N(F,G)$ is likely to be lawlike regardless of whether it is even approximately true if F and G are universals, while if they are not, the statement may 'not even be false.'

Why do we need idealization? Few, if any, universals are instantiated (or exhibited) alone or in separation — where the meaning of 'instantiation in separation' is exemplified by the case in Figure 2 — and some are never so instantiated. To discover them and the laws relating them for the construction of scientific theories, one has to separate them, which means that one has to stipulate conditions under which they are displayed purely and simply. This is the work of idealization. Moreover, nature's joints are not always sharp: some universals may overlap in the sense, for instance, the extensions of 'cat' and 'dog' may not be completely clear of each other. When I said above that stable phenomena on different levels in reality generate universals, I mean stability, not rigidity. Therefore, '*carving*', as one of the chief tasks of science, is to separate and set boundaries, which yields universals that are candidates for the relata of laws of nature.

Does not this talking of carving up nature (rather than finding out what nature itself is) commit me to the cause of social constructionism? No, not really. I do believe that there are constructive elements in our understanding of nature (i. e. in our *true* theories). The reason is simply this: idealization is indispensable in theoretical science and the result of idealization is the construction of models that do not obtain in nature. Theoretical arguments and experimental devices are often used to *approximate* the idealized models, but the models can never be literally realized. Hence, science as finding out what nature itself is, taken literally, is a false image. On the other hand, I am by no means forced by my own view on idealization to social constructionism. In fact, the very fact that I take approximation and idealization seriously excludes me from that club: the very idea of social constructionism, however one finesses it, excludes the notion of approximation and idealization. If it is entirely up to us to construct a coherent and practical system of theories which does not have to answer to any specific features of reality, why should there be anything to approximate or to be idealized away?

I have been talking as if idealization only applies to the discovery of universals and laws in science. Idealized physical systems, which are models that serve as guides for devising experimental set-ups in which the targeted lawlike behavior displays itself, are imagined for the sake of discovering laws. But in fact, such objects or systems are also frequently discovered for their own sake under appropriate idealizations. An obvious example would be ideal gas which bears the notion of idealization in its name. Even though, ultimately, idealizations which generate terms to pick out systems are ones for the systems' properties, it would not do any harm to divide idealizations into (i) material idealizations that conceptually produce predicates representing types of objects or systems and (ii) nomic idealizations that conceptually separate nomic or causal connections and, as a result, helps us to discover universals and lawlike relations among them. I will not discuss in any detail aspects of (i); for that see Suppe's discussion in connection to the semantic conception of scientific theories (1989, 81–172). I shall entertain here only one point in connection to *ceteris paribus* laws. It concerns what may be called constitutive laws of physical systems. Are not laws such as the thermodynamic laws for ideal gas or of water problematic cases for my account? For the former, the idealization includes zero molecular size and the absence of any inter-molecular forces; but Boyle's law ($pV=RT$) obviously cannot be true without the idealization. For the latter, water is a chemical compound of hydrogen and oxygen gases; but the laws for hydrogen and oxygen do not seem to be co-instantiated in water. For a short reply it suffices to claim that Boyle's law is indeed a genuine *ceteris paribus* law, if it is a law at all. (I think that it is not really a law if van der Waals's law is.) In fact both conditions in the idealization are physically impossible. It is better to see Boyle's law as a sketch of a law whose details are to be filled out by better idealized models, such as van der Waals's. And to such laws one may also add laws like Snell's law of light refraction in isotropic media (see the correct analysis of it in Cartwright 1983, 46–47). And phenomenologically, water is *not* a compound of the two gases, and therefore, the phenomenological laws of the gases are not instantiated at all in water. But microscopically, the laws of H and O are obviously co-instantiated and true in H_2O.

References

Armstrong, D. M. (1983). *What Is a Law of Nature?* Cambridge, Cambridge University Press.

Cartwright, N. (1983). *How the Laws of Physics Lie*. Oxford, Clarendon Press.

Cartwright, N. (1989). *Nature's Capacities and Their Measurement*. Oxford, Clarendon Press.

Cartwright, N. (1999). *The Dappled World: A Study of the Boundaries of Science*. Cambridge: Cambridge University Press.

Creary, L. G. (1981). "Causal Explanation and the Reality of Natural Component Forces." *Pacific Philosophical Quarterly* **62**: 148—157.

Hilpinen, R. (1976). Approximate Truth and Truthlikeness. *Formal Methods in the Methodology of Empirical Sciences* Eds. M. Przlecki, K. Szanianwski and R. Wojicki. Dordrecht, Reidel, 19—42.

Kline, D. A. and C. A. Matheson, (1986). "How the Laws of Physics Don't Even Fib." *PSA 1986* Eds. P. D. Asquith et al. East Lansing, Philosophy of Science Association. **1**: 33—41.

Laymon, R. (1980). Idealization, Explanation, and Confirmation. *PSA 1980* Eds. P. D. Asquith and R. N. Giere. East Lansing, Philosophy of Science Association. **1**: 336—350.

Laymon, R. (1985). Idealizations and the Testing of Theories by Experimentation. *Observation, Experiment and Hypothesis in Modern Physical Science* Eds. P. Achinstein and O. Hannaway. Cambridge, MA, MIT Press. 147—173.

Laymon, R. (1989). "Cartwright and the Lying Law of Physics." *Journal of Philosophy* **86**: 353—372.

Lewis, D. (1983). "New Work for a Theory of Universals." *Australasian Journal of Philosophy* **61**: 343—377.

Liu, C. (1999). "Approximation, Idealization, and Laws of Nature." *Synthese* **118**: 229—256.

McMullin, E. (1985). "Galilean Idealization." *Studies in the History* and *Philosophy of Science* **16**: 247—273.

Mellor, H. [1971]: *The Matter of Chance*. Cambridge: Cambridge University Press.

Mellor, H. [1974]: 'In Defense of Dispositions', *The Philosophical Review*, **83**, pp. 157—181.

Mellor, H. and A. Oliver [1997]. *Properties*. (Oxford Readings in Philosophy) Oxford: Oxford University Press.

Niiniluoto, I. (1984). *Is Science Progressive*. Dordrecht, Reidel.

Nowak, L. (1972). "Laws of Science, Theories, Measurement." *Philosophy of Science* **39**: 533—548.

Nowak, L. (1980). *The Structure of Idealization: Towards a Systematic Interpretation of the Marxian Idea of Science*. Dordrecht, Reidel.

Suppe, F. (1989). *The Semantic Conception of Theories and Scientific Realism*. Urbana: University of Illinois.

（作者系美国佛罗里达大学哲学系副教授）

回忆布伦塔诺*

埃德蒙多·胡塞尔 著

王俊 译

  仅仅两年时间我有幸聆听布伦塔诺的课，其间完整的学期只有1884/85和1885/86的冬季学期。在这两个学期中他讲授的是每次五小时的"实用哲学"和与这个哲学练习相关的一到两个小时的"哲学问题举要"。在与两个冬季学期相应的后续的夏季学期中他都继续讲授这一独特的小型讲座，并在七月的第一个星期结束。讲座的第一讲以"基本逻辑学和它的必要变革"为题，论述了系统化联结的关于理解力的描述心理学的基础。与之相应的关于情感领域的内容也在一个特别的章节中被探讨。另外"心理学和美学问题举要"主要提供了关于想像力表象之本质的描述性基本分析。大约在7月中旬（1886——译者注）他前往当时他非常喜欢的沃尔夫冈湖，（往St. Gilgen的）途中我应他的盛情邀请陪伴着他。正是在这个夏天，我可以随时造访他的寓所或与他共同散步和泛舟（还参加了这两年中唯一一次较大规模的郊游），我可以与他接近，尽管我们在年龄上相差甚大。当时我正好完成大学学业，在哲学上还只是刚起步（哲学是我的数学博士学位的副专业）。

  当时我对哲学的兴趣高涨，并正在踌躇之中，我是否应以数学为人生职业抑或献身于哲学，此时布伦塔诺的课起了决定性的作用。起先我去听课

---

  * 原文选自 Oskar Kraus 编的《弗兰茨·布伦塔诺：了解他的生活与学说》一书（Oskar Kraus（Hrsg.）: *Franz Brentano: Zur Kenntnis seines Lebens und seiner Lehre*, München, 1919)，第153—167页，附录二。卡尔·施通普夫和埃德蒙多·胡塞尔也参与了编写此书。——译注

纯粹出于好奇,只是为了去听一次他的课;在当时的维也纳关于他的传闻甚多,他受到无比的崇敬和赞赏,据传他不同于那些被斥为虚伪的耶稣会士、好奉承者、智者或经院哲学家的人。我见他的第一印象确与传闻有所相符。瘦高的身材和有着一头卷发的硕大的脑袋,有力而线条分明的鹰钩鼻,令人印象深刻的目光,他的言谈不仅是关于人文工作、更是发自灵魂深处的斗争,而这一切都包含在平凡的生活之内。他的一举一动,那热情洋溢的眸子中闪烁的目光,他的整个生存方式,都流露出一种宏大的使命感。他在授课时的言谈有着完美的形式,完全没有人工斧凿之迹,没有刻意卖弄才智的辞藻装饰和讲求修辞的无用之谈,而是一种冷静客观的科学话语。这一话语方式拥有一种极为高雅和艺术家式的风格,而这一风格正是他人格个性的自然流露。当他以其特有的柔和、低沉而沙哑的嗓音言谈,并配以凝重的姿势,就如同一个永恒真理的见证者和天国世界的宣告者,矗立在青年学生们面前。

不久我就抛弃一切成见而被他的人格魅力所征服。很快我就被这样一些事情所吸引,他的论述中那独一无二的明晰性和辩证法式的精确性,他的问题推衍和原理论述中可以说是紧张的内在张力,都令我为之折服。最初从他的课上我获取了一种信念,这一信念使我有勇气选择哲学作为人生职业,这种信念使我相信,哲学也是一个严肃的工作领域,哲学不仅能够而且也必须以一种严格科学的精神去探讨和处理。他以纯粹的客观性去拷问一切问题,他对待疑难的论述方式,精确而辩证地权衡不同的可能性论据,解析歧义性,向直觉体验的源头追溯一切哲学概念——所有这些都令我对他满怀钦佩和信任。在他的讲座中,极度严肃和完全忘我的言谈杜绝了一切低俗的课堂玩笑和戏谑之词。他避免使用一切形式的情绪化命题,因为这些命题经常是以激烈的语言方式换取强词夺理的思想简化。而在日常谈话中,当他心情愉快时也是充满激情和情趣横溢的。令人难忘的哲学练习的功效是最有说服力的。(我能回忆起的有如下题目:休谟:"关于人类理解力的论文"和"论道德律";Helmholtz 的讲话:"感知的事实";Dubois-Reymonds 的"自然认识的界限"。)布伦塔诺是苏格拉底"助产术"的大师。他知道如何通过提问和反问去引导在不确定中摸索的初学者,去激起严肃探索的勇气,将关于真理体验不明晰的开端向明晰的思想和认识转化;另一方面,他能像那些泛泛的空谈家那样思考,除了设置游戏外不得罪任何人。在练习课之后他乐于将作报告者和三到四个最勤奋的听课者带回家中,在那里 Ida Brentano 太太①已经预备好了晚餐。在此不会涉及家常闲聊。研讨课的主题被进一步深入探讨,布伦塔诺不知疲倦地继续讲授,提出新的问题或在课的整体之上开启一个广阔的视界。用餐之后 Ida 太太很快离开,因为她对此已感厌烦,之后腼腆的学生们才会放肆地伸手自取食物,对此布伦塔诺毫不在意。有一次恰好他们家的密友、著名政治家 E. V. Plener 造访,出现在这个聚会上,而布伦塔诺竟没有为此分散注意力,在这样的夜晚他完全属于他的学生和讨论的主题。

在他的学生看来,布伦塔诺是很容易交流的。他喜欢邀请别人共同散步,在途中他回答学生们提出的哲学问题,而完全不受城市街道上嘈杂的干扰。对他的学生来说,他是富有献身精神的,不仅在科学上更是人格上的楷模,他是学生们最知心的咨询人和教导者。对那些他认为是值得信赖的朋友们,他也会谈及他的政治和宗教信仰以及个人命运。他对日常政治毫无兴趣,但是一个"大德意志"的理念却是他的心头大事,这一理念基于古老的"南德意志"观念的思想,这个古老的观念伴他成长,如同他对普鲁士人的反感一样,这一古老的观念也是他长久以来固有的。我们在此事上从未取得过一致。对他来说普鲁士的方式从来就不是富有人性的和有价值的社会形式,而我由于从中获益甚多,已学会了高度褒扬这一方式。与此对应,他却缺少对普鲁士历史本质上的伟大意义的敏感性。与此相似的是他对新教的态度,他退出天主教后也绝不与新教亲近。作为哲学家他独立于天主教的教条之外;与新教理念的关系在此也无足轻重,在历史政治见解上人云亦云,这不是布伦塔诺的方式。就我所听到的,关于天主教教义本身,他从来都是抱以极大的关注去谈论。有时他会通过宗教—伦理的效力去反驳那

---

① 1880 年布伦塔诺与 Ida 结婚,Ida 于 1895 年去世。——译注

些不理智的、轻视这一效力的言论。在哲学上,有神论的世界观将他与旧教会联系在一起,他深受此世界观的影响,以至于非常乐于谈论上帝和永生的问题。他的两个小时的关于神证论的讲座(这一讲座是关于形而上学的大型讲座的一部分,他早年在维尔茨堡,后在维也纳都讲授过)是经过非常审慎的考虑的;正当我离开维也纳时,他又重新投入研究与此相关的问题。据我所知,这些问题直到他的晚年仍伴随着他。

在那几年里,他特别关注那些描述心理学的问题,这些问题是上面提及的讲座的主题,关于感知心理学研究的部分内容在几年前才得以发表,其内容来自于我们于维也纳和 St. Gilgen 的令人难忘的谈话(至少主要线索是相符的)。在关于基本逻辑学的课上,他特别详细清晰地在创造性的新结构中论述了统一体的描述心理学,并深入考察了波尔查诺的"无穷尽悖论";他还论述了诸如"体验和非体验"、"明晰和不明晰"、"清楚和不清楚"、"本真和非本真"、"具体和抽象"等表象的差异,在接下来的夏天里他还进行了如下尝试:从根本上探究一切存在于传统判断背后的、描述性的、在判断的内在本质中自我显现的阶段。他特别关注由此直接引出的想像力的描述问题(也是上述他的一个讲座的主题),特别是想象表象和感觉表象的关系。这些课总是特别令人激动,因为在诸如关于实用哲学的课上(或是关于逻辑学和形而上学的课上,在那些课上我只能做少量的笔记),总是在探究过程中引出问题,尽管有一些批评的、辩证式的表述在某种意义上是有教条性质的,即由固定的终极真理和始终有效的原理必然引起并已引起的此种印象。从那时起我就一直有此种印象:事实上布伦塔诺完全视自己为一种永恒哲学的创造者。他力求一种完全确定和持久的方法,满足如数学般严格的最高标准;他相信,在他清晰精练的概念中,在他体系化安排和确立的原理中,在他对反对观点的全方位反诘中,已经赢得了令人满意的真理。但是与他主张的理论不同,如我一直以来所确信的,他并不顽固地一味坚持它们。对于一些早年的看似可爱的命题,后来他都放弃了。他从来没有停步不前。然而在对于直观的分析的深入探究和独创中,他从直观到原理的转化相对草率的:清晰概念的确立,所探究问题的原理性建构,解决之可能性的体系化整体结构,在其中通过批判而作出正确的选择。如果我对他的哲学方式的评价正确,即在他的每一个发展阶段中,他总是以相同的方式拥有稳定的原理,这些原理由缜密而经过深思熟虑的论据支持;有了这些论据他感到自己能应对一切陌生的理论。对那些思想家如康德和康德之后的德国唯心主义者来说,原初直观和先验观点的价值完全高于诸如逻辑方法和科学原理,对此他并不赞同。当一个哲学家的一切原理在非科学的方式下被严格接受,甚至他的基本概念几乎全部未达到"明晰性和清楚性"时,他还是能被认为是伟大的;他的伟大并非来自于他的原理的逻辑完满性而是来自于那些含义丰富但是模糊、未被解释的基本原初体验之中,因此是存在于带有目标性的逻各斯的前逻辑之中——总而言之是存在于一种全新的思考动机中,是为了一切哲学工作最终目标而确立的思考动机,尽管这一目标距离在原理性的严格理解中发挥作用尚十分遥远:布伦塔诺并不赞同这种观点。他完全沉浸在最严格哲学科学的严肃观念之中(对他来说,这一观念体现了精确的自然科学的方式),他视德国唯心主义体系为一种退化堕落。从我认识布伦塔诺以来,我一直坚信,他是一位在现时代关注一种严格科学性哲学的研究者:那些唯心主义体系在本质上与那些笛卡尔之前的哲学无异,他们以一种幼稚的观点看待问题,却同时被认为是最有价值的。对于那些充满张力的问题发端进行科学的严格探讨,对此康德和其后的德国唯心主义者未能提供令人满意和持久的方案。这种方案能使这些问题发端能真正重新被理解,并一直在它们的直观结构中自我调适,能肯定的一点是,它完全异质于那些唯心主义体系,而在哲学的最尖锐的问题视域中显露出来,它通过由其自身特点所决定的哲学方法来建构和阐释,从而达到它的终极目标。

此外布伦塔诺令人钦佩的过人之处在于逻辑的原理建构,他的哲学中外型有序、持久而开放的最终效用是以此为基础的:他自身作为原创思想家,从直觉的根源攫取力量,向七十年代已变得毫无创造力的德国哲学提供一种具有崭新的原初力量的契机。在此无法估量他的方法和理论能有多么深远的影响。在其他思想的形成过程中这些契机往往能引出与他的观点完全不同的衍生，而这正证明了它们具有根源性原初力量的活力。尽管并非他所愿，因为据说他对自己的哲学很有信心，而事实上他的自信也是相当强的。由内在确定性引出正确的道路和独立的科学化哲学，这一确定性没有任何动摇。他有一种发自内心、不可推卸的使命感，即进一步传布他所确信的那种在体系化基本理论内的哲学。我将他这种对这一使命的深信不疑的信念称之为他人生的原始特征。离开这一信念人们很难理解和正确评价布伦塔诺其人。

因此对他的理解首先涉及的是对他深邃的理论效力的众说纷纭，这对一个学派来说是有积极意义的：不只是拓宽那些已取得的认识，更是进一步深化他的思想。当然他敏感地反对每一种对他固有信念的偏离，面对这些相关异议他会变得很激动，并有些固执地坚持那些经过深思熟虑才得出的结论和成果，他借助于他那大师级的辩证法获得胜利——这一辩证法与那些异议者引以为根基的原初体验相对，然而并不圆满。没有人能比他更多地引导出自觉的自由思考，而且当这些思考是针对他自己内心固有的信念时，这一过程就显得更为艰难。

带着这一信念，作为一种新哲学的开创者，他毫无疑问是有巨大价值的（而当时我对此知之甚少），布伦塔诺由此再次取得了在维也纳的正式教职。他谈了很多关于希望，那些希望总是向新事物敞开，也抱怨那些从未实现的承诺。对他而言难以忍受的是，不能再承担培养博士生的工作，在系里不能出头说话，更有甚者，对待教职论文的消极态度使他被认为是最不受欢迎的私人讲师。他经常带着极大的痛苦谈及这些。然而由于他不仅在维也纳，更在整个奥地利所具有的决定性影响，他的教学活动在这种不利情况下并未受损（从他夏季学期的课上所实行的"自愿限制"可见一斑）。他关于实践哲学的课精彩而从传统上看也相当完美，每个冬天总有上百个法律系的一年级新生和来自其他所有系的听众来听课——尽管几周之后这个庞大的数字会急剧减少，因为在这个课上所布置的常规作业就不是任何人都能完成的。而那些有才华的年轻人总是能一直坚持参加他的课和完成练习，并且相信，为此他已经殚精竭虑。

在那几年他对自己衰弱的神经多有怨言,甚至是在 St. Gilgen 期间,那里原本是他的精神得到休养恢复之地。他一直在寻找高强度精神工作之余的片刻歇息,然而生活的其他方面由于他洋溢的发掘热情也并不轻松。作为一位才智出众的国际象棋棋手他参加了维也纳国际象棋俱乐部(对于他的才智,有人说他曾极度专注于思想的端倪,以求能获胜),由此而能暂时地在一种他酷爱的游戏中得到放松。在其他时间里他刨木头或者画画,他总是全身心地投入所做之事。在我们前往 St. Gilgen 的途中,他拿出自己亲手刨制的国际象棋,以便在游戏中度过漫长的旅途。在 St. Gilgen 他非常热衷于修改润饰或中途接手他太太的肖像画,然而作为一位出色的女画家,他的太太事后不得不伸出援手有时还要重新返工。在 1886 年他同太太一起为我画了一幅画像:"一幅和蔼可亲的画像"——就如感觉敏锐的艺术史家 Theodor Vischer 所评价的那样。带着这份热情在 St. Gilgen 的每个下午他都要玩"拱形游戏"(在"花园"里,即在所租小屋后面靠近湖边的一小块草地)。他对登山毫无兴趣,而只喜欢适度地散步。无论在 St. Gilgen 还是在维也纳,他的生活方式都是极为简单的。另外人们不需要跟他极为熟稔或长时间地观察他的生活习惯,就能感受到流言的荒唐之处——流言传说他是因为第一位太太的财产才与她结婚的。对财富的享受、奢侈、美食、享乐的生活方式他完全不在行。他不吸烟,饮食很有节制,完全不在意不同食物的口味差别。我经常在用餐时间还待在他家,却从未听到过他对饮食显示出特殊兴趣的任何言谈。当我们先于他太太一些时候到达 St. Gilgen 时,不得不在一个很差的旅馆中用餐,但他对此却毫不在意并总是表现得很满足,他只热衷于他的思想和讨论。他要求最最简单的餐谱,如同他独自乘火车时也总是满足最低等的车厢。他就那样站立着,身上的服装简朴还经常是穿破了的。在这些方面他十分节俭,只求能满足生存,而在行善方面他却十分慷慨。在对待年轻人时,他一方面沉稳持重,另一方面也非常亲切热情,经常为它们学习的经济来源乃至道德行为操心。在此人们能感觉沉浸在他的高尚指引及其持久向上的力量之中,甚至在空间上与他相隔甚远也能感觉到这种力量。那些投入地听他的课的人,在课上不只是被事物的原理、更是被他人格深处的那种纯粹的道德所吸引。他是如此坦率真诚！令我难忘的是我们在静谧的夏夜,在沃尔夫冈湖畔散步,此时他经常会谈及他自己。他像孩童般地坦率,就如他拥有天才的纯真。

我与布伦塔诺通信不多。在一封信中,我曾请求他接受在我的《算术哲学》一书(我在哲学方面的处女作)上的献词,他回信表达了热忱的谢意,但同时严肃地提醒道:对于他的反对者心怀的怨恨,我不该对此操心。但我仍然将这部作品的题词献给了他,但是寄出献词样本后一直没有得到回信。直到14年之后布伦塔诺才发现我真地将这本书的题词献给他,而对我表示了衷心的感谢;很明显他并未仔细地看这本书或者只是按他的方式浏览了一下。对我来说他当然是高高在上的,我试图更好地理解他,以便由此得到一些敏锐的启发。

关于我们之间没有建立频繁的通信联系,还有一些更深的原因。从一开始作为深受他鼓舞的学生,我就一直将他敬奉为老师,然而我并没有成为他的学派中的一员。但是我知道,按照自己的方式行进,这会让他感到非常不快,尽管行进的道路是从他那里引出的。此后他会轻易地有失偏颇,而我成了他的对立面,这是令人痛心的。有些人,他们从内心里被那些未经解释而强势的思想动机所驱使,或者追求并满足于那些抽象而无法把握的体验,他们并不乐意接受一些行为,比如说对已有的原理表示怀疑和不赞同,或对某人(甚至是布伦塔诺那样的逻辑学大师)的理论持保留意见。自身的含混性已使人们受够了困扰,对于逻辑的局限——这正是研究和思考的推动力量——我们已不需要更多新的论据和辩证式的反驳。那些预设的方法、概念、命题,很遗憾必须经过怀疑然后在悬疑之中被排除掉,人们不能清楚地进行反驳,自身也无法确定无疑地设立任何可以企及的东西,这正是一种不幸。在我的成长过程中情形就是如此,这表现为某种疏远;这不仅仅只是我老师个人的异化,这种异化在其身后很难与科学建立联系。但我必须承认,他一直都抱有这个意图。他竭尽全力重新建立一种科学的联系。他感到,我庞大的工作方法对他的影响在这十年中从未降低,相反只会越来越大。我在自身的发展中也认识到,那种来自于他的推动的力量和价值有多么重要。

担任私人讲师期间在一个暑假中我曾拜访过他一次,那时在多瑙河畔的 Schönbühl①;不久之前他在此购买了一家意大利酒店,并改建为住宅。当时见到他的情形令人难忘。我走近房子时看到一群泥瓦工,一个敞着衬衫、穿着沾满石灰的裤子、戴着宽边软帽、手里与其他人一样拿着抹子的瘦高个站在下面:像一个当时人们在大街小巷随处可见的意大利工人,那就是布伦塔诺。他热情地迎接我,向我介绍他的改建构想,抱怨那些无能的工头和泥瓦工人,由此他必须事事亲自经手过问并参与劳作。但不久我们便又沉浸在哲学讨论中了,他向来如此。

1908 年在佛罗伦萨,在他位于 Via Bellosgauardo 的美丽居所里我才再次见到他。回想那些日子总是令我感动不已。让我感触颇深的是,当时双眼已近乎失明的他从阳台上向我和我的太太介绍佛罗伦萨无与伦比的景色风光,带着我们参观位于景色优美的道路边的两处伽利略居住过的别墅。从外貌上我觉得他几乎没什么变化,只是头发有些斑白,眼睛失去了以往的光泽神采。然而现在这双眼睛所流露的是一种神圣的意味,当然很大部分是来自于哲学思考的。令人感到辛酸的是,能够再一次与人谈论哲学竟使他如此欢心愉悦;他这样一个将教导他人作为生活必需的人,却不得不在佛罗伦萨孤独地苟且度日,在这里他无从发挥个人才能,偶尔有能倾听和理解他的人从北方来,会令他喜悦不已。那几日对于我来说,仿佛又重回几十年前在维也纳的学习时光。我感到自己在他面前,在这样一位卓越和充满精神力量的大师面前,又重新变回成一个羞怯腼腆的初学者。我更乐于倾听,就如同我自己在讲述。他的言谈仍然清晰和有条不紊。而他听我讲述有关现象学的研究方法的意义和我早先与心理主义的斗争时,也一直不曾打断我。我们之间一直未能取得观点上的一致,对此也许我应承担一定的责任。

---

① 布伦塔诺在此购买了一家酒店并改为住房,他称之为"新阿沙芬堡",因为据说 Schönbühl 的景色环境与他记忆中位于故乡阿沙芬堡的祖屋十分相似。(Brigitte Schad 编:《阿沙芬堡的布伦塔诺家族:遗物中关于家族史的未刊文献》,Aschaffenburg,1984。)——译注

一种内在的念头使我固执地认为,他是在思考方式的固有风格中,使用那些死板的概念和论据的固定结构,去重新理解他的基本体验建构的必要性——对这种基本体验我深有体会。

这种细微的不一致并未损害那段美好的时光;在那段时间里他的第二任夫人 Emilie[①] 无微不至地关照我们。她自然妥帖、充满关爱地照顾布伦塔诺的晚年生活,并完全融入他当时的生活之中。他乐意尽量陪伴着我;我对他的感激之情——即他人格和理论的活生生的力量对我产生的影响——难以忘却,这令他颇为感动。晚年的他变得更加充满爱心和宽容,从他身上我发现的不是抑郁不振的衰老——这应归功于他的第一和第二故乡以及他与生俱来的伟大秉赋。他一直生活在他的理念世界和哲学的完满之中,如他所说,他的哲学在这数十年中得到了巨大的发展。这使他笼罩在一种容光焕发的气息之中,如同他不再属于这个世界,如同他生活的另一半存在于一个更高尚的世界——对于这个更高尚的世界他笃信不疑,他用毕生的时间在原理之中阐释它的哲学含义。当时我在佛罗伦萨见到他的最后一面,深刻地印入我的灵魂最深处:他总是生活在我前面,那是一幅来自于更高尚世界的图景。

---

① 1897 年布伦塔诺与第二任太太 Emilie Rueprecht 结婚。第二次婚姻对布伦塔诺来说是极大的幸运,Emilie 不仅贤惠能干,而且当布伦塔诺因眼部手术在最后十年几乎失明时,她协助他进行科学工作,为此她学习了希腊文。(《阿沙芬堡的布伦塔诺家族:遗物中关于家族史的未刊文献》)——译注

图书在版编目(CIP)数据

外国哲学.第十七辑/《外国哲学》编辑委员会编.
北京:商务印书馆.2005
ISBN 7-100-04259-3

Ⅰ.外… Ⅱ.外… Ⅲ.哲学—外国—丛刊
Ⅳ.B1-55

中国版本图书馆 CIP 数据核字(2004)第 101200 号

所有权利保留。
未经许可,不得以任何方式使用。

外 国 哲 学
第十七辑

商 务 印 书 馆 出 版
(北京王府井大街36号 邮政编码100710)
商 务 印 书 馆 发 行
北京民族印刷厂印刷
ISBN 7-100-04259-3/B·618

2005年9月第1版　　　开本 787×960　1/16
2005年9月北京第1次印刷　印张 18 1/2
定价:26.00元